Your Life Matters

by John W. Stanko

Your Life Matters
by John W. Stanko

ISBN 978-1-63360-038-6
For Worldwide Distribution
Printed in the U.S.A.

PurposeQuest Ink
P.O. Box 8882
Pittsburgh, PA 15221-0882
412.646.2780

TABLE OF CONTENTS

INTRODUCTION

Early in my walk with the Lord, I heard that if I read one chapter from Proverbs every day along with five psalms, I would finish both books every month or twelve times in a year. That appealed to the administrative side of my thinking, and I successfully read Proverbs like that for years, but Psalms was more of a struggle. I would do well in the months when the psalms were short, but when the psalms got longer, I struggled to find the time or maintain my interest.

I have been an instructor for Geneva College at the Center for Urban Biblical Ministry in Pittsburgh since 1998 and I have taught a number of different classes. In 2012, I taught the Psalms for the first time and then repeated the course in 2014. It was then that the lights went on for me as I taught the Psalms. Until I taught from the Psalms, I did not realize that there was a theme and that the order or progression of the individual psalms contributed to that theme. In other words, the editor of the book played almost as important a role as the authors of the psalms themselves.

The book of Psalms is actually broken into five parts or books: Book 1 from 1 to 41: Book 2 from 42 to 72; Book 3 from 73 to 89; Book 4 from 90 to 106 and Book 5 from 107 to 150. Without going into a lot of detail, it is important for you to understand that the Book of Psalms was probably compiled and edited during the time when Israel was captive in Babylon during the sixth century BC so the sub-books were compiled and edited over time. Since the Jews were in Babylon for 70 years, we can assume that the entire book took shape during that period. We have no idea who the editors were. Of course the individual psalms were mostly written prior to that Babylonian exile, and a few were even written by Moses. That means the Psalms were written over many centuries, and compiled when Israel was in great distress.

Here is a general theme for each of the five books and the thinking of the editors as they did their work:

1. Book 1 – "How could this have happened to us? It's our enemy's fault; God, we want you to judge and destroy them."
2. Book 2 – "How could this have happened to us? Well, maybe we had a role in it, but it's still our enemy's fault. They hate us and therefore they hate you, Lord, as well. So we suggest, Lord, that You destroy them."
3. Book 3 – "You know, we may have had a bigger role in our captivity than we first thought. We have sinned, but surely our sins don't deserve all this. God, remember us and do what You did for us in days gone by when You rescued us from our enemies."
4. Book 4 – "This captivity is our fault. We have sinned, just like our forefathers. You are a great God and we remember all that you did for us as a people, but You are under no obligation to do it it again, except for Your grace."
5. Book 5 – "God is with us and in His mercy, He is going to restore us to our land. We are preparing to return so we can worship, sing and serve the Lord in Jerusalem, our holy city! Our return is because He is gracious to His people and faithful to His word!"

Now the summary above is simplistic and no one book exactly fits the description I have provided. Yet if you keep those themes in mind, the entire book makes more sense and you see that it is as much more than a collection of poems and songs. Of course, the psalms also point to the coming Messiah, and you will recognize that the Lord Jesus actually quoted these psalms as He endured His rejection and suffering. Therefore, the Book of Psalms is also a prophetic voice of and for the suffering Messiah and King of Israel. We now look back and realize it is Him speaking in the psalms because we have the benefit of hindsight. The writers may or may not have known what they were saying when they penned those individual poems and songs, but they had to know something about the glories that were to come in Christ.

In the next 365 days, I am recommending that you read the five psalms for the day. I will focus on one verse or passage from that daily reading. If you don't have time to read all five psalms, then at least read the one on which I am writing that day. If you don't have time to read even one, then this devotional can still give you a quick Bible study without the reading. By the way, in the months that have 31 days, we will look at verses from Psalm 119, the longest psalm.

On each day, I will take one verse or passage from one of those five psalms and include another passage from another book of the Bible or a prayer for you to pray. I encourage you to have a journal close by while you read and pray to record your own insights and reflections. As usual, each day in my devotionals stands alone, so if you miss reading a day or a week, you can pick right back up where you left off and not have missed any of progression, because there is none.

I actually found it difficult to choose 366 verses from Psalms to use in this devotional because many of the psalms are short entries with one theme; the individual verses do not stand alone well without the others. Therefore, some days will have a passage with multiple verses from a psalm while other days will feature only one verse from another. There are more than 2,400 verses in the entire book, and we will cover about 15-20% of them in this study.

Finally, I chose the title because it has a double meaning where the book of Psalms is concerned. On one hand, the psalms focus on the life struggles of both the community of Israel and its leaders and followers. The psalms clearly show that all of life matters to the Lord as His people cry out to him in the midst of their fears, tribulations, and confusion. On the other hand, the Psalms cover all the issues that matter in life, things like suffering, joy, weeping, victory, setbacks, frustration, generosity, and worship. From this we can conclude that life matters to the Lord in the midst of all the life situations His people encounter as they serve and follow Him. You are reading the ancient psalms to apply the lessons to your life, thus the title *Your Life Matters: Daily Reflections from the Book of Psalms.*

There you have an overview of what you will be receiving every day that you read this devotional. I pray that this study will empower and enrich you when you need it most. I also pray that God will take what I write, you will read it, and then be able to think, "That was just for me." Thank you for reading along with me, and may the Lord bless the reading and study of His word!

John W. Stanko
Pittsburgh, PA
May 2016

January 1

Faith in Action

Today's Reading: Psalms 1-5

"For the Lord watches over the way of the righteous, but the way of the wicked leads to destruction" - Psalm 1:6.

This verse mentions "way" twice, one for the righteous and one for the wicked. All people are walking one of those two ways. The Lord expects you to be on His way, and that way is the road marked "faith." The word *way* and a life of faith imply movement and progress in the right direction. James 2:17 describes the way for God's people: "In the same way, faith by itself, if it is not accompanied by action, is dead." There is **always** something you can do in faith, otherwise your faith is useless. Your life matter today is to determine what faith action you can take concerning a particular situation you are facing. What is that action? Be specific, and don't say you don't have time. Let's start the year off with a prayer, shall we? *Father, I thank You for your Word and the chance to study it. I commit these readings to you, and I pray that you will equip and empower me to learn and apply the lessons You have for me, and I will be able to apply what I learn by Your grace. I commit this year and this study to You!*

January 2

Vindication

Today's Reading: Psalms 6-10

"Let the Lord judge the peoples. Vindicate me, Lord, according to my righteousness, according to my integrity, O Most High" - Psalm 7:8.

It can be difficult to wait for the Lord to vindicate you when you have been wrongly accused or someone criticizes or maligns you. Two common responses to when your reputation is sullied is to take legal action or to counterattack. Yet the psalmist in today's verse chose to trust that God would be the One to vindicate him, a strategy that Jesus employed as Peter explained: "When they hurled their insults at him, he did not retaliate; when he suffered, he made no threats. Instead, he entrusted himself to him who judges justly (1 Peter 2:23). Both Jesus and the psalmist chose to wait for God to do set things right according to His own time and in His own way. Pray this prayer today: *Lord, I put You in charge of my image and my defense. I choose not to defend myself, but will wait for You to do so - or not!*

January 3

Your Thought Life

Today's Reading: Psalms 11-15

"How long, Lord? Will you forget me forever? How long will you hide your face from me? How long must I wrestle with my thoughts and day after day have sorrow in my heart? How long will my enemy triumph over me?" - Psalm 13:1-2.

When you are suffering, there are two questions that generally arise: why and how long will it last? David was sorrowful as he battled thoughts of God's possible unfaithfulness amidst the seemingly endless duration of his pain. In this case, David's battle was not external but in his mind and that is where your greatest battle takes place as well. Paul wrote that this work of renewing your mind is like hand-to-hand combat, as he described in 2 Corinthians 10:5: "We demolish arguments and every pretension that sets itself up against the knowledge of God, and we take captive every thought to make it obedient to Christ." Are you willing to take on this battle to bring your thought life into alignment with God's reality and will? If so, then pray this prayer: *Lord, today I choose to believe that You are faithful, and I commit to wrestle with my thought life to make sure it accepts and meditates on Your truth.*

January 4

A Spacious Place

Today's Reading: Psalms 16-20

"He reached down from on high and took hold of me; he drew me out of deep waters. He rescued me from my powerful enemy, from my foes, who were too strong for me. They confronted me in the day of my disaster, but the Lord was my support. He brought me out into a spacious place; he rescued me because he delighted in me" - Psalm 18:16-19.

Time and again in the book of Psalms, the writers wrote and sang about their trouble and how the Lord rescued and delivered them. In today's passage, the psalmist stated that the Lord brought him into what he referred to as a "spacious place." What does a spacious place represent for you? Ministry or professional growth? A larger family? Greater influence or wealth? A role where you can be who God made you to be, surrounded by people who appreciate and don't envy or limit you? In your journal, take a few minutes to write about what an ideal "spacious place" would look like for you. Then trust the Lord to help you find such a place!

January 5

His Kingdom Rule

Today's Reading: Psalms 21-25

"The earth is the Lord's, and everything in it, the world, and all who live in it; for he founded it on the seas and established it on the waters" - Psalm 24:1-2.

God is the Lord over all people and all things, whether those people acknowledge Him or not. The things over which He rules include every area of life and culture such as business, education, social work, banking, government, church, entertainment, music, and science. Since He is Lord, He has the right to rule and declare His will as he sees fit. The Lord Jesus' first words when He began His ministry were, "Repent, for the kingdom of heaven has come near" (Matthew 4:17). In that one statement, Jesus expressed His mission on earth and that was to proclaim, embody, and establish God's government over what already belonged to the Father. When you repent of building your own kingdom and come to the Lord, you accept your role to extend God's Kingdom rule into the spheres mentioned above, according to your purpose assignment. What is your Kingdom assignment? Do you see that you are here to do more than attend church services? Do you understand that you are God's Kingdom representative where you work, in your family, and in your neighborhood? What implications does being a representative have for your attitude and behavior?

January 6

The Flood, Your Flood

Today's Reading: Psalms 26-30

"The Lord sits enthroned over the flood; the Lord is enthroned as King forever. The Lord gives strength to his people; the Lord blesses his people with peace" - Psalm 29:10-11.

Have you ever watched video footage of a flood or tsunami? If you have, you know it's an awesome and frightening event, as you watch the water pick up boats and cars and carry them like they are toothpicks. Today's passage tells you that the Lord presided over Noah's flood as King. The same King who controlled Noah's Flood sits as King over the flood waters in your life. That knowledge should give you peace and comfort in the midst of flood-like situations that overwhelm and terrify you. Jesus exhibited God's power over your flood when He rebuked the wind and waves that were about to overtake the disciples. With just one word, He calmed the seas! Is there a flood in your life right now? Thank Him today for both empowering you to cope with your situation and also controlling your flood-like circumstances.

JANUARY 7

HOPEFUL AND OPTIMISTIC

Today's reading: Psalms 31-35

"The Lord foils the plans of the nations; he thwarts the purposes of the peoples. But the plans of the Lord stand firm forever, the purposes of his heart through all generation" - Psalm 33:10-11.

It is easy to listen to media reports and become pessimistic about the state of the world and its future. Someone once said, however, that God is playing chess with the nations, for He matches their every move! The enemies of God may win some short-term battles, but God has already won the war, and the final victory will be declared for all the world to behold at the Second Coming of Jesus. Therefore, you can be hopeful and optimistic, not based on what you see but according to the faith you have in the truth found in today's passage. God's purposes will stand regardless of what victories the nations along with their philosophies and false religions seem to win. When Elijah was depressed about the state of the world, he said to the Lord, "I have been very zealous for the Lord God Almighty. The Israelites have rejected your covenant, torn down your altars, and put your prophets to death with the sword. I am the only one left, and now they are trying to kill me too" (1 Kings 19:14). The Lord responded, "Yet I reserve seven thousand in Israel—all whose knees have not bowed down to Baal and whose mouths have not kissed him" (1 Kings 19:18). Ask God to give you His perspective today, like He did to Elijah, so you can put your faith not in what you see but in what God sees!

JANUARY 8

ANGER'S PURPOSE

Today's Reading - Psalms 36-40

"Refrain from anger and turn from wrath; do not fret—it leads only to evil" - Psalm 37:8.

Anger is a normal human emotion that God gave you to spur you on to *righteous* action. Anger can become a problem whenever you do two things: 1) internalize it, which leads to your mind running wild with anxiety as you replay the situation that offended you and proceed to develop and rehearse revenge scenarios; or 2) express it improperly through angry words or actions intended to hurt others emotionally or physically. Your job is to control your anger and quickly channel it in positive ways. It will help to remember what Paul wrote: "In your anger do not sin: Do not let the sun go down while you are still angry" (Ephesians 4:26). That verse indicates that you can be angry and not sin. Can you see that anger is intended to motivate you to do something, and it's what you do that can be the problem, not the anger itself? Have you been trying to suppress your anger instead of facing it?

JANUARY 9

GOD-RELIANT

Today's Reading: Psalms 41-45

"I put no trust in my bow, my sword does not bring me victory; but you give us victory over our enemies, you put our adversaries to shame" - Psalm 44:6-7.

It is a lifelong journey to learn how to be God-reliant and not self-reliant. The more talented or experienced you are, the more your tendency to think, "I've got this," and to act accordingly. The psalmist in Psalm 44 was probably skilled using the bow and sword, but he learned to put no trust in them, but instead placed his confidence in the Lord. In what area do you need to put your trust completely in the Lord? Where are you facing a situation that you have handled it in the past, but today you are learning to trust in God's strength and His timing for your victory? Have you begun to put your trust in your gift or skill instead of the God of your gift or skill? If you are being delivered from your reliance on self, then pray this prayer today: *Lord, I choose to be God-reliant and learn to trust You to help me overcome my enemies and win the victory in every area of life.*

January 10

Be Realistic

Today's reading: Psalms 46-50

"God is our refuge and strength, an ever-present help in trouble. Therefore we will not fear, though the earth give way and the mountains fall into the heart of the sea, though its waters roar and foam and the mountains quake with their surging" - Psalm 46:1-3.

The writer of Psalm 46 was realistic and understood that God would not keep him out of trouble but instead would protect him in the midst of trouble. This is an important distinction because if you think God will not allow something to happen and it happens, you can become disillusioned with and even bitter against the Lord. Today's passage indicates that the tribulation in your life can be traumatic, similar in effect to some of the worst natural disasters you can imagine. It is during those times, however, that you come to know God as your refuge and strength. Without tough times, you would only know those aspects of God's character in theory and not reality. Paul and Barnabas encouraged the saints with these words. You should be encouraged by them as well: "Then they returned to Lystra, Iconium and Antioch, strengthening the disciples and encouraging them to remain true to the faith. "'We must go through many hardships to enter the kingdom of God'" (Acts 14:21-22).

JANUARY 11

CHOOSING TO GIVE

Today's Reading: Psalms 51-55

"I will sacrifice a freewill offering to you; I will praise your name, Lord, for it is good" - Psalm 54:6.

The act of giving is not only a duty but also an act of worship that you should freely embrace. Your attitude should not be that you **have** to give but rather that you ***get*** to give. In today's verse, David wrote that he was giving a freewill offering - not something God directed him to do but something David chose to do of his own volition. Paul taught about this attitude toward giving:

> Each of you should give what you have decided in your heart to give, not reluctantly or under compulsion, for God loves a cheerful giver. And God is able to bless you abundantly, so that in all things at all times, having all that you need, you will abound in every good work (2 Corinthians 9:8-9).

What is your attitude toward giving? Are you a cheerful giver? Is it something you feel compelled to do or choose to do?

JANUARY 12

FEAR IS THERE

Today's Reading: Psalms 55-60

"When I am afraid, I put my trust in you" - Psalm 56:3.

Notice that David did not write "*if* I am afraid" but rather "*when* I am afraid." Fear is present in your life, but is a master of disguise, often appearing as rational thought. Therefore, you should go on a search-and-destroy mission to identify where it is operating in your life and limiting your performance, not being surprised when you find it. For example, you may be thinking, "I don't have enough time." That may better be stated as "I'm *afraid* I don't have enough time to do that well" or "I'm *afraid* I will fail, so I won't even try." Second Timothy 1:7 says, "For God did not give us a Spirit of fear but of power and love and self-control" (NET). What could you do today if you were not afraid? Are you ready to confront and eradicate your fears today? Ask the Spirit's help so you can uncover fear and replace it with a spirit of boldness.

January 13

Private Worship in a Public Setting

Today's Reading: Psalms 61-65

"I have seen you in the sanctuary and beheld your power and your glory. Because your love is better than life, my lips will glorify you. I will praise you as long as I live, and in your name I will lift up my hands." - Psalm 63:2-4.

David was reflecting on God's love, but he was doing it inside the sanctuary, probably in the Tabernacle of David, a tent where he had placed the ark of the covenant to make it accessible to all the people, not just the priests (see 1 Chronicles 16 and Acts 15:15-18). In that setting, David glorified God with his lips, uttered words of praise, and lifted up his hands. David's example indicates that worship is to be public and corporate - not just private - and that worshippers are to use their mouths, minds and bodies (in this case, hands) as they worship. Where does corporate worship occur in modern times? It takes place in local churches and the writer of Hebrews taught how important local church meetings are for the believer: "[you are] not [to be] giving up meeting together, as some are in the habit of doing, but [rather] encouraging one another—and all the more as you see the Day approaching" (Hebrews 10:26). Are you regularly attending church? When you do, do you involve your whole being, spirit, emotions and body?

JANUARY 14

VOWS TO GOD

Today's reading: Psalms 66-70

***"I will come to your temple with burnt offerings and fulfill my vows to you—vows my lips promised and my mouth spoke when I was in trouble"* - Psalm 66:13-14.**

A pastor once said that God will collect on promises we make in times of war during times of peace. What exactly did he mean? When you are in a tough place, you can say, "God if you get me out of this, I will do such and such" or "If you help me, I will never do this or that again." You cannot see God, however, and you can easily forget those promises when the pressure is removed from your life. When the crisis passes, God may remind you about those promise you made to Him. We read in Acts 18:18 that Paul, "Before he sailed, he had his hair cut off at Cenchreae because of a vow he had taken." Have you made any promises to God on which you have not made good? Have you made a pledge to give to a cause, and then backed out of your commitment? Have you vowed to read or pray more? If so, then today is a good day to ask His forgiveness and to start fulfilling the vows you chose to make.

JANUARY 15

MONEY LOVE

Today's reading: Psalms 71-75

***"But as for me, my feet had almost slipped; I had nearly lost my foothold. For I envied the arrogant when I saw the prosperity of the wicked"* - Psalm 73:2-3.**

It can be difficult to understand why good things happen to seemingly bad people and why they have the resources and opportunities for success that seem to elude you. The psalmist confessed that he had almost succumbed to envy when he beheld what others had. The good news is he did not, and you must not either! Paul wrote about this tendency in 1 Timothy 6:6-10:

> But godliness with contentment is great gain. For we brought nothing into the world, and we can take nothing out of it. But if we have food and clothing, we will be content with that. Those who want to get rich fall into temptation and a trap and into many foolish and harmful desires that plunge people into ruin and destruction. For the love of money is a root of all kinds of evil. Some people, eager for money, have wandered from the faith and pierced themselves with many griefs.

Are you envious of someone who has more than you but seems to be less spiritual? Has the love of money gotten hold of your heart? What can you do to set yourself free?

January 16

Responsible to Teach

Today's reading: Psalms 76-80

"He decreed statutes for Jacob and established the law in Israel,which he commanded our ancestors to teach their children, so the next generation would know them, even the children yet to be born, and they in turn would tell their children" - Psalm 78:5-6.

The Lord established a strategy for how His good news will be spread, and that strategy is simply one generation teaching the next. You have an obligation to teach what you know in some capacity, which may take the form of teaching your children, grandchildren, nieces and nephews, neighborhood or church children, or children in another land through missions work. Your teaching duty may not be restricted to children, however, but may also include adult Sunday School or even teaching encounters through books, broadcasting or online programs that you write and develop. Do you accept your duty and responsibility to teach the next generation? If so, pray this prayer: *Lord, I accept my responsibility to be a teacher in order to pass along Your ways and good news to others, especially those younger than I. Show me how and where I can do this and I will gladly accept the task.*

January 17

Remember the Poor

Today's Reading: Psalms 81-85

"Defend the weak and the fatherless; uphold the cause of the poor and the oppressed. Rescue the weak and the needy; deliver them from the hand of the wicked" - Psalm 82:3-4.

God requires that His people remember the poor through practical acts of kindness, which includes giving alms and special benevolent offerings. Remembering the poor may also involve protecting them from those who would infringe on their rights and take advantage of them. This may require speaking up for those who cannot speak for themselves. When Paul was explaining his call to the Jerusalem elders, he wrote this concerning their response to his explanation: "They agreed that we should go to the Gentiles, and they to the circumcised. All they asked was that we should continue to remember the poor, the very thing I had been eager to do all along" (Galatians 2:9b-10). Are you remembering the poor? Are you eager to do something on their behalf? What more can you do? *Lord, I thank You for the blessings I have, and I want to be a good steward of the opportunities You give me to share what I have with others. Forgive me when I have been insensitive to the needs of others, and give me a heart for the poor and seal my resolve to do more to help them according to Your will. I want to do this, Lord, for those in my own country as well as those in other countries. Allow my gifts to make a difference in the lives of others so they know that You love them. Amen.*

January 18

Your Anointing

Today's reading: Psalms 86-90

"Once you spoke in a vision, to your faithful people you said: 'I have bestowed strength on a warrior; I have raised up a young man from among the people. I have found David my servant; with my sacred oil I have anointed him'" - Psalm 89:19-20.

David was anointed, which means the Spirit was with him to help him do God's will. Jesus was also referred to as the Christ, which means the Anointed One as Luke described: "How God anointed Jesus of Nazareth with the Holy Spirit and power, and how he went around doing good and healing all who were under the power of the devil, because God was with him" (Acts 10:38). You are anointed when you function in your purpose, and your purpose work and anointing are not restricted to church work. They are present in your life wherever God assigns you a task, and that may be at work, in school, in a foreign land or with a particular group of people who have a special need. Where do you sense God's anointing in your life? What are you doing when you sense it? Do you understand that God's anointing may be with you when you are working in what some would call a secular setting?

January 19

God Is Speaking

Today's reading - Psalms 91-95

***"Today, if only you would hear his voice, 'Do not harden your hearts as you did at Meribah, as you did that day at Massah in the wilderness, where your ancestors tested me; they tried me, though they had seen what I did'"* - Psalm 95:7b-9.**

God can speak through others; His Word; the preached Word; a still, small voice; or through circumstances. This passage warns you not to harden your heart whenever and however God is speaking to you. Notice that in today's verses, God is speaking directly through the author to the reader, and the author recognized that he was hearing from the Lord. This passage is then quoted three times in Hebrews 3 and 4 by another author who was speaking on the Lord's behalf. The point is that God is always speaking and "broadcasting" His messages, many times using others to get the message to you. The questions are: Are you listening, what is He saying, and how are you recording it to keep it before you? Be listening today and make sure you stay open and don't harden your heart.

January 20

Give Thanks

Today's reading: Psalms 96-100

"Enter his gates with thanksgiving and his courts with praise; give thanks to him and praise his name" - Psalm 100:4.

It is common to hear those saints who are a bit older thank the Lord for giving them another day. As you get older, you should appreciate life and the grace of God that has gotten you that far. It is a good thing to be mindful that this is God's doing, and to give thanks to the Lord, for it helps you focus on your blessings and the goodness of God in the midst of life's uncertainties. Paul instructed the church in Ephesians 5:20 to "always [be] giving thanks to God the Father for everything, in the name of our Lord Jesus Christ." Do you have an attitude of gratitude? Do you see God in the things of life, and acknowledge His presence and grace? Spend some significant minutes today and every day thanking God for your life and the people and things that are in it.

JANUARY 21

YOUR SELF-TALK

Today's reading: Psalms 101-105

"Praise the Lord, my soul, and forget not all his benefits" - Psalm 103:2.

David had a serious talk with his own soul, directing it to praise God and remember His benefits. Have you noticed that you are in a constant dialog with yourself? This is called self-talk. It is important that when you do something less than perfect, you don't engage your self-talk by saying, "You are stupid" or "You never were any good at that." David suggested what the content of your self talk should focus on God's goodness to you while praising His holy name. One way to guide your inner talk is to have a robust dialog with others according to Revelation 12:11: "They triumphed over him by the blood of the Lamb and by the word of their testimony." Are you sharing with others how good God is to you? Are you rehearsing God's goodness in your mind according to what you have, or do your thoughts focus on what you don't have or how bad things are?

JANUARY 22

HOPE FOR THE FUTURE BY REMEMBERING THE PAST

Today's reading: Psalm 106-110

***"But they soon forgot what he had done and did not wait for his plan to unfold"* - Psalm 106:13-14.**

It can be difficult to wait for God to reveal His will for your life, especially when you don't know what is ahead or how long you have to go on waiting. You can help yourself in the process by remembering God's faithfulness to you in the past, recounting how

He acted previously. If God has never failed you, then chances are He is not about to start now! Doing that should help you as you wait for Him to paint the big picture that reveals where you fit in and what He wants you to do. These words from Isaiah can also help you while you are in God's waiting room: "But those who hope in the Lord will renew their strength. They will soar on wings like eagles; they will run and not grow weary, they will walk and not be faint" (Isaiah 40:31). Hope in the Lord and never lose sight of the fact that He cares for you. *Father, I thank You that you do care for me and You always have. Forgive me when I have doubted Your love and faithfulness. Help me to know how long I should wait and what I should do while I am waiting. Lord, I promise to remember what You have done for me by sharing it with others, and thanking You for Your love on a regular basis.*

January 23

The Fear of the Lord

Today's reading: Psalms 111-115

"The fear of the Lord is the beginning of wisdom; all who follow his precepts have good understanding. To him belongs eternal praise" - Psalm 111:10.

In the midst of the psalms that mostly declare God's praise, this verse in Psalm 111 resembles a verse found in Proverbs: "The fear of the Lord is the beginning of knowledge, but fools despise wisdom and instruction" (Proverbs 1:7). That's because praise and worship, a common theme in Psalms, are based on the fear of the Lord, a common theme in Proverbs. When you worship, you sing, clap, dance, shout, and lift your hands not because you feel like it or it is your preferred mode of worship. You do those things because they please God, acknowledging that He commands them to be performed. Have you given much thought to your demeanor and "body language" when you worship the Lord? When you worship, do you follow your own preferences or God's? Do you know what God's preferences are?

January 24
Expectations

Today's reading: Psalms 116-120

"It is better to take refuge in the Lord than to trust in humans" - Psalm 118:8.

It is inevitable that at times you will disappoint those closest to you and those closest to you will disappoint you. This can happen through a simple daily event, a casual comment, or a serious life matter in which you were counting on another person for support and help but they were unable to deliver according to your expectations. The closer the person is to you, the more painful the disappointment can be. The Apostle Paul knew this kind of pain for he wrote: "You know that everyone in the province of Asia has deserted me, including Phygelus and Hermogenes" (2 Timothy 1:15). Armed with the knowledge of this reality, you are best served if you put high expectations on the Lord who will never desert or betray you. It would also help if you adjust the unrealistic expectations you have of others meeting your needs, realizing that you are just as capable of disappointing them, thus extending grace when they fall short.

January 25
You Live in Him

Today's reading: Psalms 121-125

"The Lord will keep you from all harm—he will watch over your life; the Lord will watch over your coming and going both now and forevermore" - Psalm 121:7-8.

You probably have a story or two that speaks to the truth in today's verses – God will protect and keep you from harm. You may have had a close call or two that caused you to realize God was and is watching over you. Yet even when you know that's true, you may still be afraid of airplanes, heights, water, snakes, spiders, failure, criticism, to go on a foreign trip, or apply for a new job. Even though you know God is in control, fear can still stymie what you want or need to do. Paul preached to the Athenians, saying, "For in him we live and move and have our being" (Acts 17:28a). That means your life is like an aquarium; you are the fish and the water is the presence of God. Are you swimming freely or huddled in the corner of your tank, afraid to move out? Where has fear limited your ability to exercise faith and take action before you have all the information of how everything will work out?

January 26

Mourning Joy

Today's reading: Psalms 126-130

"Those who sow with tears will reap with songs of joy. Those who go out weeping, carrying seed to sow, will return with songs of joy, carrying sheaves with them" - Psalm 126:5-6.

What is the Lord telling you through today's verses? Your tears can lead to a harvest of joy. Jesus made a similar statement in Matthew 5:4: "Blessed are those who mourn, for they will be comforted." Why should you mourn? You can start with your own sinfulness. Then move on to mourn the injustice in the world, the persecuted church, the opportunities that are lost due to greed, disunity in the church, and the lost who don't know Christ. God does not want you to stay in a state of mourning, however, for your tears lead you to recognize that God wants you to play a role in addressing that need over which you mourn. When you realize that God has something for you to do, your will see that your tears were actually seeds that have led to a harvest. Then you will sing songs of joy and bear much fruit as you find and fulfill your God-given purpose that is designed to address those things over which you have wept.

January 27
Reconciliation

Today's reading: Psalms 131-135

"How good and pleasant it is when God's people live together in unity!" - Psalm 133:1.

There is spiritual power in harmony and reconciliation, which is why the devil, our great enemy, stirs up so much animosity, hatred and misunderstanding. You cannot control how someone else thinks or acts, but you can work on your own heart and mind as God gives you grace to do. Your job, therefore, is to make sure that none of those negative attitudes creep into any of your relationships. Where those already function, you must confront and repent from them, as Jesus directed you to do: "Therefore, if you are offering your gift at the altar and there remember that your brother or sister has something against you, leave your gift there in front of the altar. First go and be reconciled to them; then come and offer your gift" (Matthew 5:23-24). Is there anything you can do today to be reconciled with anyone from whom you are estranged?

January 28
Humility

Today's reading - Psalm 136-140

"Though the Lord is exalted, he looks kindly on the lowly; though lofty, he sees them from afar" - Psalm 138:6.

Another word for lowly is humble, and the opposite of humility is pride. Both those traits attract God's immediate attention, for He helps the humble and opposes the proud. Mary understood this truth when she praised God during her visit to her cousin Elizabeth: "He has brought down rulers from their thrones but has lifted up the humble. He has filled the hungry with good things but has sent the rich away empty" (Luke 1:52-53). The implications for you from what Mary said are clear: humble yourself and be God's friend, or be proud and risk having God humble or even humiliate you. The choice is obvious but not always easy to do. Where do you need to humble yourself, even if you believe you are right and others are wrong?

January 29

Guidance

Today's reading 141-145

"Teach me to do your will, for you are my God; may your good Spirit lead me on level ground" - Psalm 143:10.

In this psalm, David was asking God's help as he carried out his dual roles of teacher and leader in the power of the Spirit. David acknowledged that he needed the Spirit's help to do God's will, and prayed the words in today's prayer on his own behalf. Centuries later, Jesus described the Spirit's role in your life in John 16:13: "But when he, the Spirit of truth, comes, he will guide you into all the truth. He will not speak on his own; he will speak only what he hears, and he will tell you what is yet to come." Are you praying for yourself? Are you asking in faith that God will guide you, and then trusting that He is answering your prayer?

January 30

The Church

Today's reading Psalms 146-150

"For the Lord takes delight in his people; he crowns the humble with victory" - Psalm 149:4.

Some people interpret the "people" in this verse to mean individuals like you and me. Yet the context is not singular but plural. God delights in His people and those people today are His church. which Jesus paid to establish with His life. John saw the church and described it in Revelation 21:2: "I saw the Holy City, the new Jerusalem, coming down out of heaven from God, prepared as a bride beautifully dressed for her husband." This begs the questions: Are you involved in a local church? Are you utilizing your gifts to help edify her people and reach new converts? While you are special to God as an individual, the corporate church is where God's heart is, and you need to be involved in what matters to God.

January 31

Word Change

Today's reading - Psalm 119

"Turn my heart toward your statutes and not toward selfish gain" - Psalm 119:36.

Your heart is inclined toward evil, but that tendency can be reversed. God is able to change hearts including yours, but you must want the transformation to take place. It starts when you see the need for change, then in faith you ask God to change you. After that, you confront your own proclivity for self-interest by studying God's word, all the while praying for your heart to stay focused on Him. Study of God's word is important for reasons explained by the writer of Hebrews:

> For the word of God is alive and active. Sharper than any double-edged sword, it penetrates even to dividing soul and spirit, joints and marrow; it judges the thoughts and attitudes of the heart. Nothing in all creation is hidden from God's sight. Everything is uncovered and laid bare before the eyes of him to whom we must give account (4:12-13).

Are you willing to put in the time and effort necessary so that God's word can change your heart?

February 1
Critics

Today's reading: Psalms 1-5

"Lord, how many are my foes! How many rise up against me! Many are saying of me, 'God will not deliver him'" - Psalm 3:1-2.

It can be unnerving when you have enemies who criticize or even persecute you because of your stand for the Lord and His righteous standard. Yet you should be more surprised and concerned if you *don't* have enemies based on what Jesus said: "Woe to you when everyone speaks well of you, for that is how their ancestors treated the false prophets" (Luke 6:26). While you should not go out of your way to attract critics, you should not back off or back down from any stance for the Lord just because some people are upset because of it. Are you shying away from any bold public stand for Christ because you fear what others may say or are saying about you? Are you hesitant to be who God created you to be because of fear? What changes do you propose that will take you out of this fear groove?

February 2
When God Delays

Today's reading: Psalms 6-10

"But God will never forget the needy; the hope of the afflicted will never perish" - Psalm 9:18.

It may seem like God has forgotten you, but He never has and never will. He will delay in responding, however, because there are lessons He wants to teach you. What's more, God will manifest the validity of the work He has done in you by delaying so He can reveal to principalities and powers that you are obedient in the midst of trials. The Lord described this process in Deuteronomy 8:3-5:

> He humbled you, causing you to hunger and then feeding you with manna, which neither you nor your ancestors had known, to teach you that man does not live on bread alone but on every word that comes from the mouth of the Lord. Your clothes did not wear out and your feet did not swell during these forty years. Know then in your heart that as a man disciplines his son, so the Lord your God disciplines you.

Is God humbling you and how are you responding to this season in your life?

February 3

Blessings Inventory

Today's reading: Psalms 11-15

"But I trust in your unfailing love; my heart rejoices in your salvation. I will sing the Lord's praise, for he has been good to me" - Psalm 13:5-6.

There are three verbs in today's passage: *trust, rejoice,* and *sing.* The context for those three verbs to function is God's goodness, love and salvation He has extended to the psalmist. You also have a track record with the Lord, who has extended the same blessings to you as He did to David. Are you responding with the same actions? Are you trusting? How do you know you are? Are you rejoicing or bogged down in the worries of life? Are you singing, or is your gratitude strictly internal, with no outward expressions of praise? Take some time today to inventory the ways the Lord has blessed you, and then respond in faith with joy and singing! *Lord, once again You remind me that I must be mindful of Your presence in my life and of the good gifts Your presence has bestowed upon me. That includes salvation, forgiveness of sins, being made holy, my spiritual gifts and Your ongoing love and care. Help me live with a greater awareness of Your presence in my life, and I vow to praise you for Your goodness and mercy.*

February 4
Spiritual War

Today's reading: Psalms 16-20

"He trains my hands for battle; my arms can bend a bow of bronze" - Psalm 18:34.

When you become a believer, you inherit many wonderful promises that God stands behind to fulfill. You also inherit a place in God's army, which means that spiritual warfare becomes a way of life, for often you must do battle against God's enemy (who has also become yours) to realize the fulfillment of God's promises. You cannot be passive in this war, but you must aggressively do what Paul wrote about in 2 Corinthians 10:3-6:

> For though we live in the world, we do not wage war as the world does. The weapons we fight with are not the weapons of the world. On the contrary, they have divine power to demolish strongholds. We demolish arguments and every pretension that sets itself up against the knowledge of God, and we take captive every thought to make it obedient to Christ. And we will be ready to punish every act of disobedience, once your obedience is complete.

How is this war playing out in your life right now and are you an active or passive combatant?

February 5
God Pleaser

Today's reading: Psalms 21-25

"In you, Lord my God, I put my trust" - Psalm 25:1.

Perhaps you are familiar with Hebrews 11:6, which states, "And without faith it is impossible to please God, because anyone who comes to him must believe that he exists and that he rewards those who earnestly seek him." If without faith, it's impossible to please God, then with faith it's *possible* to please Him. You can bring joy and pleasure to God's heart when you cease from striving to manage your life in your own efforts, and relax, putting your trust in Him - for career, finances, relationships and ministry. Where are you trying too hard in your own efforts? Where do you need to stop and make a conscious and once-and-for-all decision to trust God? Whenever you do that, rest assured that you have pleased God! *Lord, those are not just words, for I do indeed put my trust in You. Help me to learn new levels of trust as I serve and follow You. Remind me when I take the reins of my life away from You, and forgive me when I am afraid and try to take matters into my own hands.*

February 6

Fickle Feelings

Today's reading: Psalm 26-30

"When I felt secure, I said, 'I will never be shaken.' Lord, when you favored me, you made my royal mountain stand firm; but when you hid your face, I was dismayed" - Psalm 30:5-6.

It is easy to be optimistic and make commitments when things are going well, but difficult to keep those commitments when things are not going so well. When you have money, you can pledge your unfailing generosity, but you will be tested on that vow when money is tight. What's more, you can determine what season you are in by how you feel without remembering that feelings can change, and therefore need to put your trust in the Lord regardless of how you feel. In fact, the *less* you feel, the *more* you should trust and rely on your values and previously-made vows to direct your behavior. Where are you too dependent on your feelings to direct your behavior, thereby subjecting yourself and others to your high "high" and low "lows"? Where do you need to be more consistent in your attitudes and behavior?

FEBRUARY 7

TROUBLES

Today's reading: Psalms 31-35

"The righteous person may have many troubles, but the Lord delivers him from them all; he protects all his bones, not one of them will be broken" - Psalm 34:19-20.

When I first met the Lord, I held a strange assumption about my new life in Christ: "I will never again have a flat tire!" Somehow, I thought I was exempt from car trouble because of my faith in Jesus. Needless to say, I have had a lot of car trouble since then along with troubles in many other areas of life. God has used those troubles to teach me about His love and ability to deliver me from my troubles, while teaching me trust, patience and empathy for others who are going through troubles. Are you surprised by your troubles? Do you see the role they play in your walk with the Lord? Perhaps Paul's words will help you as you endure difficult times: "Then they returned to Lystra, Iconium and Antioch, strengthening the disciples and encouraging them to remain true to the faith. 'We must go through many hardships to enter the kingdom of God'" (Acts 14:21b-22).

FEBRUARY 8

URGENCY

Today's reading: Psalms 36-40

"Show me, Lord, my life's end and the number of my days; let me know how fleeting my life is. You have made my days a mere handbreadth; the span of my years is as nothing before you. Everyone is but a breath, even those who seem secure" - Psalm 39:4-5.

As I write, I am almost 66 years of age. I am asking, "Where have the years gone?" I am not complaining, for I have lived a rich, full life, but of course I hope I have many years remaining. Today, however, may be my last day, for I am not guaranteed anything beyond this very minute. With that in mind and while looking at today's passage, I want to make the most of every day I have left, doing what is in my heart to do and being as productive as possible. Is that your attitude? Are you putting off doing things in your heart, acting like you have ten, twenty or thirty years more? If you knew that you had two years to live, what would you be doing? You must act with that kind of urgency every day if you are going to make your mark and leave a legacy for others to follow and remember.

February 9

Rumors

Today's reading: Psalms 41-45

"All my enemies whisper together against me; they imagine the worst for me, saying, 'A vile disease has afflicted him; he will never get up from the place where he lies'"
- Psalm 41:7-8.

David reported how his enemies had concocted rumors that encouraged them in their vicious attempts to destroy his reputation and life. Those rumors served to diminish David's stature and importance in their minds so they could justify their persecution and ensure their probability of victory. Rumors are a way of life and unfortunately are sometimes the most effective and efficient way of communicating, even when they contain half-truths and lies. Your role should be two-fold: Don't receive and pass on rumors with information that is hearsay and cannot be substantiated. And don't manufacture rumors, especially those that contain gossip and innuendo that can destroy or reduce people's esteem or stature in the minds of others. Remember what Paul wrote: "Therefore each of you must put off falsehood and speak truthfully to your neighbor, for we are all members of one body" (Ephesians 4:25). Are you a source of rumors, either to manufacture or disseminate them? What changes do you need to make to stop that habit?

February 10

Self-Righteousness

Today's reading: Psalms 46-50

"I have no need of a bull from your stall or of goats from your pens, for every animal of the forest is mine, and the cattle on a thousand hills" - Psalm 50:9-10.

The Lord was speaking in today's passage, confronting Israel's attitude that they were doing Him a favor when they offered sacrifices, as if God needed them. The Lord reminded them that He already owned what they were giving Him, and that He really wanted their love and heart, not their external rituals. God does not need your music, money, Sabbath rest or presence in church. He does not require your prayers or fasting. Are you like the Pharisee who came into God's presence and said, "The Pharisee stood by himself and prayed: 'God, I thank you that I am not like other people—robbers, evildoers, adulterers—or even like this tax collector. I fast twice a week and give a tenth of all I get'" (Luke 18:11-12)? If so, then you need to repent of your self-righteous attitude and learn to humbly serve the Lord, which is for your own benefit and not for God's.

February 11

Fruit

Today's reading: Psalm 51-55

"But I am like an olive tree flourishing in the house of God; I trust in God's unfailing love for ever and ever" - Psalm 52:8.

An olive tree produces a lot of olives and does so for many years. There are some olive trees at the Church of All Nations in Jerusalem that are 2,000 years old and would have been there the night Jesus prayed and sweat blood. David wrote that he was like one of those olive trees and his nourishment came from God's presence. God doesn't only want you to be a "nice" person; He also wants you to be a nice, fruitful person, just like an olive tree. Jesus said, "You did not choose me, but I chose you and appointed you so that you might go and bear fruit—fruit that will last—and so that whatever you ask in my name the Father will give you" (John 15:16). What is your fruit? What are you producing as a result of your relationship with and faith in the Lord? What do you do that when you do it, you sense God helping you produce results? How and when can you do more of that activity?

February 12
Teaching Trials

Today's reading: Psalms 56-60

"You are my strength, I watch for you; you, God, are my fortress, my God on whom I can rely" - Psalm 59:9-10.

If you haven't noticed by now, Psalms is filled with cries for help and declarations of trust because David and his people were often in serious trouble. Sometimes the trouble was their own fault and other times it was unjust persecution from their enemies. Regardless of the reason, David learned to call out to God, which is in part why the trouble came - his trials taught David to trust in the Lord. It's important that you learn to watch for, trust in and rely on the Lord just like David did as you encounter your own struggles. Later, David's son Solomon would write the words by which many have chosen to live: "Trust in the Lord with all your heart and lean not on your own understanding; in all your ways submit to him, and he will make your paths straight" (Proverbs

3:4-6). Are you relying on your own strength or God's help in your various trials of life?

February 13
Greed

Today's reading: Psalms 61-65

"Do not trust in extortion or put vain hope in stolen goods; though your riches increase, do not set your heart on them" - Psalm 62:10.

In a world where some have unprecedented wealth, it is difficult not to focus on getting money. The "have-nots" see what others have and can be envious or set their sights on getting a piece of the good life. Most ethical failures in business are based on the desire to get more money. The Apostle Paul clarified the problem when he wrote to the Ephesians: "For of this you can be sure: No immoral, impure or *greedy* person—such a person is an *idolater*—has any inheritance in the kingdom of Christ and of God" (Ephesians 5:5 emphasis added). The desire for more money stems from greed, which is a form of idolatry. Simply put, some people worship money! What are you doing to keep greed from sprouting, taking root and bearing fruit in your heart?

February 14
Priorities

Today's reading: Psalms 66-70

"A father to the fatherless, a defender of widows, Is God in his holy dwelling. God sets the lonely in families, he leads out the prisoners with singing; but the rebellious live in a sun-scorched land" - Psalm 68:5-6.

This passage tells you a lot about God's values and priorities.

Even though He dwells in holiness, He is intimately involved in the lives of His people. What does today's passage tell you that God does? He cares for widows and orphans. God places the lonely in family settings. He leads those in captivity to freedom from addictions, debt or any other enslaving habit. Yet if people stubbornly insist on doing their own thing in their own way, He leaves them alone. The implications for you are two-fold. If you are lonely, God has a new family for you - if you are willing to have those blessings. If not and you prefer to sulk in self-pity, He will leave you be. Then also, if God is interested in helping the lonely, will you allow Him to use you to help them by opening your home and heart? Can you make God's priorities your priorities?

February 15

The Needy

Today's reading: Psalm 71-75

"He will take pity on the weak and the needy and save the needy from death. He will rescue them from oppression and violence, for precious is their blood in his sight"
- Psalm 72:13-14.

God is full of compassion for the weak and downtrodden. If God is going to help them, however, He must use you and me to do so. That means we must have the same compassion and pity, and take action on God's behalf. You cannot expect or wait for God to use someone else, especially if you notice the plight of the needy, for that is another sign that God wants you to be involved. (It's difficult to accept, but some *cannot* see it like you do and therefore will not act.) The wisdom writer taught, "Whoever oppresses the poor shows contempt for their Maker, but whoever is kind to the needy honors God" (Proverbs 14:31). Where can you show kindness to the weak and needy? How can you get involved in justice and mercy issues in your country or another?

February 16
Teaching Kids

Today's reading: Psalms 76-80

***"My people, hear my teaching; listen to the words of my mouth. I will open my mouth with a parable; I will utter hidden things, things from of old—things we have heard and known, things our ancestors have told us"* - Psalm 78:1-3.**

Every one of us is to be involved in teaching the next generation, imparting to them the values, attitudes and behaviors consistent with the life of a believer. That teaching may be face-to-face classroom, but it can also occur through social media, broadcasting, or writing and publishing teaching material. With the fragmentation of the modern family, it is more important than ever that you find some role to play in imparting truth to the next generation, remembering the verse in Proverbs; "Train up a child in the way he should go, even when he is old he will not depart from it" (22:6 NASB). Do you see that you have an obligation to teach and train? What are you doing? What more can you do? Can you support others who are teaching?

February 17
Purpose Pilgrim

Today's reading: Psalms 81-85

***"Blessed are those whose strength is in you, whose hearts are set on pilgrimage"* - Psalm 84:5.**

This verse reminds you that God is your strength. To be more specific, the joy of the Lord is your strength. If you don't have God's joy, therefore, you don't have God's strength. The only substitute for God's strength is your own, and that of course is a poor replacement. Remembering what Nehemiah said, "Do not grieve, for the joy of the Lord is your strength" (Nehemiah

8:10b), examine yourself to see if you have God's joy. If not, it may mean you are not functioning in your life purpose. Notice that this verse reminds you that you must set your heart like you were on a pilgrimage, for purpose is a pursuit and not a destination. Are you prepared to seek God and His purpose today and for the rest of your days? What implications do you think this will have for your life, work, and family? *Lord, I want and need your joy, for I am tired of operating in my own strength, which is so limited. I am sometimes afraid of my own joy, and don't really trust that You are using it to guide me into Your will. I accept that I am a pilgrim on a journey to find Your will for my life. I trust that You will reveal it to me. Amen!*

FEBRUARY 18

ATTACK OF THE ENEMY

Today's reading: Psalms 86-90

"The enemy will not get the better of him; the wicked will not oppress him" - Psalm 89:22.

You can read today's verse and easily misinterpret what it actually says. You may think the enemy will never try to get the better of you or oppress you. That would be incorrect. The enemy will try and try, and sometimes seem like he has the upper hand, but ultimately God will have the victory in and through you. It is important to understand this because when you come under heavy attack, you may think, "I did something wrong" or "God has failed" or "God doesn't love me." This truth is also present in Isaiah 54:17: "'No weapon forged against you will prevail, and you will refute every tongue that accuses you. This is the heritage of the servants of the Lord, and this is their vindication from me,' declares the Lord." Have weapons been formed against you? Have tongues accused you? Are you clear that God will keep them from prevailing, not keep them from trying to prevail?

February 19

Fruitfulness

Today's reading: Psalms 91-95

"The righteous will flourish like a palm tree, they will grow like a cedar of Lebanon; planted in the house of the Lord, they will flourish in the courts of our God" - Psalm 92:12-13.

Flourish is used twice in this passage and its definition is "to achieve success, to be in a state of activity or production." Palm trees grow well in hot climates, with moderate to little rainfall. Yet they grow to stately heights and some produce dates and coconuts. This palm tree simile is one that should describe your life as you walk with the Lord in His "house" and "courts." Jesus described this process with these words: "I am the vine; you are the branches. If you remain in me and I in you, you will bear much fruit; apart from me you can do nothing" (John 15:5). What tangible fruit are you producing in your life as part of the vine? Is your fruit only internal or is it external also? What can you do to produce even more fruit?

February 20

Justice for the Poor

Today's reading: Psalms 96-100

"The King is mighty, he loves justice—you have established equity; in Jacob you have done what is just and right" - Psalm 99:4.

God values justice and desires that His people and especially His leadership be committed to establish and administer justice without bias or prejudice. In the New Testament, James, the brother of Jesus, wrote about one form of injustice: bias against the poor. Here is what he wrote:

My brothers and sisters, believers in our glorious Lord

> Jesus Christ must not show favoritism. Suppose a man comes into your meeting wearing a gold ring and fine clothes, and a poor man in filthy old clothes also comes in. If you show special attention to the man wearing fine clothes and say, "Here's a good seat for you," but say to the poor man, "You stand there" or "Sit on the floor by my feet," have you not discriminated among yourselves and become judges with evil thoughts?
>
> Listen, my dear brothers and sisters: Has not God chosen those who are poor in the eyes of the world to be rich in faith and to inherit the kingdom he promised those who love him? But you have dishonored the poor. Is it not the rich who are exploiting you? Are they not the ones who are dragging you into court? Are they not the ones who are blaspheming the noble name of him to whom you belong? (James 2:1-7).

Are you doing what you can to further justice in your world, whether it be in your family, ministry or occupation? Is there anything else you can do or be involved in to help the poor?

February 21

Praise Party

Today's reading: Psalms 101-105

"Praise the Lord, my soul, and forget not all his benefits— who forgives all your sins and heals all your diseases, who redeems your life from the pit and crowns you with love and compassion, who satisfies your desires with good things so that your youth is renewed like the eagle's" - Psalm 103:2-5.

In this psalm, David once again engaged in something called self-talk: he conversed with himself to keep his soul encouraged and focused. He was not giving himself a pep talk, but rather having a conversation outlining all God's goodness toward David. Here is a list of all the things that God had done for David; forgiven, healed, redeemed, crowned, satisfied, and renewed. David then ordered his soul to praise the Lord in response to God's many blessings. How many of those things has God also done for you? Do you praise Him for His benefits, or are you bogged down in your circumstances that are less than ideal? Remember what Paul wrote in Philippians 4:6 and then overcome your anxiety with a praise party every day: "Do not be anxious about anything, but in every situation, by prayer and petition, with thanksgiving, present your requests to God."

February 22

Tell Your Story

Today's reading: Psalms 106-110

"Let the redeemed of the Lord tell their story—those he redeemed from the hand of the foe, those he gathered from the lands, from east and west, from north and south" - Psalm 107:2-3.

The playwright Oscar Wilde once said, "Every saint has a past, every sinner has a future." You have a past, a story of how God found you, healed you and how He is using you. You also have a story of your failures and how God worked good in and through them. You have a story today that is still being written, with chapters yet to be developed and a conclusion yet to be penned. Are you willing to tell this story? If the answer is "yes," then how can you tell it? Does God want you to write a book? Make a movie? Give your testimony in person or through some other media? Are you hesitant to do this, not wanting to draw attention to yourself? If you don't produce it (whatever the "it" is for you to produce), it will deprive people of the encouragement and consolation only your story can provide. *Lord, today's entry describes me. I have been hesitant to draw attention to myself, yet if You don't use me, then who will You use to do Your will? I have a story and a purpose that You want me to share with others. I surrender to Your plan, even if that means I will be "front and center" in the minds of other people. I gave You my life. Now use it as You see fit!*

February 23
Idolatry

Today's reading: Psalms 111-115

"But their idols are silver and gold, made by human hands. They have mouths, but cannot speak, eyes, but cannot see. They have ears, but cannot hear, noses, but cannot smell" - Psalm 115:4-6.

Idolatry is a dehumanizing experience. It causes the worshiper to take on the traits of the object of worship. In today's passage, those traits would be loss of the ability to communicate effectively, or to see or hear accurately - especially spiritual things. The tendency we have was described by a theologian when he said: "The human heart is a factory of idols," so the idol doesn't have to be statue to which we bow down. Paul expanded our understanding of idolatry when he wrote: "Put to death, therefore, whatever belongs to your earthly nature: sexual immorality, impurity, lust, evil desires and greed, which is idolatry" (Colossians 3:5). Ask the Lord today to show you your heart to see if idolatry has crept in to rob you of your spiritual awareness. If it has, don't deny it but repent and allow God to restore you.

February 24
Dealing with Fear

Today's reading: Psalms 116-120

"The cords of death entangled me, the anguish of the grave came over me; I was overcome by distress and sorrow. Then I called on the name of the Lord: 'Lord, save me!'" - Psalm 116:3-4.

The psalmist was in life-threatening trouble and he has no where to turn but to the Lord. He was in emotional distress and was almost overwhelmed. The good news is that he cried out for help and God heard and saved his life. The Apostle Paul encountered his own harrowing experience when he was sailing to Rome to stand trial. An awful storm arose and threatened the ship and the lives of all onboard. Here is part of the story:

> Last night an angel of the God to whom I belong and whom I serve stood beside me and said, "Do not be afraid, Paul. You must stand trial before Caesar; and God has graciously given you the lives of all who sail with you." So keep up your courage, men, for I have faith in God that it will happen just as he told me. Nevertheless, we must run aground on some island (Acts 27:23-26).

The fact that the angel told Paul not to be afraid indicates what Paul was indeed afraid. Once the word of the Lord came to him, however, Paul relied on the word and no longer focused on the storm. Are you in a storm? Where is your focus? Do you see that God has given you an opportunity to trust Him and to apply the lessons from Paul and David to your own life?

February 25

Mercy Focus

Today's reading: Psalms 121-125

"I lift up my eyes to you, to you who sit enthroned in heaven. As the eyes of slaves look to the hand of their master, as the eyes of a female slave look to the hand of her mistress, so our eyes look to the Lord our God, till he shows us his mercy" - Psalm 123:1-2.

Today's passage is from the psalms of ascents, those psalms that pilgrims sang or recited as they made their way up to Jerusalem for one of the many religious festivals. The topic of this psalm is focus, for the pilgrims were not focusing on the danger, inconvenience, or rigors of travel, but rather on their time with the Lord during their journey. Your focus should be the same, even though there are many other entities vying for your heart and attention, things like your career, health, church and family.

While you need many things from the Lord, you need mercy on a daily basis and one way to get that mercy is to give it, as Jesus taught: "Blessed are the merciful, for they will be shown mercy" (Matthew 5:7). Where is your focus these days? Do you see your need for mercy? Are you extending mercy?

February 26

Fruit of Your Labor

Today's reading: Psalms 126-130

"Blessed are all who fear the Lord, who walk in obedience to him. You will eat the fruit of your labor; blessings and prosperity will be yours" - Psalm 128:1-2.

The psalmist stated that there is a reward for all those who fear and obey the Lord. Those who fear Him are blessed, but God also enables them to eat the fruit of their labor, as well as enjoy blessings and prosperity. The wisdom writer later wrote about blessings and prosperity: "A person can do nothing better than to eat and drink and find satisfaction in their own toil. This too, I see, is from the hand of God, for without him, who can eat or find enjoyment? To the person who pleases him, God gives wisdom, knowledge and happiness" (Ecclesiastes 2:24-26a). If that's true, and of course God's word is true, then you must ask yourself whether or not you are eating the fruit of your labor. If not, why not? Are you enjoying abundance? If not, then is there some crack in your foundation of fearing and obeying the Lord?

February 27

Anointed Work

Today's reading: Psalms 131-135

"For the sake of your servant David, do not reject your anointed one" - Psalm 132:10.

When someone was anointed in the Old Testament, they were marked with oil to indicate that God was with them to perform some special role or task. Today, anointing tends to be restricted in people's minds to church work, but you are anointed to do whatever God is with you to do, which is your life purpose. Isaiah described Cyrus, a heathen king, in the following manner: "This is what the Lord says to his *anointed*, to Cyrus, whose right hand I take hold of to subdue nations before him and to strip kings of their armor, to open doors before him so that gates will not be shut" (Isaiah 45:1 emphasis added). What are you anointed to do? What activity or role do you perform when you sense God is with you in a special way? If you are not sure, then pay attention and allow God to show you!

FEBRUARY 28

THE SPIRIT'S ROLE

Today's reading: Psalms 136-140

"How precious to me are your thoughts, God! How vast is the sum of them! Were I to count them, they would outnumber the grains of sand—when I awake, I am still with you" - Psalm 139:17-18.

God wants to reveal Himself to you but you need help to see and understand. God reveals His thoughts in His word through the illumination of the Holy Spirit, and Jesus explained how this would take place in John 16:13: "But when he, the Spirit of truth, comes, he will *guide* you into all the truth. He will not *speak* on his own; he will speak only what he hears, and he will *tell you what is yet to come*" (emphasis added). First, the Spirit will come and dwell within you. Second, the Spirit will guide you, never drive or overwhelm you. Third, He will speak to you personally and in a way you can comprehend. Fourth, the Spirit will impart God's thoughts that you need for your future development and direction. Is the Spirit revealing more of God's truth to you? If not, what are you doing to block that process? Are you spending enough time in God's word?

FEBRUARY 29

HONESTY WITH GOD

Today's reading: Psalms 141-145

"I cry aloud to the Lord; I lift up my voice to the Lord for mercy. I pour out before him my complaint; before him I tell my trouble" - Psalm 142:1-2.

You may think that you cannot be honest with the Lord or that there are certain things you cannot say to Him. Think about that for a minute. If He knows your thoughts from afar and knows your words before you speak them, then if He were going to punish you, He would do so *before* you ever say anything! Therefore, honesty with God is not for anyone's benefit but your own, to reveal your inner reality to you so God can change you. Furthermore, when you are honest with God, He will be honest with you and that is the ultimate goal - not just you venting your feelings, but for God to share His flawless perspective. This is exactly what happened in Job's situation: "Then the Lord spoke to Job out of the storm. He said: 'Who is this that obscures my plans with words without knowledge? Brace yourself like a man; I will question you, and you shall answer me'" (Job 38:1-3). Are you holding back or being honest with God? Do you need to have a conversation with Him today that starts with you talking but ends with you listening?

MARCH 1

GRACE OR WORKS?

Today's reading: Psalms 1-5

"Surely, Lord, you bless the righteous; you surround them with your favor as with a shield" - Psalm 5:12.

God's favor can also be labeled God's grace. What God does, He does because He is motivated by His character of love. When you try to earn what only God can give, you try to establish that God owes you something in response to your labors. Unfortunately, God never owes you anything. When you do good works, you do them in response to God's grace, never to earn it. Paul wrote about good works in Ephesians 2:10: "For we are God's handiwork, created in Christ Jesus to do good works, which God prepared in advance for us to do." Do you have a grace or a works mentality? Do you give or perform acts of charity expecting to get something in return, or do you do them out of the riches of the grace that is already bestowed on you?

March 2

God's Cause

Today's reading: Psalms 6-10

"You, Lord, hear the desire of the afflicted; you encourage them, and you listen to their cry, defending the fatherless and the oppressed, so that mere earthly mortals will never again strike terror" - Psalm 10:17-18.

God cares for the orphan and those in trouble, yet those are the very people who are often victimized by society through unjust laws and economic practices. It seems that God takes it personally when they are oppressed and deals directly with the oppressors so they will "never again strike terror." It makes sense that if God values the orphan and the weak, then you should value them as well. Proverbs 22:9 states, "The generous will themselves be blessed, for they share their food with the poor." Are you sharing your food with the poor? What more can you do to take up their cause, thereby pleasing God? If you are a leader, is your organization sensitive to the needs of the poor?

March 3

Discouragement

Today's reading: Psalms 11-15

"Help, Lord, for no one is faithful anymore; those who are loyal have vanished from the human race" - Psalm 12:1.

David was discouraged as he wrote this psalm and uttered a statement that only fed his discouragement. He proclaimed that only he was faithful, and that everyone else was a group of disloyal malcontents. Discouragement causes you to distort reality and leads to a downward spiral from which it is difficult to escape. Elijah also manifested this kind of discouraging talk when he said, "I have been very zealous for the Lord God Almighty. The Israelites have rejected your covenant, torn down your altars, and put your prophets to death with the sword. I am the only one left, and now they are trying to kill me too" (1 Kings 19:14). The Lord assured Elijah he was not the only one, and that there were 7,000 other faithful people in the land in addition to Elijah. Are you discouraged? To whom can you go or what can do that will help you break your discouragement cycle? What is your self talk like? Is it feeding or curtailing your discouragement?

March 4

Vindication

Today's reading: Psalms 16-20

"Hear me, Lord, my plea is just; listen to my cry. Hear my prayer—it does not rise from deceitful lips. Let my vindication come from you; may your eyes see what is right" - Psalm 17:1-2.

David was in trouble so he prayed to the Lord and then wrote down his prayer. He was looking for vindication, which is the process by which people who saw him in a negative light would eventually see that they were wrong. Rather than try to achieve his own vindication, however, David prayed that God would look and judge his situation and then provide vindication on his behalf. In other words, David decided to trust the Lord for his reputation. Jesus did the same thing according to Peter's account:

> To this you were called, because Christ suffered for you, leaving you an example, that you should follow in his steps. 'He committed no sin, and no deceit was found in his mouth.' When they hurled their insults at him, he did not retaliate; when he suffered, he made no threats. Instead, he entrusted himself to him who judges justly (1 Peter 2:21-23).

Are you trying to achieve your own vindication where you have been wrongly accused? Can you let it go and trust the Lord for your reputation today?

March 5

God's Blessing

Today's reading: Psalms 21-25

"You prepare a table before me in the presence of my enemies. You anoint my head with oil; my cup overflows" - Psalm 23:5.

God will bless you, but He won't always isolate you when He does. He will bless you in full view of those who opposed, persecuted and criticized you. What's more, your anointing will also be in their presence, similar to how it was with Daniel. God blessed Daniel, but it was in Babylon, far away from his home and culture. We read in Daniel 1:18-20,

> At the end of the time set by the king to bring them into his service, the chief official presented them to Nebuchadnezzar. The king talked with them, and he found none equal to Daniel, Hananiah, Mishael and

> Azariah; so they entered the king's service. In every matter of wisdom and understanding about which the king questioned them, he found them ten times better than all the magicians and enchanters in his whole kingdom.

Are you willing to have God use you in your own Babylon, wherever that may be? Are you willing to have your anointing devoted to bless and help those who may not be part of God's people?

March 6

Your Comforter

Today's reading: Psalms 26-30

"You turned my wailing into dancing; you removed my sackcloth and clothed me with joy, that my heart may sing your praises and not be silent. Lord my God, I will praise you forever" - Psalm 30:11-12.

God is your Comforter. When you are in pain, He will provide solace and encouragement. When you are wounded, He will heal you. If you never know wailing and times of darkness, however, you will never know Him as your Comforter. Yet you can take matters into your own hands and try to comfort yourself through any number of self-medicating actions: addictions like shopping and eating, relationships that you know are not good for you, attitudes like self-pity and anger that make you feel that life and the Lord are not fair. Peter wrote in his epistle,

> Dear friends, do not be surprised at the fiery ordeal that has come on you to test you, as though something strange were happening to you. But rejoice inasmuch as you participate in the sufferings of Christ, so that you may be overjoyed when his glory is revealed (1 Peter 4:12-13).

Are you suffering? Are you trying to make yourself feel better or are you trusting that God will do that for you, giving you joy in spite of your circumstances?

March 7

Injustice

Today's reading: Psalms 31-35

"For the word of the Lord is right and true; he is faithful in all he does. The Lord loves righteousness and justice; the earth is full of his unfailing love" - Psalm 33:4-5.

There are many who ask, "Where is God?" when they behold evil in the earth. Today's passage answers the question: He is right here! The earth is full of His unfailing love, for as bad as it seems, it would be much worse if God did not hold back the tide of evil. When Job and his friends questioned where God was in Job's situation, the Lord rebuked them and said:

> Who is this that obscures my plans with words without knowledge? Brace yourself like a man; I will question you, and you shall answer me. "Where were you when I laid the earth's foundation? Tell me, if you understand. Who marked off its dimensions? Surely you know! Who stretched a measuring line across it? On what were its footings set, or who laid its cornerstone—while the morning stars sang together and all the angels shouted for joy?" (Job 38:2-7).

Do you ever question of God's goodness in the midst of inequities? Do you see God's greatness even in the midst of sorrow and suffering? If you have, are you prepared to help correct what you see rather than insinuating that somehow God is to blame? *Lord, forgive me, for I have questioned You and Your motives in the midst of the injustices I have seen. Give me Your perspective of the situation, and then show me how I can get involved to be Your agent of healing concerning that problem.*

MARCH 8

YOUR REWARD

Today's reading: Psalms 36-40

"Commit your way to the Lord; trust in him and he will do this: He will make your righteous reward shine like the dawn, your vindication like the noonday sun" - Psalm 37:5-6.

There is definitely a reward in store for those who serve the Lord. While your reward may delay, you cannot and should not lose sight of the fact that God does reward His people as they serve Him. Paul wrote the Colossians to encourage them to trust God and serve Him with all their heart, for there is surely a reward for those who do: "Whatever you do, work at it with all your heart, as working for the Lord, not for human masters, since you know that you will receive an inheritance from the Lord as a reward. It is the Lord Christ you are serving" (Colossians 3:23-24). Are you keeping your eye on the prize of your reward for a job well done? What job or good work are you doing? What is the reward you are trusting the Lord to receive? Do you realize that part of your reward, perhaps even all of it, is the joy that you have when your way is committed to the Lord?

MARCH 9

TRANSFORMATION

Today's reading: Psalms 41-45

"Why, my soul, are you downcast? Why so disturbed within me? Put your hope in God, for I will yet praise him, my Savior and my God" - Psalm 43:5.

You can wait for someone to come along and encourage you if you are discouraged, or you can take up the task and encourage yourself! Once again we see in today's verse that your self-talk and thought life hold the keys to your attitude, mental health and ultimate behavior. David was downcast but he talked himself out of it. By ordering his soul to put its trust in God, David declared that better days were ahead when he would praise God for his breakthrough. This is similar to the concept Paul described in Romans 12:1-2: "Do not conform to the pattern of this world, but be transformed by the renewing of your mind. Then you will be able to test and approve what God's will is—his good, pleasing and perfect will." Any transformation in your life will only take place when you align your thoughts properly to God's desired outcome. Is it time you had a talk with your soul? If so, what will you tell it? How do you want it to feel and behave? Be specific and be direct, and don't give up until you talk yourself out of your funk.

March 10

Wisdom of the World

Today's reading: Psalms 46-50

"This is the fate of those who trust in themselves, and of their followers, who approve their sayings. They are like sheep and are destined to die; death will be their shepherd (but the upright will prevail over them in the morning). Their forms will decay in the grave, far from their princely mansions" - Psalm 49:13-14.

There are many forms of wisdom that appeal to man's carnal nature, some of which even sound spiritual. Often those who subscribe to that wisdom become followers and name their group after the main proponent of the philosophy or movement. Today's passage warns you of the futility in such a strategy. God desires and is worthy of your absolute allegiance, and you must not give the best of you are or what you do to any movement that ends in *-ism*. John's vision in Revelation is clear that anything or anyone that exalts itself against God's wisdom will be brought down:

> When the kings of the earth who committed adultery with her and shared her luxury see the smoke of her burning, they will weep and mourn over her. Terrified at her torment, they will stand far off and cry: "Woe! Woe to you, great city, you mighty city of Babylon! In one hour your doom has come!" (Revelation 18:9-10).

Have you become a follower in any area of life of another philosophy that has claimed your allegiance? Where has the wisdom of the world crept into your life's work?

March 11

Betrayal

Today's reading: Psalms 51-55

"If an enemy were insulting me, I could endure it; if a foe were rising against me, I could hide. But it is you, a man like myself,my companion, my close friend, with whom I once enjoyed sweet fellowship at the house of God, as we walked about among the worshipers" - Psalm 55:12-14.

It is a painful experience for a friend to betray you. It is what I call a *Star Trek* that happens when your shields are down and you aren't expecting an attack. Once it happens you can wrestle with issues of unforgiveness for a long time, sometimes having to forgive the person over and over again. When you have to repeat the process, it doesn't mean your last attempt failed. It simply means that you must go deeper and deeper in your heart to weed out the hurt and bitterness. Having felt the pain of betrayal, however, should be an incentive for you to *never* do what someone else did to you. If you do or if they perceive that you did, then you must forgive them or seek their forgiveness: "Then Peter came to Jesus and asked, 'Lord, how many times shall I forgive my brother or sister who sins against me? Up to seven times?' Jesus answered, 'I tell you, not seven times, but seventy-seven times'" (Matthew 18:21-22). Do you need to forgive a former friend who betrayed you? Have you been the betrayer and need to seek out your former friend to ask forgiveness? Where can you bring some much-needed reconciliation today?

March 12

Leadership

Today's reading: Psalms 56-60

"Do you rulers indeed speak justly? Do you judge people with equity? No, in your heart you devise injustice, and your hands mete out violence on the earth" - Psalm 58:1-2.

God is watching the ethical behavior not just of leaders who know and serve Him, but also of all leaders. God is a leadership God, which means He promotes leaders to their positions, no matter what the sphere of influence. He then expects those leaders to serve the people and not themselves, and to carry out His will. If you don't believe that, look at Jeremiah, Isaiah or the other prophets and see how often they addressed not just Israel but the other nations. The Lord even refers to Cyrus, a heathen king, as "His shepherd": "[the Lord] who says of Cyrus, 'He is my shepherd and will accomplish all that I please; he will say of Jerusalem, 'Let it be rebuilt,' and of the temple,' 'Let its foundations be laid'" (Isaiah 44:28). If you are a leader, are you mindful that God is watching you and will hold you accountable, no matter where you lead? If you are an aspiring leader, then are you learning what God expects of you when you obtain a leadership role?

March 13

Faith for Living

Today's reading: Psalms 61-65

"Trust in him at all times, you people; pour out your hearts to him, for God is our refuge" - Psalm 62:8.

Faith is not an event; it's a lifestyle. It's not a parachute to be opened in an emergency, it is the oxygen of the soul that you are to breathe every day to sustain your existence in the Lord. There is saving faith - faith that you put in Christ to forgive your sins and restore your relationship with God - and then there is living faith - the faith you must exercise to receive anything from the Lord. Faith is natural for you and you use it everyday. When you drive across a bridge, for example, you have faith that it will remain intact and that the other cars will remain on their side of the road. Faith was both an Old and New Testament requirement, as you can read in Habakkuk 2:4, "Behold, as for the proud one, his soul is not right within him; but the righteous will live by his faith." Is faith your lifestyle or something you resort to when you are in need? What evidence can you provide that it is your lifestyle? What are you believing God to do that if He doesn't do it, you will look foolish?

March 14

The Great Commission

Today's reading: Psalms 66-70

"May God be gracious to us and bless us and make his face shine on us—so that your ways may be known on earth, your salvation among all nations" - Psalm 67:1-2.

You pray for God's blessings, not simply for your own benefit, but for your ability to help spread the gospel to other people and nations. In the midst of life - raising children, doing jobs, building local churches - you still have one overriding assignment, and that is to go to the nations to declare the good news. Jesus Himself gave you what is called The Great Commission: "Therefore go and make disciples of all nations, baptizing them in the name of the Father and of the Son and of the Holy Spirit, and teaching them to obey everything I have commanded you. And surely I am with you always, to the very end of the age" (Matthew 28:19-

20). What are you doing to contribute toward a foreign missions outreach? Are you praying? Are you going? Are you giving toward those who go? Choose a nation or people group today and ask God to help you reach them with the gospel.

March 15

Self Prayer

Today's reading: Psalms 71-75

"Endow the king with your justice, O God, the royal son with your righteousness. May he judge your people in righteousness, your afflicted ones with justice" - Psalm 72:1-2.

The 150 psalms were written by numerous authors, one of whom was Solomon. In today's passage, Solomon began his psalm with a prayer, which must have been the theme for his reign, which was getting divine wisdom so he could rule well. Solomon prayed for himself that he would be able to judge the people with righteousness and justice, and God answered his prayer in a big way as reported in 1 Kings: "God gave Solomon wisdom and very great insight, and a breadth of understanding as measureless as the sand on the seashore. Solomon's wisdom was greater than the wisdom of all the people of the East, and greater than all the wisdom of Egypt" (1 Kings 4:29-30). What is your prayer for yourself? Is it working? Are you becoming or receiving that for which you pray? Do you need to pray for yourself more regularly or fervently?

March 16

Ethical Skill

Today's reading: Psalms 76-80

"And David shepherded them with integrity of heart;

with skillful hands he led them" - Psalm 78:72.

David was a great leader who, for the most part, had both an ethical compass that kept him righteous but also had skills that made him effective. For you to be truly successful, you will need both those components working in your life. Skill without ethics can make you proud, believing you can do anything and it will be successful. Ethics without skill makes you "nice" but without the ability to lead and make practical decisions. What's more, you need to work on both of those characteristics, becoming the best you can be at what you do along with knowing the rights and wrongs of your trade or business. Notice what they said about Jesus: "They were utterly astonished, saying, 'He has done *all* **things well**; He makes even the deaf to hear and the mute to speak'" (Mark 7:37). Do you do things well? How can you improve your skill level? And do you at least know and attempt to follow the basic ethical directives in Scripture about your work?

MARCH 17

HEARTBURN

Today's reading: Psalms 86-90

"I will listen to what God the Lord says; he promises peace to his people, his faithful servants—but let them not turn to folly" - Psalm 85:8.

In today's verse, the psalmist first made a commitment to listen to the Lord's voice. Do you listen to God's voice? He speaks every language, speaks through circumstances, through other people - some who know Him, some who don't - and especially through His word and His servants who preach and teach His word. The writer acknowledged that God promised peace to His people. Do you have peace? If not, is it because you are somehow not listening to the Lord? It's easy to miss His voice as two disciples who knew Jesus well did not recognize Him when He came to visit:

> When he was at the table with them, he took bread, gave thanks, broke it and began to give it to them. Then their eyes were opened and they recognized him, and he disappeared from their sight. They asked each other, "Were not our hearts burning within us while he talked with us on the road and opened the Scriptures to us?" (Luke 24:30-32).

Is your heart burning with His presence, but you don't recognize it? What's holding you back from acknowledging it? *Father, I want to know You and Your voice. Show me where fear or hardness of heart have prevented me from recognizing when You are speaking to me. I put my trust in Your ability to speak to me and make Your will clear for my life.*

March 18

A United Heart

Today's reading: Psalms 85-90

"Teach me Your way, O Lord; I will walk in Your truth Unite my heart to fear Your name" - Psalm 86:11.

I see three truths in this verse, perhaps you see more. *First,* you never lose your need to learn the ways of God. That requires you be taught by knowledgeable people who know and love the Lord. What are you studying and learning in the Lord? What are you reading? Are you part of a local church that teaches the Word? *Second,* you are accountable to do what you learn, to "walk in the truth." Jesus said, "If you know these things, you are blessed if you do them" (John 13:17). Are you doing what you know you know you should do? *Third,* God must help you have a heart that is totally devoted to serve and learn from Him as He promised to do: "And I will give them one heart, and put a new spirit within them. And I will take the heart of stone out of their flesh and give them a heart of flesh" (Ezekiel 11:19). Are you cooperating with God's work on your heart?

March 19

Stalkers

Today's reading: Psalms 91-95

"You will not be afraid of the terror by night, Or of the arrow that flies by day; Of the pestilence that stalks in darkness, Or of the destruction that lays waste at noon" - Psalm 91:5-6.

There is no lack of dangerous trends that stalk mankind. New, exotic diseases baffle experts and defy any cure. Terrorism is on the rise and seems to be in every corner of the world. Bizarre, violent behavior is present in every country. Economies seem to teeter on the verge of collapse. Yet the words of Psalm 91 remain true for those who know the Lord. Not only does this psalm promise God's protection, it also states that the righteous won't even be afraid of the stalkers. Are you afraid? Do you find your fears affecting your daily activities? Are you consumed by and fearful of the daily media reports of danger? If you are, read Psalm 91 along with the Lord's admonition to Joshua as he was about to enter the Land: "Be strong and courageous, for you shall give this people possession of the land which I swore to their fathers to give them. Only be strong and very courageous" (Joshua 1:6-7a).

March 20

Emotions

Today's reading: Psalms 96-100

"Shout for joy to the Lord, all the earth, burst into jubilant song with music; make music to the Lord with the harp, with the harp and the sound of singing, with trumpets and the blast of the ram's horn—shout for joy before the Lord, the King" – Psalm 98:4-6.

There are some who say that emotions are potentially dangerous and to be avoided when you serve the Lord. Those people must not have read the psalms, for they comprise a book of emotions – anger, joy, frustration, sadness, and gladness just to name a few. Deuteronomy 6:5 sets the standard for your worship and relationship with the Lord when it instructs you to "Love the Lord your God with all your heart and with all your soul and with all your strength." In other words, you are to serve the Lord with your entire being, and that includes your emotions. Are you hiding your emotions when you pray or worship? Has your approach to God been a "mind thing" rather than a "heart thing?" Why are you ashamed of your emotions when you come into God's presence? Do you think He will be offended? Doesn't He already know your emotional state before you come to Him?

March 21
Mercy

Today's reading: Psalms 101-105

"He does not treat us as our sins deserve or repay us according to our iniquities" – Psalm 103:10.

Our God is a God of mercy. You cannot earn, presume upon, or understand His mercy. You can only thank Him for it, never fully realizing the reason why He chooses to bestow mercy as graciously and as often as He does. His merciful heart is revealed in His encounter with the woman caught in adultery, to whom He said: "Jesus straightened up and asked her, 'Woman, where are they? Has no one condemned you?' 'No one, sir,' she said. 'Then neither do I condemn you," Jesus declared. "Go now and leave your life of sin'" (John 8:11-12). Some have believed they should sin more so that His mercy would be revealed more – which is simply foolishness – but even more have either felt like they must try to do something to earn His mercy or have actually rejected His mercy, refusing to forgive themselves for a wrong done or mistake made. How do you respond to God's mercy? Do you thank Him for it, realizing He is not obligated to give it but does out of His love? Do you in return grant mercy to others in response to His mercy toward you?

March 22

One Way

Today's reading: Psalms 106-110

"God has spoken from his sanctuary: 'In triumph I will parcel out Shechem and measure off the Valley of Succoth. Gilead is mine, Manasseh is mine; Ephraim is my helmet, Judah my scepter. Moab is my washbasin, upon Edom I toss my sandal; over Philistia I shout in triumph'"
- Psalm 108:7-9.

God is the God of all the nations and people groups. Many are in rebellion and refuse to submit, some live in ignorance of God's truth and still others who realize this do little to further the work of missions and world evangelism. In this day of tolerance, there is the opinion that there are many ways to God, but God's word indicates there is only one way: "Salvation is found in no one else [Jesus], for there is *no other name* under heaven given to men by which we must be saved" (Acts 4:12 emphasis added). What are you doing to help spread the good news of the gospel, not only in your neighborhood, but also to the ends of the earth? Why not adopt a people group or nation and pray for their salvation? Can you give money to help those who are on the front lines of missions work?

March 23

Your Breakthrough

Today's reading: Psalms 111-115

"He raises the poor from the dust and lifts the needy from the ash heap; he seats them with princes, with the princes

of his people. He settles the childless woman in her home as a happy mother of children" - Psalm 113:7-9.

God is the God of the turnaround. You can be in dire straits one day and the next you can have all you need to prosper. When you think of it, you are just one phone call, one chance meeting, one idea, one speech, one sales call, one appointment away from the breakthrough for which you are praying. When I read today's verses, I thought of what Mary said when she found out she was pregnant:

> His mercy extends to those who fear him, from generation to generation. He has performed mighty deeds with his arm; he has scattered those who are proud in their inmost thoughts. He has brought down rulers from their thrones but has lifted up the humble. He has filled the hungry with good things but has sent the rich away empty (Luke 1:50-53).

Can you thank God today for your breakthrough, even before it comes? Can you encourage yourself today that you are just that close to the fulfillment of your dreams and prayers?

March 24
Rejection

Today's reading: Psalms 116-120

"The stone the builders rejected has become the cornerstone; the Lord has done this, and it is marvelous in our eyes" - Psalm 118:22-23.

Jesus was a man who knew rejection: "He came to that which was his own, but his own did not receive him" (John 1:11). Yet even though He experienced rejection, God chose Him to be the cornerstone of salvation. It is of note that today's passage is quoted in three gospels, the book of Acts and Peter's epistle, for

God wanted all to know that man's rejection was not the final word on the matter (take the time to look them up). Your rejection by others is not the final word either, for if God has chosen you, your purpose will prevail as God promised: "If God is for us, who can be against us?" (Romans 8:31b). Have you experienced rejection from those close to you, perhaps even by the church? Be reminded today that God is with you to help you do what He created you to do. Be encouraged!

March 25

Trust Focus

Today's reading: Psalms 121-125

"I lift up my eyes to the hills—where does my help come from? My help comes from the Lord, the Maker of heaven and earth" – Psalm 121:1-2.

You may have a great job with wonderful benefits and perks. You may have earned a university degree with highest honors. Perhaps you have inherited family wealth that has made your life comfortable. You may enjoy perfect health and work out to ensure it stays that way. Yet no matter the benefits you enjoy, it's important you not put your trust or faith in your own abilities or strength. The Lord warned against this danger through the prophet Jeremiah: "Let not the wise man boast of his wisdom or the strong man boast of his strength or the rich man boast of his riches, but let him who boasts boast about this: that he understands and knows me, that I am the Lord, who exercises kindness, justice and righteousness on earth, for in these I delight,' declares the Lord" (Jeremiah 9:23-24). Where have you become self-reliant and stopped or refused being God reliant? I acknowledge, Lord, that You are my Provider, using my job as the means to provide. I confess my utter dependence on You for my daily bread!

March 26

Your Efforts, God's Help

Today's reading: Psalms 126-130

"Unless the Lord builds the house, its builders labor in vain. Unless the Lord watches over the city, the watchmen stand guard in vain" – Psalm 127:1.

This verse requires careful consideration, otherwise you will misunderstand your responsibility to accomplish God's will and produce fruit, and also confuse God's role in the process. If you continue to "wait on the Lord," you will do little or nothing. If you launch out impetuously, you will find yourself working alone without God's help. The key is to do what you can do, all the while realizing if God doesn't help you, your efforts are not enough. You never put your trust in your preparations or strength, no matter how substantial they are, because they are never enough without God's help. It is almost as if you must do all you can and only then God will do what only He can do. Are you working hard and putting your trust in that? Or are you working hard but still putting your trust in God's help?

March 27

Faithfulness

Today's reading: Psalms 131-135

"Praise the Lord, all you servants of the Lord who minister by night in the house of the Lord. Lift up your hands in the sanctuary and praise the Lord" - Psalm 134:1-2.

There were some priests who drew night duty as they served in the Temple. This psalm urged them to be diligent and faithful to perform their duties, even though the temptation may have been to sleep or slack off due to the hour when people normally rest. If God has directed you to do something, then it doesn't matter what others are doing or how many hours it takes you to complete the project. If they are sleeping, playing, enjoying leisure or sitting idly, you are to stand watch and do what the Lord wants you to do. Paul wrote, "Now it is required that those who have been given a trust must prove faithful" (1 Corinthians 4:2). In what is God asking you to be faithful? Faithful in school and studies? Faithful to serve others? Faithful to write or teach or stand with a friend?

March 28

Specific Prayer

Today's reading: Psalms 136-140

"Search me, God, and know my heart; test me and know my anxious thoughts. See if there is any offensive way in me, and lead me in the way everlasting" - Psalm 139:23-24.

The Bible is full of inspired prayers that you can employ for yourself and for others. Today's verses represent a somewhat dangerous prayer, for the psalmist was asking God to take a set of spiritual x-rays on his inner being to see if everything was as God would require it. Specifically, the psalmist was looking for anxiety and offensive ways that would prevent him from walking in eternal life, right here and right now. When you get specific with God, He gets specific with you and this prayer is specific. It reminds me of the rich young ruler who asked Jesus how he could obtain eternal life: "When Jesus heard this, he said to him, 'You still lack one thing. Sell everything you have and give to the poor, and you will have treasure in heaven. Then come, follow me'" (Luke 18:22). The young man was saddened by the answer. Is there anything you are afraid or need to ask the Lord? When you ask, be prepared to receive the answer. My goal today is to hear Your voice. Speak, Lord, for your servant is listening, ready to do what You command and direct.

March 29

Mouth Guard

Today's reading: Psalms 141-145

"Set a guard over my mouth, Lord; keep watch over the door of my lips" - Psalm 141:3.

The Bible has a lot to say about the words that come out of your mouth. Just put those words in any Bible search site and you will see what I mean. In the New Testament, James specifically addressed the problems that your mouth can cause:

> Likewise, the tongue is a small part of the body, but it makes great boasts. Consider what a great forest is set on fire by a small spark. The tongue also is a fire, a world of evil among the parts of the body. It corrupts the whole body, sets the whole course of one's life on fire, and is itself set on fire by hell (James 3:5-6).

Are you using your mouth to build others up or tear them down? Is your mouth getting you into trouble or opening doors of opportunity? Do you find yourself thinking of something to say, not saying it and being glad after you didn't? If so, then God has helped you set a guard over your mouth.

March 30

Properly-Placed Trust

Today's reading: Psalms 146-150

"His pleasure is not in the strength of the horse, nor his delight in the legs of the warrior; the Lord delights in those who fear him, who put their hope in his unfailing love" - Psalm 147:10-11.

Even when Israel had an army led by their warrior king, David, they learned to put their trust in the Lord. Once the Lord directed David to attack the Philistines head on but then the Philistines returned for another round. David could have just gone back into battle using the same tactics, but He sought the Lord:

> Once more the Philistines came up and spread out in the Valley of Rephaim; so David inquired of the Lord, and he answered, "Do not go straight up, but circle around behind them and attack them in front of the poplar trees. As soon as you hear the sound of marching in the tops of the poplar trees, move quickly, because that will mean the Lord has gone out in front of you to strike the Philistine army." So David did as the Lord commanded him, and he struck down the Philistines all the way from Gibeon to Gezer (2 Samuel 5:22-25).

David trusted in the Lord more than his experience or military skills. Have you learned to do the same? Are you seeking God's help with things that you already know how to do? If not, how is that working for you? What changes do you need to make?

March 31

Oxygen for the Soul

Today's reading: Psalm 119

"Sustain me, my God, according to your promise, and I will live; do not let my hopes be dashed" - Psalm 119:116.

The psalmist had put his hope in the Lord and asked the Lord to keep those hopes alive and not let them be dashed. Someone once said that hope is oxygen for the soul. Hope is wishing for something for which there is no specific promise from God that He will do it, but there is also no reason why He will not do it. You can wish for a new car and then one day you have faith that you will get that car. In a sense, hope is an optimism that God will do good for you regardless of what you are encountering at the moment. It is also described in Psalm 138:8b, when the psalmist wrote, "The Lord will accomplish what concerns me." Are you optimistic? What do you have hope that God will do for you? Do you act like you have hope or are you pessimistic about the present and the future?

April 1

Decision to Rest

Today's reading: Psalms 1-5

"I lie down and sleep; I wake again, because the Lord sustains me.I will not fear though tens of thousands assail me on every side" - Psalms 3:5-6.

When you read the psalms in sequential order, you begin to realize that there was a crisis causing the writers to write and the editors to order the psalms as they did. In Psalm 3, we see that King David and the monarchy were in danger when David was badly outnumbered while fleeing from his rebel son, Absalom. Yet in the midst of it all, David found time to write and pray, and to make his affirmations of trust and hope in God. When David said he could sleep and not fear when thousands came against him, he wasn't exaggerating. If David could create, write, pray, trust and sleep in the midst of his life's problems, can you do the same? All those actions were decisions within his power to make, and he followed through with the evidence of his obedience This is reminiscent of the peace Jesus had in the midst of His storm: "The disciples went and woke him, saying, 'Master, Master, we're going to drown!' He got up and rebuked the wind and the raging waters; the storm subsided, and all was calm" (Luke 8:24). Have you made the decision to be at rest, even though there is turmoil all around you? Is your mind at peace even though war is raging all around you? What steps can you take to find and keep that peace? *Lord, I am not at peace because I have not surrendered my life to You. I still want to take back control, and worry and fret over the things that are going on around me. I trust You today to handle the things I cannot control.*

APRIL 2

KEEPING A JOURNAL

Today's reading: Psalms 6-10

***"When I consider your heavens, the work of your fingers, the moon and the stars, which you have set in place, what is mankind that you are mindful of them, human beings that you care for them?"* - Psalm 8:3-4.**

David took time to reflect and think, and when he did, he received insight into God, man, and the relationship between the two. Perhaps David did this when he was a shepherd boy, or maybe while he was king, or waiting to become one. Whenever it happened, David spent reflective time and then wrote about his conclusions. It is interesting how often in the Bible the Lord directed people to write things down. Here is one such directive: "Appoint three men from each tribe. I will send them out to make a survey of the land and to write a description of it, according to the inheritance of each. Then they will return to me" (Joshua 18:4). Do you have a journal? Do you faithfully use it? What can you do to help carve out some thinking, reflecting and journaling time? Do you see the benefit of doing so? If not, then you will probably not make an effort to do more of it.

APRIL 3

SAFETY

Today's reading: Psalms 11-15

***"You, Lord, will keep the needy safe and will protect us forever from the wicked, who freely strut about when what is vile is honored by the human race"* - Psalm 12:7-8.**

Today's passage contains a vivid description of modern society: the evil strut about freely because what is vile is honored. The problem is that as they strut, they persecute and dishonor those who walk in righteousness. The promise in the verse, however, provides comfort: The Lord always protects His people in the midst of the madness. Jesus reiterated this promise when He said: "I have given them your word and the world has hated them, for they are not of the world any more than I am of the world. My prayer is not that you take them out of the world but that you protect them from the evil one" (John 17:4-5). Are you nervous over the state of the world? Has it caused you to alter your lifestyle, or do you just keep your fear silently in your heart, afraid when you step out of the comfort zone you know? The good news is that God is watching and has promised to protect you. What will you do differently now that you are reminded of that truth?

April 4

Your Role

Today's reading: Psalms 16-20

"To the faithful you show yourself faithful, to the blameless you show yourself blameless, to the pure you show yourself pure, but to the devious you show yourself shrewd. You save the humble but bring low those whose eyes are haughty"
- Psalm 18:7-9.

In a sense, you help direct how God responds to you by first responding to Him in the similar manner. If you are faithful, God shows Himself faithful. If you are blameless, He is blameless. If you are devious, He responds as shrewd. If you are humble, He saves you. If you are proud, He brings you low. This list is not meant to be exhaustive but only points out the role you have in your relationship with Him. Therefore, if you are not happy with how God is revealing Himself to you, then perhaps the problem rests with you. Are you experiencing lack? Then perhaps you are not being generous. Are your prayers not being answered? Then maybe you are not listening to God first and foremost, so He is not listening to you. Take some time today and reflect on the truth in this passage, and then do some serious self-evaluation to see if you are contributing to your current state of a less-than-satisfactory relationship with the Lord in any area of life.

April 5

God's Perspective

Today's reading: Psalms 21-25

"My God, my God, why have you forsaken me? Why are you so far from saving me, so far from my cries of anguish? My God, I cry out by day, but you do not answer, by night, but I find no rest" - Psalm 22:1-2.

These verses are probably familiar because Jesus uttered these words while dying on the cross. Jesus recited the first verse and any Jew listening would have recognized that this was a cry of David in which he reiterated his confidence that he would survive his trials and praise the Lord. It is permissible to be honest with the Lord and to pour your heart out to Him. The purpose, however, is not to stay in your perspective as you cry out, but to obtain God's perspective concerning your situation, and then to reiterate your hope in Him. Perhaps it would be good for you to go to the account of Jesus' death during which He uttered this phrase in Matthew 27, and be challenged to do what the writer of Hebrews instructed you to do:

> Consider him who endured such opposition from sinners, so that you will not grow weary and lose heart. In your struggle against sin, you have not yet resisted to the point of shedding your blood. And have you completely forgotten this word of encouragement that addresses you as a father addresses his son? . . .Therefore, strengthen your feeble arms and weak knees (Hebrews 12:4-5, 12).

April 6

Integrity

Today's reading: Psalms 26-30

"Test me, Lord, and try me, examine my heart and my mind; for I have always been mindful of your unfailing love and have lived in reliance on your faithfulness" - Psalm 26:2-3.

David prayed and asked the Lord to scrutinize his mind and heart to make sure it was in compliance with what God required. David was making sure his integrity was intact - that he was being who he claimed to be and not just a talker. Talk is cheap and some believe if they are sincere when they say something then they have done what God wanted, even if they don't follow through. That was not good enough for David and it should not be for you either. Peter and the disciples did this very thing when they said to Jesus, "But Peter declared, 'Even if I have to die with you, I will never disown you.' And all the other disciples said the same" (Matthew 26:35). A few hours later, they did indeed betray the Lord in spite of their bold declaration. Are you walking in integrity? Do you have the goods to back up what you say you are and promise you will do? Where are you allowing sincerity and good intentions to override your need to actually follow through?

April 7

In the Battle

Today's reading: Psalms 31-35

"The righteous cry out, and the Lord hears them; he delivers them from all their troubles" - Psalm 34:17.

It seems like the psalmists were constantly in a lot of trouble, not always of his own doing. In today's verse, the writer penned a truth that was not just relevant in his life but also in the life of all the saints: they cry out, God hears and delivers them. The challenge is that the deliverance is often *through* the trouble and not *out* of the trouble. This is further explained in Hebrews 11:34b: ". . . whose weakness was turned to strength; and who became powerful in the battle, routing foreign armies." People were not spared *from* battle but were strengthened *in* the battle. Is your expectation that God will keep you from trouble? Do you find God instead giving you strength for and in the battle? Can you make peace with the fact that this is how God operates? Are you in a battle right now? Then have faith that God will deliver you as you fight your way through.

April 8
Speak Up

Today's reading: Psalm 36-40

"So I remained utterly silent, not even saying anything good. But my anguish increased; my heart grew hot within me. While I meditated, the fire burned; then I spoke with my tongue" - Psalm 39:2-3.

There are times you should remain silent, but only if you have nothing to say. If you have something to say that can help others and don't say it, then you are being irresponsible. Usually fear is the culprit, keeping you from saying something that may offend or upset another person. Your words can cause turmoil, but they can also build others up, or prevent someone from going down on a wrong path or having a bad attitude. Jeremiah faced the same dilemma when he said, "But if I say, 'I will not mention his word or speak anymore in his name, his word is in my heart like a fire, a fire shut up in my bones. I am weary of holding it in; indeed, I cannot'" (Jeremiah 20:9). Where have you been silent, but your heart is burning within you with a conviction that you need to speak up and speak out? What is the cost to you and others for your silence? What can you do to change the situation?

April 9
Your Creativity

Today's reading: Psalms 41-45

"My heart is stirred by a noble theme as I recite my verses for the king; my tongue is the pen of a skillful writer" - Psalm 45:1.

Many people don't write or create more often because they cannot picture themselves sitting at a computer, writing for hours at a time. Yet today's verse sets them free to recite rather than write their stories and lessons. Paul wrote most of his letters by dictating them to someone else, only signing off in his own handwriting at the end. Luke interviewed others and compiled his gospel from their accounts. Are you among those who are fearful or hesitant to express your creative insights and ideas? Then fear no more. Find someone to whom you can dictate your concepts and ideas, and let your creativity flow! After a few hours, you will see something begin to take shape that can turn into a book project. What steps can you take to move your ideas from your heart to the place where people can enjoy and learn from them?

April 10
Envious

Today's reading: Psalms 46-50

"Do not be overawed when others grow rich, when the splendor of their houses increases; for they will take nothing with them when they die,their splendor will not descend with them" - Psalm 49:16-17.

In today's world, wealth has increased at a rapid rate but so has poverty. The Internet and media shows highlight the lifestyles of the rich and famous, and it is easy to become a bit envious (or a lot envious) of those who have so much, especially when you have so much less. The psalmists today cautioned their generation against being 'overawed' when others gain much. To put things in perspective, the writers reminded the readers that the wealthy are going to die and they will take nothing with them. Jesus gave similar advice:

> What good will it be for someone to gain the whole world, yet forfeit their soul? Or what can anyone give in exchange for their soul? For the Son of Man is going to come in his Father's glory with his angels, and then he will reward each person according to what they have done (Matthew 16:26-27).

Are you envious of the wealthy? Are your eyes set on the temporal or the eternal? Are you working to earn what will not and can not last, or are you investing in eternal things that cannot perish?

APRIL 11

THE BLAME GAME

Today's reading: Psalms 51-55

"For I know my transgressions, and my sin is always before me. Against you, you only, have I sinned and done what is evil in your sight; so you are right in your verdict and justified when you judge" - Psalm 51:3-4.

David acknowledged that he was wrong, and had sinned against the Lord. There was no blame shifting, no victim mentality, and no rationalizing his sin - David accepted responsibility for what he had done. It is rare to hear anyone be so forthright in holding themselves accountable, for we are all like our parents, Adam and Eve, who played the blame game from the beginning of their Fall: "The man said, 'The woman you put here with me—she gave me some fruit from the tree, and I ate it.' Then the Lord God said to the woman, 'What is this you have done?' The woman said, 'The serpent deceived me, and I ate'" (Genesis 3:12-13). Do you admit when you are wrong? When you are, do you say, "I'm sorry" or "I'm sorry, *but*..." and then go on to list all the reasons why it wasn't *really* your fault? Is there something for which you need to apologize and ask forgiveness without trying to justify or rationalize what you did?

April 12

Sing and Make Music

Today's reading: Psalms 56-60

"My heart, O God, is steadfast, my heart is steadfast; I will sing and make music. Awake, my soul! Awake, harp and lyre! I will awaken the dawn" - Psalm 57:7-8.

These verses are not particularly inspirational, and represent what one would expect from a book that emphasizes praise and worship. Yet the heading of the psalm makes these verses remarkable. David penned them while he was hiding in a cave when Saul was searching to destroy him! In the midst of the pressure and tension, David made a commitment to sing and make music. He was not going to allow the circumstances to dictate his attitude; instead, he was going to determine what kind of attitude he would have, and then follow through on his commitment. Paul imitated this response to adversity in his own ministry experience:

> After they had been severely flogged, they were thrown into prison, and the jailer was commanded to guard them carefully. When he received these orders, he put them in the inner cell and fastened their feet in the stocks. About midnight Paul and Silas were praying and singing hymns to God, and the other prisoners were listening to them (Acts 16:23-25).

Have you allowed your life situation to affect your praise and worship? Are you part of a local church? Are you following through on your commitments to serve the Lord in spite of any setbacks you may have experienced?

APRIL 13

KINGDOM RULE

Today's reading: Psalms 61-65

"Truly my soul finds rest in God; my salvation comes from him. Truly he is my rock and my salvation; he is my fortress, I will never be shaken" - Psalm 62:1-2.

David wrote this in a time when he was under assault, which happened to him quite often in his role as warrior king. David came to many conclusions during those dangerous times. First, his true rest was not in escape but in the Lord. Second, his salvation came from God and not his military prowess. Third, God was his fortress, not those he could build or design with his military experience. Armed with those conclusions, David proclaimed that he would *never* be shaken. This reminds me of what is written in Hebrews: "Therefore, since we are receiving a kingdom that cannot be shaken, let us be thankful, and so worship God acceptably with reverence and awe, for our 'God is a consuming fire'" (Hebrews 12:28-29). Have you thought out what attitude you will have when things are tough? If you are shaken, then perhaps you are not living under God's kingdom rule as you should? If you don't have rest, maybe your thinking is off and this is causing you to seek refuge in something or someone other than God?

APRIL 14

REMEMBER

Today's reading: Psalms 66-70

"He turned the sea into dry land, they passed through the waters on foot—come, let us rejoice in him" - Psalm 66:6.

When the psalmist wrote this psalm, Israel was scattered and in exile. As he reflected on their condition, he decided to remember the past works of God to help Israel rejoice in where they were. You would do well to do the same thing. When you reflect on God's past goodness and mercy, it encourages you and gives you hope that God will once again move miraculously on your behalf. In the book of Deuteronomy, the Lord commanded Israel to "remember" what He had done 16 times, and here is one example: "Remember the days of old; consider the generations long past. Ask your father and he will tell you, your elders, and they will explain to you" (Deuteronomy 32:7). Spend some time today remembering what God has done for you. Talk about it, write about it, tell others about it. Allow the past to lift your spirits today as you reflect on memories of God's goodness.

April 15

The Will of God

Today's reading: Psalms 71-75

"You guide me with your counsel, and afterward you will take me into glory" - Psalm 73:24.

God is a God of guidance. If He wants you to do His will - and of course He does - then He must reveal to you what His will is. God is a great communicator and does not lack the means to reveal Himself to you. He can use His word, other people, or life's circumstances. The key to understanding God's will is committing to do it, whatever it is, before you know what it is. In other words, you surrender your "veto power" and say 'yes,' trusting that whatever He shows you is good and in your best interests. This principle is found in John 7:17 when Jesus answered the question, "How do we know if you [Jesus] are from God? [Jesus answered] 'Anyone who chooses to do the will of God will find out whether my teaching comes from God or whether I speak on my own.'" Are you struggling with the will of God as you consider a certain issue or decision? Have you made a commitment to do it before you know what the 'it' is? Do you believe that God will make it clear? *Lord, I want and need to know Your will for my life. I ask You today to reveal it to me, and I trust that You not only hear me but will also answer. I have tuned my heart to hear, and will not allow fear or doubt to hinder hearing Your response!*

April 16

Worry

Today's reading: Psalms 76-80

"In spite of all this, they kept on sinning; in spite of his wonders, they did not believe" - Psalm 78:32.

Israel saw many miracles as they left Egypt to enter the Promised Land. Yet each time they confronted a crisis, they had short-term memory loss and panicked, challenging the Lord to prove Himself again and again. They did not put their trust in Him and worried they would die in the Wilderness. You and I can have the same problem, for even though we have seen God do great things, we also can worry and fret over our current situation. We have faith that God raises the dead, yet we also have amnesia concerning His goodness and freak out over a bad doctor's report or a job loss. Jesus taught His disciples not to worry in His first sermon: "Therefore I tell you, do not worry about your life, what you will eat or drink; or about your body, what you will wear. Is not life more than food, and the body more than clothes?" (Matthew 6:25). If He were preaching today, He would add transportation and health care to the no-worry list. Are you a worrier? Do you see worry as not just a bad habit, but a sinful one? Perhaps today is a good day to begin living a worry-free life? *Father, I trust You. I acknowledge that worry and fear have often robbed me of the joy You want me to have as I trust You for provision and protection. You are a good Provider, and I ask Your forgiveness for my anxiety, and I renew my faith today in You.*

April 17

Price of Disobedience

Today's reading: Psalms 81-85

"If my people would only listen to me, if Israel would only follow my ways, how quickly I would subdue their enemies and turn my hand against their foes!" - Psalm 81:13-14.

Occasionally in the Psalms, it is the Lord speaking and not the psalmists themselves. In this passage, the Lord laments His people's disobedience, reiterating His desire to help and deliver them if they would only listen to His voice. He had given them over to their stiff-necked ways, however, and they were not about to repent and turn to Him. There is always a price to pay for disobedience. You must always ask yourself if some of your dilemmas are a result of your own disobedience in some area of life. What's more, some of what you have considered spiritual warfare may not be that at all, and your obedience could bring about God's swift intervention on your behalf. Are you struggling financially? Relationally? Occupationally? Then take a close look today, with God's help, and see if you can engage God's quick help by obeying His word and will for your life in that particular area.

April 18

Walk in the Light

Today's reading: Psalms 86-90

"Blessed are those who have learned to acclaim you, who walk in the light of your presence, Lord" - Psalm 89:15.

The word *acclaim* is not often used as a verb, but it means "to praise enthusiastically and often publicly." What's more, the people who acclaim the Lord and who walk in the light of His presence are called blessed. What does it mean to walk in God's light? John explained it in his epistle when he wrote:

> God is light; in him there is no darkness at all. If we claim to have fellowship with him and yet walk in the darkness, we lie and do not live out the truth. But if we walk in the light, as he is in the light, we have fellowship with one another, and the blood of Jesus, his Son, purifies us from all sin. If we claim to be without sin, we deceive ourselves and the truth is not in us. If we confess our sins, he is faithful and just and will forgive us our sins and purify us from all unrighteousness (1 John 1:5b-9).

Are you walking in the light by confessing your sins? Do you deny it when you are wrong or make excuses just like Adam and Eve did when they sinned? Or do you accept responsibility for your shortcomings? If you do, then the Bible says you are a blessed person!

APRIL 19

PRAISE AND WORSHIP

Today's reading: Psalms 91-95

"Come, let us sing for joy to the Lord; let us shout aloud to the Rock of our salvation. Let us come before him with thanksgiving and extol him with music and song" - Psalm 95:1-2.

There is certainly nothing wrong with private devotionals in which you spend time worshiping and praising the Lord. The context of this passage, however, is for "us" to sing for joy, and that means a group of people worshiping in a corporate setting. Jesus gave His life for the church; it is the apple of His eye. If Jesus felt church was that important, you should too. And part of the dynamic of gathering is to experience the combined singing, clapping and joy of many voices joined together in one accord. Paul instructed the church with these words: "Let the message of Christ dwell among you richly as you teach and admonish one another with all wisdom through psalms, hymns, and songs from the Spirit, singing to God with gratitude in your hearts" (Colossians 3:16). Are you part of a worshiping local congregation? Do you attend regularly and make your gifts available to the leadership and members? Do you actively worship when you do attend, putting aside all worry and distractions to joyfully join your voice with others?

APRIL 20

THE KINGDOM

Today's reading: Psalms 96-100

"Say among the nations, 'The Lord reigns.'
The world is firmly established, it cannot be moved;
he will judge the peoples with equity" - Psalm 96:10.

The redeemed have credibility when they say to the unredeemed, "The Lord reigns," only when He truly reigns in the lives of His people. When Jesus started His ministry, He preached this message: "'The time has come,' he said. 'The kingdom of God has come near. Repent and believe the good news!'" (Mark 1:15). Jesus came preaching the Kingdom and He expects you and I to do the same thing. That means that God wants to establish His government in your life, in the life of the Church and then in every ethnic group on earth. Are you a 'Kingdom person'? Have you accepted Jesus as both Savior *and* Lord? Are you working to have His rule extend to every area of your life? Then are you helping to extend His rule to other areas, like where you work? Finally, are you helping others who are proclaiming the Kingdom as missionaries in other lands?

APRIL 21

YOUR HUMANITY

Today's reading: Psalms 101-105

"As a father has compassion on his children, so the Lord has

compassion on those who fear him; for he knows how we are formed, he remembers that we are dust" - Psalm 103:13-14.

The Lord is comfortable with your humanity, perhaps more comfortable with it than you are. He knows you and He still wants to use you, as you are today and as you will be in the future. Some people are convinced that God must do major reconstruction on their lives before He can use them. The good news is that He is ready to use you now for His purpose. That means you can stop beating yourself up that you are not in a 'better' place than you are, and that you can stop delaying your purpose work until a more opportune moment. Are you hard on yourself that you aren't more spiritual, intelligent or prepared to serve the Lord? Are you even open to the fact that God wants to use you today, just as you are? What have you been putting off that you can and should embrace today as a work that God wants you to start and complete *now*?

April 22
Hatred

Today's reading: Psalms 106-110

"May his days be few; may another take his place of leadership. May his children be fatherless and his wife a widow" - Psalm 109:8-9.

There is a human emotion often revealed in the psalms that is unpleasant to talk and think about, and that emotion is hatred. In today's passage, David prayed about an enemy who had opposed him. David cried out to God to do bad things to that enemy. You may recoil at such talk, but there are important things to realize here. First, David did not take revenge; he entrusted that job to the Lord. Second, David was honest with the Lord and did not gloss over his feelings, telling God what he thought God would want to hear. Third, David recognized that there was evil in the world and he went to a good God to help him deal with and sort it out. Jesus taught about how to treat your enemies when He said: "You have heard that it was said, 'Love your neighbor and hate your enemy.' But I tell you, love your enemies and pray for those who persecute you" (Matthew 5:43-44). Do you have any enemies about whom you need to talk to God? Are you masking your strong emotions, even hatred, because you don't want to admit you have them? Lord, I admit that I am ambivalent at times about my emotional side. Help me to accept them as part of how You created me, and then help me harness them for Your service.

April 23
Generosity

Today's reading: Psalms 111-115

"Good will come to those who are generous and lend freely, who conduct their affairs with justice. . . . They have freely scattered their gifts to the poor, their righteousness endures forever; their horn will be lifted high in honor"
- Psalm 112:5, 9.

God loves a generous person. The Bible is full of exhortations to be generous, reminding you how God rewards those who remember the poor. That assumes you know who the poor are, are in touch with their needs, and have the willingness to help. If you have time, do a search of the word *poor* in the book of Proverbs and you will see for yourself some of God's promises for the generous person. A few of my favorites are: "Whoever is kind to the poor lends to the Lord, and he will reward them for what they have done" (Proverbs 19:17) and "Those who give to the poor will lack nothing, but those who close their eyes to them receive many curses" (Proverbs 28:27). Do you know any poor in your country or another? What do you do to help the poor? How can you increase your awareness of the needs of the poor and then increase your level of assistance?

APRIL 24

YOUR PROMISES

Today's reading: Psalms 116-120

***"I will fulfill my vows to the Lord in the presence of all his people"* - Psalm 116:7.**

There are times when you make commitments, only to find later that circumstances make them difficult to fulfill. Some are small things like, "I'll call you soon" and then you don't call the person, or "I'll be praying for you" and then neglect to pray. Some are more major commitments such as, "I am going to pray 30 minutes every day" or "I pledge to give $1,000 toward that church project." Still others are songs sung in church: "I seek You only, Lord" or "You are my all," only to find that you don't live up to your promise to seek or remain true. Jesus told a short parable to emphasize the importance of not saying the right thing but doing it: "'What do you think? There was a man who had two sons. He went to the first and said, 'Son, go and work today in the vineyard.' 'I will not,' he answered, but later he changed his mind and went. Then the father went to the other son and said the same thing. He answered, 'I will, sir,' but he did not go. Which of the two did what his father wanted?' 'The first,' they answered' (Matthew 21:28-31). Are there promises you have hanging over your life that you have not fulfilled? What are you prepared to do about them? Remember, it's better to not promise and do than to promise and not do.

APRIL 25

YOUR HELPER

Today's reading: Psalms 121-125

"I lift up my eyes to the mountains—where does my help come from? My help comes from the Lord, the Maker of heaven and earth" - Psalm 121:1-2.

The psalmist reflected on where his help came from, and he concluded it came from the Lord. He looked to the mountains the Lord created and realized the same God who created them created him. The writer also knew that his help did not come from within - his intelligence, wits, skill or business acumen - but rather from an outside source. This perspective caused him to humble himself and recognize the Lord's role as his provider and helper. Do you have this same humble perspective? Have you reflected lately on how well God takes care of you? Are you humbled in the realization of how well God has taken care of you? Do you fret or rest in the truth that the same God who made everything you see also created you? If He can make and maintain the universe, then He can certainly continue to maintain you. Thank Him and rejoice in Him today!

APRIL 26

YOUR MERCY NEEDS

Today's reading: Psalms 126-130

"Out of the depths I cry to you, Lord; Lord, hear my voice. Let your ears be attentive to my cry for mercy" - Psalm 130:1-2.

It is easy to cry out for mercy when you have messed up or when you are in over your head or "out of the depths" as the psalmist phrased it. Then you are acutely aware of your need for God's grace that you don't deserve. It is much more difficult to maintain your sense of need when everything is going well. Yet your need for mercy is just as great when things are going well as when they are not going so well. The wisdom writer addressed this tendency in Proverbs 18:23: "The poor plead for mercy, but the rich answer harshly." When you are aware of your need, you tend to answer softly and tread quietly. When you don't see the need, you can become insensitive to the needs of others. Jesus guaranteed one surefire way to get the mercy you need, and that was to see your need for it and ask: "But the tax collector stood at a distance. He would not even look up to heaven, but beat his breast and said, 'God, have mercy on me, a sinner'" (Luke 18:13). Are you in touch with your need for mercy on a daily basis? Has that awareness affected how you pray, and how you talk or respond to others? *Father, I was in need of mercy, I am still in need on a daily basis. I thank You for your mercy toward me, and I ask You to keep my need fresh in my mind, so I can extend mercy to others.*

April 27

Mind Your Business

Today's reading: Psalm 131-135

"My heart is not proud, Lord, my eyes are not haughty; I do not concern myself with great matters or things too wonderful for me" - Psalm 131:1.

I was in Zimbabwe, about to follow a dynamic, animated and hilarious speaker at a church conference. The people were on their feet cheering him on and I was actually considering both changing my message along with my delivery when the Spirit "spoke" to me. He told me to "stay within myself," which I did and delivered the word the Lord had given me. Today's verse urges you to "stay within yourself" as well by minding your own business and not concerning yourself with matters that don't concern you. When you are proud, you think you know more than you do and you can begin to judge others and comment on things for which you have no experience, insight and gifting. Are you staying focused on the business and people that matter most to you, or have you strayed into fretting about things that are none of your business? Do you see that this is a matter of pride and that the answer is to humble yourself and tend your own matters? *God, I humble myself today and confess that I have spoken authoritatively and harshly about things for which I have little or no understanding. Forgive me for my arrogance!*

April 28

He Will Save You

Today's reading: Psalms 136-140

"Though I walk in the midst of trouble, you preserve my life. You stretch out your hand against the anger of my foes; with your right hand you save me" - Psalm 138:7.

David always seemed to be in trouble, some of it through his own doing and some of it because of his God-assigned purpose. Regardless of the source of his trouble, he always looked to the Lord, crying out to Him for help and deliverance. What's more, God heard his cry for help, even when David was to blame for his troubles! God did the same for Samson, who made a mess of his life, yet prevailed one last time as his hair grew back after his encounter with Delilah: "Then Samson prayed to the Lord, 'Sovereign Lord, remember me. Please, God, strengthen me just once more, and let me with one blow get revenge on the Philistines for my two eyes'" (Judges 16:28). If Samson and David can cry out to God even when they failed, so can you! Don't hesitate to turn to him when you are in trouble, regardless of its source. He will come and save you!

April 29

Entrusted to Him

Today's reading: Psalms 141-145

"Let the morning bring me word of your unfailing love, for I have put my trust in you. Show me the way I should go, for to you I entrust my life" - Psalm 143:8.

People ask me if I am afraid to travel, especially if it's to a place that has been in the news due to some unrest or violence. My standard response is, "I gave my life to the Lord, I didn't loan it to him to take back whenever it was convenient. If He chooses to take me home in my bed or on a plane, that's up to Him." My prayer has been the prayer of David in today's verse: Show me the way I should go for I trust You, Lord." Paul understood this thinking, for he wrote to Timothy, "That is why I am suffering as I am. Yet this is no cause for shame, because I know whom I have believed, and am convinced that he is able to guard what I have entrusted to him until that day" (2 Timothy 1:12). Are you living in fear or have you entrusted your life, which includes your family, reputation, career, finances, and future, to the Lord? Are you trusting that God will show you the way you should go, and then are you proactively walking out what you think that way is?

April 30

Leadership Perspective

Today's reading: Psalms 146-150

"Do not put your trust in princes, in human beings, who cannot save. When their spirit departs, they return to the ground; on that very day their plans come to nothing" - Psalm 146:3-4.

While almost all the psalms are written by leaders, the conclusion toward the end of the book is "don't put too much hope in leaders, for they are mortal and will die, just like everyone else." There are other lessons for followers in this passage: don't put your leaders on a pedestal and don't expect them to be your 'salvation,' for they are only human, no matter how gifted. For leaders, the lessons in this passage are: plan for your successor, for you will not live or rule forever, and don't take yourself more seriously than you should. When the residents of Lystra tried to honor Paul and Barnabas as gods, here's how those two leaders reacted:

> But when the apostles Barnabas and Paul heard of this, they tore their clothes and rushed out into the crowd, shouting: "Friends, why are you doing this? We too are only human, like you. We are bringing you good news,

> telling you to turn from these worthless things to the living God, who made the heavens and the earth and the sea and everything in them" (Acts 14:14-15).

Where do you need to adjust your thinking and expectations, whether you are a leader, follower or both?

May 1

Contentment

Today's reading: Psalms 1-5

"Many, Lord, are asking, 'Who will bring us prosperity?' Let the light of your face shine on us. Fill my heart with joy when their grain and new wine abound" - Psalm 4:6-7.

It seems that David's generation was similar to every generation, in that people were seeking prosperity by any and every means possible. David was countering their materialistic pursuits with a declaration that God was enough for him. Let's look at Eugene Peterson's translation called *The Message* to get his insight into this passage: "Why is everyone hungry for *more*? 'More, more,' they say. 'More, more.' I have God's more-than-enough, more joy in one ordinary day than they get in all their shopping sprees." In other words, David was content in the Lord. Paul also learned about contentment when he wrote, "But if we have food and clothing, we will be content with that" (1 Timothy 6:8). Are you content with what you have or are you frantically working to get more? Are you in debt to maintain a particular lifestyle or are you living within your means, with enough to be generous toward others? Where is your source of joy - things or the Lord? *Father, I have fallen into the "more" syndrome, thinking that things will make me happy. Things have not made me happy; they have just made me hungry for more things! Forgive me for seeking satisfaction in things that will pass away. From this point on, I will seek my joy in eternal things and trust you for the material things. Amen.*

May 2
Comfort Others

Today's reading: Psalms 6-10

"All night long I flood my bed with weeping and drench my couch with tears. My eyes grow weak with sorrow; they fail because of all my foes" - Psalm 6:6-7.

Obviously David was in great distress when he wrote this psalm due to circumstances that are not identified. The interesting thing is that, in the midst of his pain, David took time to write down what he was thinking and feeling, under the direction of the Holy Spirit. The writing must have served as a catharsis of sorts, but then also has provided comfort for the last 3,000 years for those who identify with David's pain. This points out part of why you are going through what you are: you are to use your experience to help others. Paul understood that he suffered in part so that he could comfort others:

> For just as we share abundantly in the sufferings of Christ, so also our comfort abounds through Christ. If we are distressed, it is for your comfort and salvation; if we are comforted, it is for your comfort, which produces in you patient endurance of the same sufferings we suffer. And our hope for you is firm, because we know that just as you share in our sufferings, so also you share in our comfort (1 Corinthians 1:5-7).

What can you do today to comfort someone who is in pain by sharing your own testimony? Can you visit someone, share your testimony and pray for them?

May 3
Run and Hide?

Today's reading: Psalms 11-15

"In the Lord I take refuge. How then can you say to me: 'Flee

like a bird to your mountain. For look, the wicked bend their bows; they set their arrows against the strings to shoot from the shadows at the upright in heart. When the foundations are being destroyed, what can the righteous do?'" - Psalm 11:1-3.

David was always facing some kind of opposition and trouble, and in today's passage some of his advisers were urging him to run away and hide. There were times when David did that, but then there were times when he stood his ground, fought or faced the danger. Whatever his strategy, his life philosophy can be summed up in verse one: "In the Lord I take refuge." The apostle Paul also had to face dangerous situations and sometimes he fled while at other times he stood his ground. Paul's philosophy can be found in Philippians 3:10-11: "I want to know Christ—yes, to know the power of his resurrection and participation in his sufferings, becoming like him in his death, and so, somehow, attaining to the resurrection from the dead." What is your life philosophy where danger and death are concerned? Is the Lord truly your refuge? What proof can you provide that bears out your trust in Him?

May 4

Controlling God

Today's reading: Psalms 16-20

"To the faithful you show yourself faithful, to the blameless you show yourself blameless, to the pure you show yourself pure, but to the devious you show yourself shrewd. You save the humble but bring low those whose eyes are haughty" - Psalm 18:25-27.

Someone once said, "God is playing chess with man; He matches his every move." This passage indicates there is some truth to that saying. God responds to people in the way that they respond both to Him and also to others. God is willing to show Himself faithful, blameless, pure or shrewd, and He ultimately saves those who are humble. If you are not satisfied with how God is revealing Himself to you, then you may be playing some role in the problem. The good news is that if you humble yourself, God will respond and save you from whatever you are facing: "For this is what the high and exalted One says—he who lives forever, whose name is holy: 'I live in a high and holy place, but also with the one who is contrite and lowly in spirit, to revive the spirit of the lowly and to revive the heart of the contrite" (Isaiah 57:15). Where can you do a better job of affecting God's response to you by repenting and changing your attitude or behavior?

May 5

Being Taught

Today's reading: Psalm 21-25

"Guide me in your truth and teach me, for you are God my Savior, and my hope is in you all day long" - Psalm 25:5.

You and I need to be taught the truth and that is why we need to be part of a local church. We need to hear the Word regularly from someone who is capable of teaching God's word and God's ways with skill and accuracy. What's more, that need never ends, but the problem can be that the longer you are in a church, the easier it is to get disillusioned due to the weakness and failure of leadership and followers. When the church problems manifest themselves, it is easy to pick up and go home, sometimes staying home without either returning to church regularly or being involved when you go. The writer of Hebrews stated the problem this way: "And let us consider how we may spur one another on toward love and good deeds, not giving up meeting together, as some are in the habit of doing, but encouraging one another—and all the more as you see the Day approaching" (Hebrews 10:24-25). Who is teaching you God's word? Where are you being taught? How often? Do you know God's word better today than you did a year ago? What will you do to continue your growth in the next year?

May 6

Seeking the Lord

Today's reading: Psalms 26-30

"My heart says of you, 'Seek his face!' Your face, Lord, I will seek" - Psalm 27:8.

Seeking the Lord is not a passive exercise. It requires diligence and fervor. What's more, seeking the Lord requires asking good questions if you expect to get good answers. What's more, saying, "God, I will do whatever you want me to do" is meaningless if you are a serious seeker. "God, what do You want me to do?" is a much better question to ask and to keep on asking, while you reiterate your commitment to do whatever it is that God wants. If you keep on asking the Lord the same questions, however, you will keep getting the same answers, so you need regularly to come up with some different questions. Proverbs 2 directs you to seek Him like you would seek buried treasure if you were guaranteed you would find it: "Indeed, if you call out for insight and cry aloud for understanding, and if you look for it as for silver and search for it as for hidden treasure, then you will understand the fear of the Lord and find the knowledge of God" (Proverbs 2:3-5). Are you seeking the Lord correctly? Are you asking good questions? Do you keep asking until you get an answer?

May 7

Don't Play with Your Food

Today's reading: Psalm 31-35

"Taste and see that the Lord is good; blessed is the one who takes refuge in him" - Psalm 34:8.

David urged his readers to try the Lord, to put their complete trust in Him. The implication is perhaps that some people David knew were *not* doing that, that they were *not* tasting and then living off His goodness. You are not expected to dabble in the things of God, but to be consumed by them - in fact, at times actually to consume them. Ezekiel was directed to eat the scroll with God's words on them: "And he said to me, 'Son of man, eat what is before you, eat this scroll; then go and speak to the people of Israel.' So I opened my mouth, and he gave me the scroll to eat. Then he said to me, 'Son of man, eat this scroll I am giving you and fill your stomach with it.' So I ate it, and it tasted as sweet as honey in my mouth" (Ezekiel 3:1-3). Have you been playing with God's food, or are you consuming it? What is God asking you to eat, to get down into your innermost being? Are you hesitating or can you take refuge in Him as you eat and trust Him totally?

May 8

Giving Philosophy

Today's reading: Psalms 36-40

"The wicked borrow and do not repay, but the righteous give generously . . . . They are always generous and lend freely; their children will be a blessing" - Psalm 37:21, 26.

I heard someone say one time that God doesn't evaluate the gift you give by how much it is, but by how much you have left after you give. Generosity is not about giving large gifts, but rather giving abundantly according to what you have, not what you don't have. Paul explained his philosophy of generosity when he was preparing to receive the offering for the Judean poor from the Corinthian church:

> Our desire is not that others might be relieved while you are hard pressed, but that there might be equality. At the present time your plenty will supply what they need, so that in turn their plenty will supply what you

> need. The goal is equality, as it is written: "The one who gathered much did not have too much, and the one who gathered little did not have too little" (2 Corinthians 8:13-15).

Are you giving generously according to what you have? Would you say you are a generous person? Would others say you are? What do you have to give besides money?

May 9

Depression

Today's reading: Psalms 41-45

"Why, my soul, are you downcast? Why so disturbed within me? Put your hope in God, for I will yet praise him, my Savior and my God" - Psalm 42:5.

The psalmist was experiencing some mental depression for whatever reason, and was confronted with two choices. He could either cooperate with his depression, welcoming it as an inevitability of life. This would have contributed to his mental downward spiral. His second option was *not* to accept his depression and talk himself out of it with some healthy and accurate self talk. The psalmist chose the second option and confronted his depression head on, reminding himself of his relationship with God and its power to lift him from gloom. While some depression has medical causes, in this case, it was the result of faulty thinking, and the writer opted not to accept it but to fight back. The Lord spoke to Cain, prescribing the same procedure as the psalmist employed when Cain was angry and discouraged: "Then the Lord said to Cain, 'Why are you angry? Why is your face downcast? [7] If you do what is right, will you not be accepted? But if you do not do what is right, sin is crouching at your door; it desires to have you, but you must rule over it'" (Genesis 4:6-7). Do you need to confront your depression or mood? What do you need to say to yourself to get yourself back on the right track?

May 10

Proper Perspective

Today's reading: Psalms 46-50

***"Though while they live they count themselves blessed— and people praise you when you prosper— they will join those who have gone before them, who will never again see the light of life"* - Psalm 49:18-19.**

The "they" in this verse are those who prosper. Modern media showcases the lives of the rich and famous and it is easy to become jealous and even covet what they have - beautiful homes, travel to exotic places, magnificent furnishings, clothing and jewelry, showing up at fancy events. David's wisdom pointed out, however, that no one is getting out of here alive, including the prosperous. Their wealth cannot provide eternal life, so for you to envy them and want what they have is short-sighted and dangerous. James was clear in his instructions about envy: "For where you have envy and selfish ambition, there you find disorder and every evil practice" (James 3:16). Search your heart and ask yourself, "Am I envious of what others have?" Do you look at the depictions of the rich and yearn for their lifestyle, even if it's only some aspect of that life? Do you have a proper perspective on your and their ultimate end, along with what (and Who) the source of eternal life is?

May 11

Cast Your Cares on Him

Today's reading: Psalms 51-55

***"Cast your cares on the Lord and he will sustain you; he will never let the righteous be shaken"* - Psalm 55:22.**

Have you ever had someone say in response to your problem, "You just need to give it to the Lord."? It can be annoying and even difficult to comprehend how you can hand off a visible problem to an invisible God. What they are really saying, and what the psalmist was communicating in this verse, is that you must first take your cares to the Lord in prayer and pray until your burden is lifted – until you feel like God has heard and has indicated He has it under control. Then you must resist every and any temptation to worry, fret, or be anxious as reflected by not eating, sleeping or carrying out your day-to-day duties. Peter wrote the same thing as the psalmist in his first epistle: "Cast all your anxiety on him because he cares for you" (1 Peter 5:7). What are you holding on to that you need to cast upon the Lord? What is stopping you? Which part of the process do you need to engage: the prayer or the follow through, or both? *Lord, worry is such a natural response to my daily challenges, but it's the wrong response! Forgive me for my doubt and refusal to take my needs to You in prayer, and then ignoring Your promise that You have everything under control. Today, I choose to cast all my cares on to You!*

May 12

Revenge

Today's reading: Psalms 56-60

"Break the teeth in their mouths, O God; Lord, tear out the fangs of those lions! Let them vanish like water that flows away; when they draw the bow, let their arrows fall short" - Psalm 58:6-7.

The psalmists were not hesitant to cry out for vengeance against those who had done them wrong. This may seem "un-Christian" or vindictive, but that's probably not the case. The psalmists were not carrying out vengeance on their own behalf, but were crying out to God. They were being brutally honest in the midst of situations where the wicked were triumphing and prospering at their expense. The writers were looking to God for answers and for deliverance. If you notice, almost each psalm of lament ends in words of hope, reiterating God is in control. Paul came to the same conclusion that the Old Testament writers did when he wrote the Roman church: "Do not take revenge, my dear friends, but leave room for God's wrath, for it is written: 'It is mine to avenge; I will repay,' says the Lord" (Romans 12:19). Do you seek your own revenge, even if it's a quick comeback to a verbal insult? Do your prayers contain the same honesty as the psalmists? Have you settled the fact that God is the avenger and not you?

May 13

Making and Keeping Vows

Today's reading: Psalms 61-65

"For you, God, have heard my vows; you have given me the heritage of those who fear your name" - Psalm 61:5.

A vow is a promise or a commitment to do something. It starts with a sense that a course of action is right for you, so you speak to confirm your agreement with that sense. It can be as simple as "I'll call you" or as complex as "I'm going back to school." When you make these vows, God is listening and is willing to help you fulfill them. When you break those promises, God considers it a serious breach of integrity. The interesting thing is that often you make vows when you sing in church: "I surrender all" or "I will seek You with all my being" are also vows, even though they are put to music. Are you a person who makes and keeps your vows? Do you under-promise and over-deliver, meaning you say little but then follow through on the impression you had of what you need to do, especially for others? Is your word your bond, or do you say things to make yourself and others feel better, with little capability or intention of following through?

May 14

The Big Difference

Today's reading: Psalms 66-70

"Praise be to the Lord, to God our Savior, who daily bears our burdens" - Psalm 68:19.

God just doesn't bear your burdens - discouragements, failures, disappointments, sins, pain - every once in a while. He does so on a daily basis. He is always on watch and knows you inside and out, so He can give you just what you need when you need it. The challenge is that sometimes you think you need money, for example, and God sends someone with an encouraging word! You may then say, "Lord, thank You, but I'd rather have the cash!" God knows best, however, and is deserving of praise in all circumstances and situations because He knows exactly what you need. Paul wrote, "Rejoice always, pray continually, give thanks in all circumstances; for this is God's will for you in Christ Jesus" (1 Thessalonians 5:17-18). Can you see the difference that Paul did not say to thank God ***for*** all circumstances, but ***in*** them? Can you thank God today in faith because He is bearing your burdens, whether or not it feels like He is? Can you decide to rejoice in Him even if the circumstances are not to your liking?

May 15

Is God Enough?

Today's reading: Psalms 71-75

"Surely in vain I have kept my heart pure and have washed my hands in innocence. All day long I have been afflicted, and every morning brings new punishments" - Psalm 73:13-14.

The psalmist in today's passage was struggling with whether or not it was worth it to pursue righteousness and do right, for bad things seemed to be happening no matter how much good he did. As you have seen in this devotional study so far, this is a repeating theme in the book of Psalms. The question being asked is: What do the righteous receive in return for their obedience and godly behavior? The answer is that they get God Himself – His presence and encouragement in the midst of their trials. The psalmist answered his own lament in verse 73:28: "But as for me, it is good to be near God. I have made the Sovereign Lord my refuge; I will tell of all your deeds." Is God's presence in your life your goal? Is that good enough or do you regret and even resent that you don't have more stuff, less suffering or other more tangible benefits to show for your obedience?

May 16
Faith Logic

Today's reading: Psalms 76-80

"I cried out to God for help; I cried out to God to hear me. When I was in distress, I sought the Lord; at night I stretched out untiring hands, and I would not be comforted" - Psalm 77:1-2.

In today's reading of Psalms 76-80, it is impossible to find verses that speak of anything but grief and sorrow. The people of God were in exile and the psalmist was crying out to God for clarity and restoration. He was writhing in agony as he tried to make sense of how the people of God could be in such trouble when their God, the God of the Exodus, the God of the Red Sea, the God who had delivered Israel in the past, was seemingly silent and inactive in Israel's distress. Perhaps you are facing a life situation that seems to defy "faith logic" for you put your trust in the Lord and things didn't quite work out, or the result did not seem consistent with God's promises. Are you doing what the psalmist did: repeatedly bring it before the Lord in prayer? Are you reminding God of His past deeds and promises that seem to be light years away from where you are? Are you going to God for answers, even though He seems to the One who brought or allowed the circumstances that led to the questions you are asking?

May 17

Righteous and Faithful

Today's reading: Psalms 81-85

"Love and faithfulness meet together; righteousness and peace kiss each other. Faithfulness springs forth from the earth, and righteousness looks down from heaven" - Psalm 85:10-11.

While the psalmists often lamented their current state of affairs, they always ended their pleas for help with affirmations in God's goodness. They also began to look forward to a king who was yet to come who would take up the cause of the righteous and establish justice. Of course we now know the king they were anticipating is Jesus, and He epitomizes what is described in today's passage. He was faithful on earth and the Righteousness who came down from heaven. Now you are to follow His ways and operate in a righteousness that is not your own as you behave in a faithful manner that pleases God and blesses other people. Paul wrote, "You have been set free from sin and have become slaves to righteousness" (Romans 6:18). Are you a slave to righteousness? Do you mirror Jesus' heart and actions to those around you? Are you known for your faithful, consistent and godly behavior at work, school, church or neighborhood?

May 18

Rejoice and Celebrate

Today's reading: Psalms 86-90

"Blessed are those who have learned to acclaim you, who walk in the light of your presence, Lord. They rejoice in your name all day long; they celebrate your righteousness" - Psalm 89:15-16.

"Blessed, rejoice, light, celebrate" are the key words I notice as I read today's verses. You are a *blessed* person if you know the Lord. God gives *light* to your way so you know His will and understand His ways. Knowing and having all this should cause you to *rejoice* all day long and *celebrate* His righteousness. Do you manifest those characteristics and behaviors? Is joy the of the Lord a hallmark of your persona and attitude? Is God's light shining on you to show you the way you need to go on a daily basis? Are you light to those around you? Are you celebrating God's goodness toward you? If not, what is keeping you from entering into these things? Read John 15:10-11: "If you keep my commands, you will remain in my love, just as I have kept my Father's commands and remain in his love. I have told you this so that my joy may be in you and that your joy may be complete." Then work to ensure that God's joy is in you and remove anything that may be standing in its way.

May 19

No Condemnation

Today's reading: Psalms 91-95

"When I said, 'My foot is slipping,' your unfailing love, Lord, supported me. When anxiety was great within me, your consolation brought me joy" - Psalm 94:18-19.

The psalmist made a confession that he was more than a little anxious on occasion. That anxiety did not disqualify him from God's presence, but made God's presence all the more important to him. What's more, God was not offended by that most human of emotions and granted him help in his time of trouble. There are some - and I hope you are not among them - who feel like they cannot come to the Lord as they are, but rather as they *think* He would want them to be. God is more comfortable with your humanity than you are and knows your thoughts before you articulate them. Your honesty is not for His benefit but for yours, so when you confess your anxiety, for example, He does not condemn you, but gives you peace. Perhaps you need to be reminded of what Paul wrote: "Therefore, there is now no condemnation for those who are in Christ Jesus, because through Christ Jesus the law of the Spirit who gives life has set you free from the law of sin and death" (Romans 8:1-2). Are you fearful of God's condemnation if you are honest in His presence? What do you need to tell or confess to the Lord today? Do you see that your honesty with God is for your benefit?

May 20

The Lord Reigns!

Today's reading: Psalms 96-100

"The Lord reigns, let the nations tremble; he sits enthroned between the cherubim, let the earth shake. Great is the Lord in Zion; he is exalted over all the nations. Let them praise your great and awesome name—he is holy" - Psalm 99:1-3.

As the psalmists grappled with the present state of Israel and cried out for help and understanding, they always came to the same conclusion. Even though circumstances were not to their liking and were sometimes beyond comprehension, the Lord still ruled and reigned, and ultimately His promises would be fulfilled for His people. That conclusion always led them to one response, and that was praise and worship. It is an easy thing to praise the Lord when you get a raise, a promotion or a good report from the doctor. It is a bit more challenging when the report or situation is not to your liking. A prophet penned a commitment to praise even when the crops failed: "Though the fig tree does not bud and there are no grapes on the vines, though the olive crop fails and the fields produce no food, though there are no sheep in the pen and no cattle in the stalls, yet I will rejoice in the Lord, I will be joyful in God my Savior" (Habakkuk 3:17). Has your fig, grape or olive harvest failed, along with all your other efforts? Have your flocks disappeared? If you can praise the Lord in the midst of that, then you have come to the same conclusion that the psalmist did: The Lord reigns!

May 21

What A Difference a Day Can Make

Today's reading: Psalms 101-105

"He brought out Israel, laden with silver and gold, and from among their tribes no one faltered. Egypt was glad when they left, because dread of Israel had fallen on them" - Psalm 105:27-38.

Israel had been in Egypt for 430 years, and they had been in slavery most of that time. Then one day, after Pharaoh had refused to release them, he relented and the people of God began the trek know as the Exodus, through the Red Sea to the Promised Land. When they came out of Egypt, the Egyptians were so glad to see them go after the Plagues that they gave the Jews silver and gold as departing gifts. "The Israelites did as Moses instructed and asked the Egyptians for articles of silver and gold and for clothing. The Lord had made the Egyptians favorably disposed toward the people, and they gave them what they asked for; so they plundered the Egyptians" (Exodus 12:35-36). The point is that Israel's situation changed overnight as they went from slaves to wealth. Your situation can change overnight as well, for you are just a phone call, chance meeting or idea away from your breakthrough after a long period of being down and out. How can you stay in a state of expectancy for a breakthrough when things have been down in your world for so long? Can you thank God for your breakthrough even though you have no idea how or when it will come?

May 22

Response to Thirst

Today's reading: Psalms 116-120

"By the waters of Meribah they angered the Lord, and trouble came to Moses because of them; for they rebelled against the Spirit of God, and rash words came from Moses' lips" - Psalm 116:32-33.

The reference in today's passage is to the story in Exodus 17:1-7 when the people grumbled against the Lord and complained to Moses because they were thirsty. They demanded that Moses give them water because they wanted their leader to provide for all their needs. This was an unrealistic demand and, what's more, the Lord had already proved He would provide, yet the people did not believe or remember. If you are experiencing lack, are you blaming the leadership of your company, school or church for your problems? If you are a leader, are you trying to do more for the people than you can really do? Or, if you are a leader, are you angry with the people instead of taking their demands and complaints to the Lord for His direction and counsel, as Moses did? What is the Lord trying to teach you in the midst of your life situation where there is no water?

May 23

Transformed through Worship

Today's reading: Psalms 111-115

"Those who make them will be like them, and so will all who trust in them" - Psalm 115:8.

The *them* in this verse are idols, and the warning is a sobering one. Those who make idols will become just like *them*. What is an idol like? It depends on what that idol is, but the scary aspect of this truth is the transforming affect of the idol that comes through worship to the worshipper. The good news is that you will become more like the Lord if you worship Him, but if you direct that need to worship to anything or anyone else, you are transformed in the wrong way. It has been said that man's heart is an idol factory and that statement was correct. We can make idols of our looks, money, job, intellect, hobbies, denomination, children, heritage, government, or ideology, just to name a few. The Bible is clear on how to relate to idolatry: "Therefore, my dear friends, flee from idolatry" (1 Corinthians 10:14). Do you have any idols in your life that rival for your affection and worship of God? There is only one thing to do if you have any, and that is destroy them now, or risk the wrong kind of spiritual transformation.

May 24

Discipline

Today's reading: Psalms 116-120

"The Lord has chastened me severely,
but he has not given me over to death" - Psalm 118:18.

God is your Father, and one thing that all fathers should do is discipline their children. In today's verse, the psalmist indicated his discipline had been quite severe. This brings to mind the passage in Hebrews 12:8-11, which has this to say about discipline:

> Endure hardship as discipline; God is treating you as his children. For what children are not disciplined by their father? If you are not disciplined—and everyone undergoes discipline—then you are not legitimate, not true sons and daughters at all. Moreover, we have all had human fathers who disciplined us and we respected them for it. How much more should we submit to the Father of spirits and live! They disciplined us

> for a little while as they thought best; but God disciplines us for our good, in order that we may share in his holiness. No discipline seems pleasant at the time, but painful. Later on, however, it produces a harvest of righteousness and peace for those who have been trained by it.

Is God disciplining you? Have you lost sight of your need for discipline because you have walked with Him for a while? Can you joyfully submit to God's training at this point in your life?

May 25

Off Duty

Today's reading: Psalms 121-125

"He will not let your foot slip—he who watches over you will not slumber; indeed, he who watches over Israel will neither slumber nor sleep" - Psalm 121:3-4.

God is always on duty, so to speak, and He never has to take a break to refresh or rest. That means you can be off duty and entrust things to Him while you are. That is easier said than done, however, for you cannot see God at work, so the temptation is to stay on duty through worry, sleepless nights, playing the lottery, telling others your troubles, and many other ways of taking matters into your own hands. Both Jesus and Paul modeled what today's passage suggests when they were asleep while the boat they were in was being battered by storms:

> Suddenly a furious storm came up on the lake, so that the waves swept over the boat. But Jesus was sleeping. The disciples went and woke him, saying, "Lord, save us! We're going to drown!" He replied, "You of little faith, why are you so afraid?" Then he got up and rebuked the winds and the waves, and it was completely calm (Matthew 8:24-26).

Is your boat going through a storm? Are you frantically rowing to save it or are you calmly trusting the Master of the waves and wind to fulfill what He promised in Psalm 121?

May 26

Ask Forgiveness

Today's reading: Psalms 126-130

"If you, Lord, kept a record of sins, Lord, who could stand? But with you there is forgiveness, so that we can, with reverence, serve you" - Psalm 130:3-4.

God is in the sin-forgiveness business, which is of course good news for all mankind. Today's verses imply several things. First, the Lord does not keep a record of sins. Once He forgives, He forgets as well, and does not keep a cumulative record. Second, if that is how the Lord keeps records, then you should do the same for your own mistakes and sins. Third, you should keep the same kind of records for others, which means once they ask forgiveness, you should let it go and not keep it fresh. Fourth, there is an aspect of forgiveness that is tied to asking, so you need to ask others and the Lord to forgive you when you sin. Paul instructed believers to examine themselves before they ate of the Lord's table to see if there were any sins they needed to deal with before eating: "So then, whoever eats the bread or drinks the cup of the Lord in an unworthy manner will be guilty of sinning against the body and blood of the Lord. Everyone ought to examine themselves before they eat of the bread and drink from the cup" (1 Corinthians 11:27-28). Do you need to take care of any sin business with the Lord or with others to obtain forgiveness? Are you keeping sin records on yourself or others? Is it time to destroy the files and start fresh? *Yes, it is time to destroy my memory files on all those who have hurt or offended me. I choose to forgive anyone who has done me wrong, and I extend them mercy because I need mercy as well.*

May 27
Self-Denial

Today's reading: Psalms 131-135

"Lord, remember David and all his self-denial" - Psalm 132:1.

David was God's chosen and anointed one. That did not exempt him, however, from some serious challenges and tribulation, some of it through his fault, but most of it opposition that helped develop and shape David into an even more effective leader. In today's verse, the psalmist commended David to the Lord's attention, reminding the Lord of all that David had been through, which the writer described as "self-denial." Self-denial is a way of life for the believer, for self is the greatest obstacle any believer has in his or her walk of holiness. Jesus knew this and urged His followers to make this self-denial not something that happened to them but something they did to themselves: "Whoever wants to be my disciple must deny themselves and take up their cross and follow me" (Mark 8:34). Where can you do a better job of self-denial? Listening to others when you want to talk about yourself? Interrupting your schedule for someone in need? What other ways can you think of where you can improve in that particular practice?

May 28
Our, Not My

Today's reading: Psalms 136-140

"He remembered us in our low estate His love endures forever. and freed us from our enemies. His love endures forever" - Psalm 136:23-24.

This psalm was probably part of the Temple worship, for it sings of "our" and not "my." There must be a time when you come together with God's people when everyone celebrates their life in Christ that has set them free from sin and death. Yet it is easy to become disillusioned, even bitter, with the church, its members and leadership. That is never an excuse, however, to shun gathering for worship on the Lord's Day or any other time when the church assembles. Paul had to address a dysfunctional church situation in Corinth, but his answer was not to stay home:

> In the following directives I have no praise for you, for your meetings do more harm than good. In the first place, I hear that when you come together as a church, there are divisions among you, and to some extent I believe it. No doubt there have to be differences among you to show which of you have God's approval. So then, when you come together, it is not the Lord's Supper you eat, for when you are eating, some of you go ahead with your own private suppers. As a result, one person remains hungry and another gets drunk (1 Corinthians 11:17-21).

Have you allowed the church's problems to keep you from attending? Can you see that these problems were present 2,000 years ago and the answer is not to withdraw, but to find a place where you can worship and celebrate your life in Christ as fellow believers?

May 29

The Love of God

Today's reading: Psalms 141-145

"Lord, what are human beings that you care for them, mere mortals that you think of them? They are like a breath; their days are like a fleeting shadow" - Psalm 144:3-4.

In God's grand scheme, your life doesn't amount to much when you compare it to the universe and to the billions who exist and have existed. Yet this truth generated praise and worship in David's heart when he considered the fact that God does care for each person, including him (and you). God knows your name, what you are going through, what your purpose is and your failures, both now and the ones to come. This truth goes along with what Paul wrote in Romans 8:31b-35:

> If God is for us, who can be against us? He who did not spare his own Son, but gave him up for us all—how will he not also, along with him, graciously give us all things? Who will bring any charge against those whom God has chosen? It is God who justifies. Who then is the one who condemns? No one. Christ Jesus who died—more than that, who was raised to life—is at the right hand of God and is also interceding for us. Who shall separate us from the love of Christ? Shall trouble or hardship or persecution or famine or nakedness or danger or sword?

There is no need to pose any additional questions, just answer the ones Paul posed in this Romans' passage.

May 30

Storm Master

Today's reading: Psalms 146-150

"Praise the Lord from the earth, you great sea creatures and all ocean depths, lightning and hail, snow and clouds, stormy winds that do his bidding" - Psalm 148:7-8.

Weather can be an awesome and terrifying encounter for humans, but God is in control of it all, according to today's passage. All of creation is commanded to praise the Lord in light of this power over the nature He created. It is of note that the "winds do his bidding,'" which brings to mind one of the encounters with wind that Jesus had:

> A furious squall came up, and the waves broke over the boat, so that it was nearly swamped. Jesus was in the stern, sleeping on a cushion. The disciples woke him and said to him, "Teacher, don't you care if we drown?" He got up, rebuked the wind and said to the waves, "Quiet! Be still!" Then the wind died down and it was completely calm. He said to his disciples, "Why are you so afraid? Do you still have no faith?" (Mark 4:38-40).

Are the winds of life swamping your boat? is it time you called on the Master of the storm to calm things down? Better yet, call on Him to quell the storm of fear in your own heart, and have faith that the winds are indeed doing His bidding in your world

MAY 31

STUDY THE WORD

Today's reading: Psalms 116-120

"Cause me to understand the way of your precepts, that I may meditate on your wonderful deeds" - Psalm 119:27.

The Bible and especially the psalms have great Spirit-led prayers that you can use today in your walk with the Lord. Today's verse is one of those prayers. The psalmist asked the Lord for help so he could understand God's ways and commands. God must open your mind to comprehend His word and to gain insight into His person. Are you praying for that to happen? If you are, then are you spending any amount of time not just reading His word, but also studying it? The Jews in Berea modeled this practice when Luke reported: "Now the Berean Jews were of more noble character than those in Thessalonica, for they received the message with great eagerness and examined the Scriptures every day to see if what Paul said was true" (Acts 17:11). Don't just have good intentions to study the Word and know Him better, get some help developing a plan to do so and then follow it!

JUNE 1

BLESSED

Today's reading: Psalms 1-5

"Blessed is the one who does not walk in step with the wicked or stand in the way that sinners take or sit in the company of mockers, but whose delight is in the law of the Lord, and who meditates on his law day and night" - Psalm 1:1-2.

These are the first verses in the book of Psalms, and they set the stage for the message of the entire book. After the failure of the monarchy and Israel's exile to Babylon, the psalms were compiled, and this is a clue to the book's message: The Law or Torah is the key to an individual's success and Israel's restoration while they waited for their new king. It is interesting that when Jesus began His ministry, one of the first words He spoke was "blessed," thus positioning Himself as Israel's new Psalmist and King who had come to fulfill the Law and rule Israel: "Blessed are the poor in spirit, for theirs is the kingdom of heaven" (Matthew 5:3). In the context of Psalm 1 and what Jesus said, what does it mean to be 'poor in spirit'? Do you delight in His law and meditate on it night and day? Is your life foundation God's word or some other philosophy or denominational teaching?

JUNE 2

STRATEGY FOR VICTIMS

Today's verse: Psalms 6-10

"But you, God, see the trouble of the afflicted; you consider their grief and take it in hand. The victims commit themselves to you; you are the helper of the fatherless" - Psalm 10:14.

If you have been a victim - and to some extent everyone has - then the worst thing you can do is to try and make things right in your own strength from your own perspective of what you need.

The best thing to do is to trust the Lord because when you do, he takes your grief into His own hands! It also seems that the Lord has a special "hot line" for those who suffered and are suffering from a lack of fatherly care or presence – they get His immediate and undivided attention. These verses are reminiscent of Hannah when she found herself childless:

> In her deep anguish Hannah prayed to the Lord, weeping bitterly. And she made a vow, saying, "Lord Almighty, if you will only look on your servant's misery and remember me, and not forget your servant but give her a son, then I will give him to the Lord for all the days of his life, and no razor will ever be used on his head" (1 Samuel 1:10-11).

Are you burdened with grief? Childless? Fatherless? Penniless? Are you a victim of some abuse or crime? Then do what Hannah did and commit your way to the Lord, standing on the promise of today's verse as you commit yourself to Him.

June 3

Slander and Slurs

Today's reading: Psalm 11-15

"Lord, who may dwell in your sacred tent? Who may live on your holy mountain? . . . whose tongue utters no slander, who does no wrong to a neighbor, and casts no slur on others" - Psalm 15:1, 3.

Psalm 15 asks a question and then provides the answers in the following verses. In verse three, the one who can dwell in God's presence is the person who controls his or her tongue. What does the psalmist mean by godly speech? That talk includes not slandering or 'casting slurs' on another person. A slur is a "disparaging remark" and slander is "oral communication of false and malicious statements that damage the reputation of another." Paul wrote about the need for clean speech in Ephesians 4:29:

"Do not let any unwholesome talk come out of your mouths, but only what is helpful for building others up according to their needs, that it may benefit those who listen." Are you using your mouth to build up or tear down others? What can you do to be more positive and proactive with your words? Do you need to go back and repair any damage done to others by what you said?

June 4

What's in Your Heart?

Today's reading: Psalms 16-20

"May he give you the desire of your heart and make all your plans succeed" - Psalm 20:4.

We have been taught not to trust our hearts, for they can be deceitful - and that's true. Yet just because they "can be" doesn't mean they are, and God can use your heart to guide your paths. Not every heart matter is a trick, for God put some things in your heart to do so that you are inclined toward His will in a naturally supernatural way. What's more, the Holy Spirit's presence in your life helps give you His mind and heart, so your desires cannot all be out of whack. Paul wrote: "For who has known the mind of the Lord so as to instruct him? But we have the mind of Christ" (2 Corinthians 2:16). What has been in your heart to do or be for many years, and just won't go away? Can you accept that it isn't going away because God put it there, and you need to act on it? If the Spirit is in you to give you the mind of Christ, why is it so difficult for you to accept that you now have that mind?

June 5

God's Will

Today's reading: Psalms 21-25

"Who, then, are those who fear the Lord?

He will instruct them in the ways they should choose" - Psalm 25:12.

If your desire is to know God's will, then you will do so, for you cannot do what you do not know. This requires that you sincerely desire to know His will, which can be tricky because it involves trust and overcoming fear. If you truly commit to God's will *before* you know what it is, your next step is to overcome the fear that He will have you do something radical or totally out of character for you. The promise remains, however, that if you ask, then He will reveal His will, as Isaiah explained:

> Although the Lord gives you the bread of adversity and the water of affliction, your teachers will be hidden no more; with your own eyes you will see them. Whether you turn to the right or to the left, your ears will hear a voice behind you, saying, "This is the way; walk in it" (Isaiah 30:20-21).

Is fear of the answer keeping you from seeking God's will? Do you really believe He can reveal and you will hear His will? Are you afraid of what He will show you, thus shutting yourself off from truly hearing?

JUNE 6

DO GOOD TO ENEMIES

Today's reading: Psalms 26-30

"Do not drag me away with the wicked, with those who do evil, who speak cordially with their neighbors but harbor malice in their hearts. Repay them for their deeds and for their evil work; repay them for what their hands have done and bring back on them what they deserve" - Psalm 28:3-4.

David once again cried out that God would deal with those who were evil. Some are uncomfortable with the psalmists' cries for vengeance, but at least they were not taking matters of revenge into their own hands! They were crying out for God to do it. What's more, this set the stage for Jesus' ministry, whose hallmark was forgiveness toward those same evil people who plagued David and the psalmists:

> And if you lend to those from whom you expect repayment, what credit is that to you? Even sinners lend to sinners, expecting to be repaid in full. But love your enemies, do good to them, and lend to them without expecting to get anything back. Then your reward will be great, and you will be children of the Most High, because he is kind to the ungrateful and wicked. Be merciful, just as your Father is merciful (Luke 6:34-36).

Do you have any enemies to whom you can do good today? What can you do that will distinguish you as a follower of Jesus in your kind treatment and attitude toward those who treat you poorly?

June 7

Opposition

Today's reading: Psalms 31-35

"But I trust in you, Lord; I say, "You are my God." My times are in your hands; deliver me from the hands of my enemies, from those who pursue me" - Psalm 31:14-15.

The first book of Psalms, which is comprised of Psalm 1 to 41, is filled with verses that chronicle David's persecution and opposition as the king. One may not think David would not have encountered so much trouble, for God had powerfully and sovereignly chosen David and was with him. Yet God's choice did not exempt David from all kinds of problems, some of them by his own doing. You may be going through hell, so to speak, as you do God's will, and that has caused you to doubt whether or not you heard from the Lord and are on the right path. Yet the presence of opposition is not an indication you are out of God's will, but rather a confirmation that you are in it! James wrote: "Consider it pure joy, my brothers and sisters, whenever you face trials of many kinds, because you know that the testing of your faith produces perseverance. Let perseverance finish its work so that you may be mature and complete, not lacking anything" (James 1:2-4). Have you allowed your time of testing to cast doubt on you're the way you are walking? Have you had second thoughts about whether or not you have heard from the Lord? Be encouraged today that you are on the right path!

June 8

Loneliness

Today's reading - Psalms 36-40

"My friends and companions avoid me because of my wounds; my neighbors stay far away" - Psalm 38:11.

It's easy for people to avoid you when are going through difficulty, and they do so for many reasons. One is that they lack empathy and just don't understand what you are going through. Another is that they don't want to say the wrong thing, so they say no thing. Perhaps they think your predicament is your own fault, so they distance themselves because they are being judgmental. And sometimes people don't want to be around when you feel bad because you will make them feel bad. Whatever the reason, people can and will disappoint you, especially when you are in need. Paul experienced this kind of but he also knew the comfort of loyalty and friendship: "May the Lord show mercy to the household of Onesiphorus, because he often refreshed me and was not ashamed of my chains" (2 Timothy 1:16). Have you experienced betrayal or loneliness lately? Are you bitter or resentful? Do you have the opportunity today to be a loyal friend to someone else, even though others have betrayed or abandoned you?

JUNE 9

HEART TO HEART

Today's reading: Psalms 41-45

"Sometimes I ask God, my rock-solid God, 'Why did you let me down? Why am I walking around in tears, harassed by enemies?' They're out for the kill, these tormentors with their obscenities, Taunting day after day, 'Where is this God of yours?'" - Psalm 42:9-10, The Message.

Today's passage from a different translation captures the conversational tone of many psalms as the psalmist pours his heart out to the Lord. It is impossible to offend the Lord with your honest, transparent prayers, for God knows what's on your heart before you utter a word. The honesty is not for His benefit but for yours! What's more, we see once again that the righteous were in trouble, this time from people who were tormenting the psalmist, wondering why God wasn't helping him in his distress. The writer had to work through this seeming contradiction by means of a heart-to-heart talk with God. Moses also had honest talks with the Lord, as reported in Numbers 11:14-15: "I cannot carry all these people by myself; the burden is too heavy for me. If this is how you are going to treat me, please go ahead and kill me—if I have found favor in your eyes—and do not let me face my own ruin." Is it time you had a heart-to-heart talk with the Lord? What do you need to tell Him? What confusion do you need to set before Him?

JUNE 10

WEALTH

Today's reading: Psalms 46-50

"People, despite their wealth, do not endure; they are like the beasts that perish" - Psalm 49:12.

Our society has a strange love affair with wealth. We want it, honor it, hoard it, spend it, ruthlessly pursue it, but it is always a fickle partner that goes to the highest bidder. What's more, it cannot really bring what its seekers want most - peace and contentment. In fact, when you think about it, money and wealth are a lot of trouble, for you have to spend a lot to protect what you have – and it can still all disappear through no fault of the owner. Read this rather harsh warning directed toward the wealthy:

> Now listen, you rich people, weep and wail because of the misery that is coming on you. Your wealth has rotted, and moths have eaten your clothes. Your gold and silver are corroded. Their corrosion will testify against you and eat your flesh like fire. You have hoarded wealth in the last days. Look! The wages you failed to pay the workers who mowed your fields are crying out against you. The cries of the harvesters have reached the ears of the Lord Almighty. You have lived on earth in luxury and self-indulgence. You have fattened yourselves in the day of slaughter (James 5:1-5).

Having read today's verses, do you still want to devote more time to gaining wealth? Can your pursuit of wealth give you what you truly need? If not, then why agonize over gaining it? And how much is enough where wealth is concerned?

JUNE 11

THE WILL AND THE HELP

Today's reading: Psalms 51-55

"Create in me a pure heart, O God, and renew a steadfast spirit within me" - Psalm 51:10.

This seems like a prayer that anyone could or should pray, but on closer examination, it is a dangerous prayer that could lead to a tumultuous answer. The psalmist was praying that God would do whatever He had to do to change the psalmist on the inside, in his heart. What's more, the psalmist was praying for a steadfast spirit or, in other words, patience and diligence. The psalmist was giving God permission to rework and reshape his inner being. Paul described this inner work of Christ when he wrote in Philippians 2:13: "For God is working in you, giving you the desire and the power to do what pleases him." God gives you the will to do His will and then gives you whatever help you need to do it! That's a good deal. What would God have to work in your life to give you a pure heart and a steadfast spirit? Is there anything stopping you from praying today's prayer? Can you see that this prayer is one of total surrender?

June 12

Private Devotions

Today's reading: Psalms 56-60

"But as for me, I will sing about your power. Each morning I will sing with joy about your unfailing love. For you have been my refuge, a place of safety when I am in distress" - Psalm 59:16.

David understood the importance of establishing a rhythm for his day, and that rhythm began with a time of worship or devotions. Many have insisted that this is the only pattern to follow, but I do not agree. It's important that you establish a daily pattern or rhythm that works for you, and that may mean that you have your devotions in the evening or morning, according to when you function best. If I don't get to devotions in the morning, then I tend not to get to them. There were times when Jesus had to spend His time with the Father at night: "One of those days Jesus went out to a mountainside to pray, and spent the night praying to God" (Luke 6:12). Do you have a regular time for your devotional expression? What is keeping you from that regular discipline? Are you an early morning or late night person?

JUNE 13

SCHEMING OR PLANNING?

Today's reading: Psalms 61-65

"They plot injustice and say, 'We have devised a perfect plan!' Surely the human mind and heart are cunning" - Psalm 64:6.

God put the ability in people to plan, but of course the Fall caused mankind to plan and scheme how to take care of themselves. This planning branched out into people's desire to reach God on their own terms instead of God's. This is exemplified by the story known as the Tower of Babel in Genesis 11. When God saw their scheme, He said, "If as one people speaking the same language they have begun to do this, then nothing they plan to do will be impossible for them. Come, let us go down and confuse their language so they will not understand each other" (Genesis 11:5-6). God was not threatened by their planning. He knew they were plotting something that would require Him to judge them for their disobedience (God had told them to spread out; they wanted to stay put). Jesus came to restore mankind's ability to plan but to do it for righteous and not selfish ends. Do you see planning as spiritual or unspiritual? What could you accomplish for the Lord if you had a 10- 15- or 25-year plan? Are you planning to achieve God's purpose or your own?

JUNE 14

YOUR BURDEN-BEARER

Today's reading: Psalms 66-70

"Praise be to the Lord, to God our Savior, who daily bears our burdens" - Psalm 68:19.

David broke into praise when he realized that God is both a long-term Savior as well as a short-term Helper who bore his burdens, not just every once in a while, but daily! What does it mean that God bears burdens? It means that He carries something so you don't have to. This can only happen, however, when you allow Him to be your burden-bearer; otherwise, you are left with a heavy load. Jesus said in Matthew 11:28-30: "Come to me, all you who are weary and burdened, and I will give you rest. Take my yoke upon you and learn from me, for I am gentle and humble in heart, and you will find rest for your souls. For my yoke is easy and my burden is light." If you have a heavy yoke or burden, then you have to ask yourself, "Whose yoke am I carrying?", because it cannot be the assignment that Jesus gave you. Are you under a heavy yoke today? What can you do to transfer that yoke to Jesus, the Burden-Bearer?

June 15

Mourning

Today's reading: Psalms 71-75

"When my heart was grieved and my spirit embittered,I was senseless and ignorant; I was a brute beast before you" - Psalm 73:21-22.

The psalmist made an honest confession that he was beside himself with an emotional breakdown over some issue that caused him to mourn and grieve. Some people do not allow themselves to mourn, not just the loss of a loved one, but any loss - job, life status, the potential of what could have been if someone else had not messed up, or what could have been if the mourner himself or herself had not messed up. It is painful to mourn, but absolutely necessary if the mourner is to get to the other side of healing and emotional health. Paul instructed believers about mourning when he wrote: "Brothers and sisters, we do not want you to be uninformed about those who sleep in death, so that you do not grieve like the rest of mankind, who have no hope" (1 Thessalonians 4:13). You can mourn because the situation you are mourning is in God's hands and you have hope. You do have hope don't you, or have you lost it over some situation? Have you resisted mourning, thinking it is somehow not proper behavior for a believer? Will you give yourself permission to mourn today until the season of mourning ends? *Thank You, Lord, for giving me an opportunity to grieve the loss of something or someone important to me. I trust You to heal my heart but until You do, I will continue to mourn, realizing it is part of my healing process. I have confidence that how I feel will change one day, but until I do, I will entrust this situation to You as I mourn the loss.*

June 16

Bible Hope

Today's reading: Psalm 76-80

"I will remember the deeds of the Lord; yes, I will remember your miracles of long ago" - Psalm 77:11.

The psalmist was in a tough place, as they often were, and he determined to take solace and encouragement from the miracles God performed for Israel in ages past. In other words, the psalmist went to the Scriptures to find help in time of trouble. If you are going through a tough time, you can certainly draw on the past for help by remembering what God has done for you. If you cannot find help there, however, you can and should go to the Bible to find consolation and support from what God did for others centuries ago. Your thinking should be, "If He did it for them, He can do it for me!" Paul referred to this role the Bible should have in your life when he wrote: "For everything that was written in the past was written to teach us, so that through the endurance taught in the Scriptures and the encouragement they provide we might have hope" (Romans 15:4). Do you have a favorite character in the Bible from whom you draw strength and instruction? Are you using the Word as your personal cheerleader and oxygen tank when you are down or having trouble breathing in encouragement?

June 17

In Jesus

Today's reading: Psalms 81-85

"Love and faithfulness meet together; righteousness and peace kiss each other" - Psalm 85:10.

The Psalms are about Jesus, even though David and others wrote them out of the reality of their own experience and need. In Jesus, we have a God who understands the human dilemma and the frailty of mankind. In Jesus, we have a man who became like you and me in all things except sin, and showed how to live a life pleasing to God. He not only gave the Law but He lived it in such a way so as to fulfill the Law. In Him, the *righteousness* of God in Christ and the *peace* with God gained through the cross of Christ did indeed come together or *kiss* each other. Jesus lived the psalms, prayed the psalms, and epitomized the message of the psalms to show us the way to relate to God as pilgrims in this world. Paul wrote this about Jesus:

> Who, being in very nature God, did not consider equality with God something to be used to his own advantage; rather, he made himself nothing by taking the very nature of a servant, being made in human likeness. And being found in appearance as a man, he humbled himself by becoming obedient to death—even death on a cross! (Philippians 2:6-8).

Take some time to meditate on today's verses, and then thank Jesus that He is your righteousness and that His death on the cross brought you peace with God the Father.

June 18

Anointing of Joy

Today's reading: Psalms 86-90

"Bring joy to your servant, Lord,

for I put my trust in you" - Psalm 86:4.

There are some people who don't trust joy. They claim it is an emotion and cannot be trusted as a reliable source of guidance or confirmation. If joy comes, that's all well and good, but duty, rationality, and freedom from emotions are preferable when worshiping, making decisions, and walking out discipleship. If all that's true, then why did David pray that God would bring him joy? If joy is not to be trusted, why did Jesus have and follow His joy? If joy is so unreliable and fickle, why would God create you with joy in doing certain things and then *not* allow you to follow or savor that joy? We read about Jesus in Hebrews 1:9, "You have loved righteousness and hated wickedness; therefore God, your God, has set you above your companions by anointing you with the oil of joy." Jesus was anointed with joy, and that joy led and fed Him as He carried out His earthly mission. If Jesus had, expressed and followed joy, you can be assured that God has the same pattern for you to follow. Are you seeking and following your joy? Are you praying for it as David did?

June 19

Your Father's Discipline

Today's reading: Psalms 91-95

"Blessed is the one you discipline, Lord, the one you teach from your law; you grant them relief from days of trouble, till a pit is dug for the wicked" - Psalm 94:12-13.

God is always teaching and disciplining His people, and here the psalmist indicated why He is doing that. He does it to prevent us from getting into trouble down the road. He also does it so that the righteous will be protected and preserved, set apart is the exact phrase, until such time as God is ready to judge the wicked. This also protects the righteous so they will not be judged along with wicked. Paul reiterated this principle when he wrote, "Nevertheless, when we are judged in this way by the Lord, we are being disciplined so that we will not be finally condemned with the world" (1 Corinthians 11:32). Are you experiencing discipline from your Heavenly Father's hand? What does this discipline look like? Are you chafing under or resistant to this discipline? Can you accept it in faith that it is in your long-term best interests for your Father to do this? Can you not just endure it, but see that you are blessed because of it, and even thank God for it? *Lord, the Bible is right: no discipline is pleasant, but it's necessary. I accept Your work in my life and important, and thank You for it.*

JUNE 20

DECIDE TO REJOICE

Today's reading: Psalms 96-100

"Light shines on the righteous and joy on the upright in heart. Rejoice in the Lord, you who are righteous, and praise his holy name" - Psalm 97:11-12.

We return once again to the topic of joy. In these verses, we see that joy shines on the righteous, coming from an source outside of the recipient. It is not dependent on circumstances and is not a decision on the part of the joyful. It is a decision, however, to rejoice – to allow the joy to show on your face and in your demeanor. Paul outlined how this joy and peace can shine down on a righteous person:

> Rejoice in the Lord always. I will say it again: Rejoice! Let your gentleness be evident to all. The Lord is near. Do not be anxious about anything, but in every situation, by prayer and petition, with thanksgiving, present your requests to God. And the peace of God, which transcends all understanding, will guard your hearts and your minds in Christ Jesus (Philippians 4:5-7).

Spend a few minutes today reflecting on this concept of joy and the process that Paul outlined in Philippians. Are you rejoicing?

Do others know you have joy? As God shines joy on you, do you reflect it to others? Are you anxious? Do you pray with thanksgiving? Do you have the peace that passes all understanding?

June 21

Another Way to Rejoice

Today's reading: Psalms 101-105

"Give praise to the Lord, proclaim his name; make known among the nations what he has done.Sing to him, sing praise to him; tell of all his wonderful acts. Glory in his holy name; let the hearts of those who seek the Lord rejoice. Look to the Lord and his strength; seek his face always" - Psalm 105:1-4.

Yesterday we looked at the concept of rejoicing, which is making your joy evident through words, demeanor, and song. Today's passage also mentions rejoicing, ordering those who seek the Lord to rejoice while adding another way to rejoice, and that is to share your testimony to as much of your world as possible. In other words, your devotion and worship cannot be a private matter, but must be carried out publicly to encourage others to join you – or at least to listen. A great example of this is found in Acts:

> They called the apostles in and had them flogged. Then they ordered them not to speak in the name of Jesus, and let them go. The apostles left the Sanhedrin, rejoicing because they had been counted worthy of suffering disgrace for the Name. Day after day, in the temple courts and from house to house, they never stopped teaching and proclaiming the good news that Jesus is the Messiah (6:40-42).

Are you in a worse situation than the apostles were? If not, then you have no excuse *not* to be doing what they did – rejoicing and proclaiming the reason for their joy!

June 22

The Words of God

Today's reading: Psalms 106-110

"The Lord says to my lord: 'Sit at my right hand until I make your enemies a footstool for your feet'" - Psalm 110:1.

Jesus quoted this verse when He was teaching the people in Mark 12:35-37:

> While Jesus was teaching in the temple courts, he asked, "Why do the teachers of the law say that the Messiah is the son of David? David himself, speaking by the Holy Spirit, declared: "'The Lord said to my Lord: 'Sit at my right hand until I put your enemies under your feet.' David himself calls him 'Lord.' How then can he be his son?'" The large crowd listened to him with delight.

Notice that Jesus acknowledged that David wrote this psalm. Then He recognized that the Holy Spirit had inspired David's words, speaking through David in the words of the psalm. Finally, the people so enjoyed Jesus' insight into the Word that they listened with absolute delight. Do you have the same high view of Scripture? Do you see the Bible as the words of God? If you have the privilege of speaking and teaching God's word, do people delight to listen to you as Jesus gives you insight into His word? If you sit under a teacher of God's word, are you being fed from the Word or are you tolerating poor teaching in the interest of tradition or family ties?

June 23

Light in Darkness

Today's reading: Psalms 111-115

"Even in darkness light dawns for the upright, for those who are gracious and compassionate and righteous" - Psalm 112:4.

God is able to protect His own flock no matter what the circumstances are. God preserved Noah and his family during the Flood. He protected the Jews when the plagues were tormenting Egypt. The Lord protected Shadrach, Meshach and Abednego in the fiery furnace. He also protected Daniel in the lions' den:

> At the first light of dawn, the king got up and hurried to the lions' den. When he came near the den, he called to Daniel in an anguished voice, "Daniel, servant of the living God, has your God, whom you serve continually, been able to rescue you from the lions?" Daniel answered, "May the king live forever! My God sent his angel, and he shut the mouths of the lions. They have not hurt me, because I was found innocent in his sight. Nor have I ever done any wrong before you, Your Majesty" (Daniel 6:19-23).

Like Daniel, are you facing the lions over some stand you have taken for the Lord, some persecution like a job loss, broken relationship or economic oppression? Are you afraid because of your opposition? Learn from the examples mentioned here, and don't fear, for God can make your light shine no matter how dark it gets!

June 24

Addictions

Today's reading: Psalms 116-120

"Truly I am your servant, Lord; I serve you just as my mother did; you have freed me from my chains" - Psalm 116:16.

The psalmist had a family heritage of serving the Lord, yet the psalmist also had a testimony that he had been in bondage or chains at some point in time, perhaps even while he was serving the Lord. It is possible to love and serve the Lord and still become or continue to be addicted to something as simple as television reality shows or more serious like drugs or pornography. God is able to break your chains no matter how strong they are, because He is stronger, but you must want to be set free - God will not separate you from your friends if you are that attached to them. Jesus set a man free and if this man could be set free, then you can be set free as well:

> This man lived in the tombs, and no one could bind him anymore, not even with a chain. For he had often been chained hand and foot, but he tore the chains apart and broke the irons on his feet. No one was strong enough to subdue him. Night and day among the tombs and in the hills he would cry out and cut himself with stones (Mark 5:3-5).

Are you addicted to something or do you have an overpowering negative habit? Cry out to the Lord today and He will set you free, but only if that is what you want to be free.

June 25

Go Where God Is

Today's reading: Psalms 121-125

"I rejoiced with those who said to me, 'Let us go to the house of the Lord.' Our feet are standing in your gates, Jerusalem" - Psalm 122:1-2.

This psalm is one of a collection or series known as the psalms of ascent (Psalms 120-134). Many believe these psalms were recited by pilgrims while they made their way to Jerusalem as the Lord had commanded them to do three times every year. God did not seem to mind putting the people through the rigors of travel in order to engage His presence in Jerusalem. Even today, when the Lord wants to speak to His people, He often has them go on a trip, for then they are out of their comfort zone and more aware of their environment and His voice. Jesus was with His disciples in Jerusalem but then directed them to go north to Galilee, even though He could have spoken to them in Jerusalem: "Then the eleven disciples went to Galilee, to the mountain where Jesus had told them to go. When they saw him, they worshiped him; but some doubted. Then Jesus came to them and said . . ." (Matthew 28:16-18a). Has God put it on your heart to go somewhere where God promised that He will meet you? Are you trying to talk yourself out of going? Are you thinking that what He has to say to you He can say where you are right now, so you don't have to go?

June 26

Waiting on the Lord

Today's reading: Psalms 126-130

"I wait for the Lord, my whole being waits, and in his word I put my hope. I wait for the Lord more than watchmen wait for the morning, more than watchmen wait for the morning" - Psalm 130:5-6.

There is no more misunderstood or misused concept in your walk with God than "waiting on the Lord." Most people consider waiting on the Lord the same as waiting on a train or bus. They passively wait, looking down the tracks or road to see if the transportation is coming. If it doesn't come, then they are exempt from any responsibility or action. That is not waiting; that is abdicating responsibility. Re-read the verses above and notice how the psalmist's entire being was waiting. He as searching and all his energy and faculties were focused on that task. If you are waiting on the Lord for a new job, then spend your time now getting ready for that job, as Abraham Lincoln once said: "I will study and get ready, and perhaps my chance will come." Where are you passively waiting and instead should be actively pursuing a goal while you wait for your God-given breakthrough? Where are you waiting for God to do what only you can do? Is your waiting an opportunity for growth or a dereliction of duty?

June 27

Psalms and Revelation

Today's reading: Psalms 131-135

"All you Israelites, praise the Lord; house of Aaron, praise the Lord; house of Levi, praise the Lord; you who fear him, praise the Lord. Praise be to the Lord from Zion, to him who dwells in Jerusalem" - Psalms 135:19-21.

The psalms are a mixture of individual and corporate expressions of and exhortations to praise. In today's passage, we see a corporate exhortation that covers the nation, families, tribes, and all who feared the Lord. The end goal of everything in Psalms is praise, which is a focus on God that transcends circumstances to His majesty and goodness. When you look at psalms from that perspective, you see that it mirrors the message of Revelation, which is also a picture of praise and worship as the ultimate human expression:

> After this I looked, and there before me was a great multitude that no one could count, from every nation, tribe, people and language, standing before the throne and before the Lamb. They were wearing white robes and were holding palm branches in their hands. And they cried out in a loud voice: "Salvation belongs to our God, who sits on the throne, and to the Lamb." All the angels were standing around the throne and around the elders and the four living creatures. They fell down on their faces before the throne and worshiped God (Revelation 7:9-11).

Is praise and worship the end of your spiritual devotion and seeking? Are you focused on God or on yourself and your world of family and work/ministry? Do you have both corporate and individual expressions of praise in your spiritual repertoire?

June 28

Fleeing God's Presence

Today's reading: Psalm 136-140

"Where can I go from your Spirit? Where can I flee from your presence?" - Psalm 139:7.

Adam and Eve tried to flee from God's presence, comically hiding in a bush with fig-leaf coverings as God walked in the Garden. They were afraid after their sin and tried their best to hide. Jonah also attempted to run from God, in his case to avoid carrying out God's directive to fulfill His prophetic purpose in Nineveh: "But Jonah ran away from the Lord and headed for Tarshish. He went down to Joppa, where he found a ship bound for that port. After paying the fare, he went aboard and sailed for Tarshish to flee from the Lord" (Jonah 1:3). Fear is the reason those three tried to flee from God's presence, and fear will cause you to do the same thing, actually blocking God's voice in your heart that is there to direct your steps. Are you hiding from God, afraid because of your sin or because you are afraid of your purpose? Do you see how silly that is? You know that God knows where you are, so why go through the futility of avoiding His love or His will?

June 29

Prayers for Kids

Today's reading: Psalms 141-145

"Then our sons in their youth will be like well-nurtured plants, and our daughters will be like pillars carved to adorn a palace" - Psalm 144:12.

David was a fabulous writer, so talented that we still recite his poetry and put his lyrics to music 3,000 after his death! In today's verse, he penned two similes for offspring that I incorporated into my prayers for my own children - that my son would be a well-nurtured plant and my daughter like a pillar carved for a palace! I then took that prayer to go beyond my family to the children youth in my church. Another passage that makes a great prayer for your children is found in Isaiah 44:3-5:

> For I will pour water on the thirsty land, and streams on the dry ground; I will pour out my Spirit on your offspring, and my blessing on your descendants. They will spring up like grass in a meadow, like poplar trees by flowing streams. Some will say, 'I belong to the Lord'; others will call themselves by the name of Jacob; still others will write on their hand, "The Lord's," and will take the name Israel.

On whose behalf can you start praying these prayers? For your children? Grandchildren? Nieces and nephews? Friends?

June 30

Rejoice in His Love

Today's reading: Psalms 146-150

"Let them praise his name with dancing and make music to him with timbrel and harp. For the Lord takes delight in his people; he crowns the humble with victory. Let his faithful people rejoice in this honor and sing for joy on their beds" - Psalm 149:3-5.

The Lord just doesn't tolerate you, He delights in you! He watches over you and bestows honor on you as you humble yourself to submit to His will and rejoice in His ways. If this truth doesn't exhilarate you and fill you with joy, then you may not fully comprehend either what God's love means or the significance of the favor you have with Him. Paul grasped God's great love for His people when he wrote:

> No, in all these things we are more than conquerors through him who loved us. For I am convinced that

> neither death nor life, neither angels nor demons, neither the present nor the future, nor any powers, neither height nor depth, nor anything else in all creation, will be able to separate us from the love of God that is in Christ Jesus our Lord (Romans 8:37-39).

Take some time today to reflect on the fact that God takes great joy in His love for and relationship with you. Ask Him to reveal to you any hindrance like a sense of rejection or failure that would keep you from a full appreciation of His love for you. Then work to remove that blockage so you can rejoice in His love for you!

July 1

Vivid Prayers

Today's reading: Psalms 1-5

***"Arise, Lord! Deliver me, my God! Strike all my enemies on the jaw; break the teeth of the wicked"* - Psalm 3:6-7.**

David was in trouble, and he was not praying what I call "Now-I-lay-me-down-to-sleep" prayers. He was praying fervently and aggressively because he knew the danger he was in and realized God was the only One who could help and save him. Do you realize that you are in the same kind of danger in which David found himself? You have an enemy that doesn't just want to hurt you; He wants to destroy you and cause your faith to be destroyed. Peter warned about this danger when he wrote,

> Be alert and of sober mind. Your enemy the devil prowls around like a roaring lion looking for someone to devour. Resist him, standing firm in the faith, because you know that the family of believers throughout the world is undergoing the same kind of sufferings (1 Peter 5:8-9).

Do you see the nature of the spiritual war you are engaged in when you follow Jesus? Are you praying aggressive prayers that have vivid descriptions of what you need the Lord to do? *Father,*

I have been reluctant to fight for my spiritual inheritance and blessings. I expected You to give them to me without having to invest energy or effort in the process. I see that was wrong and commit to fight for what is mine, realizing the battle will only enhance my appreciation and value of what You give me.

JULY 2

YOUR PURPOSE

Today's reading: Psalms 6-10

"What is mankind that you are mindful of them, human beings that you care for them? You have made them a little lower than the angels and crowned them with glory and honor. You made them rulers over the works of your hands; you put everything under their feet" - Psalm 8:4-6.

God determined that mankind would rule over the works of His hands and therefore gave man a mandate to do so: "God blessed them and said to them, "Be fruitful and increase in number; fill the earth and subdue it. Rule over the fish in the sea and the birds in the sky and over every living creature that moves on the ground" (Genesis 1:28). The Fall of Adam and Eve marred this dominion, but Jesus came to restore all things, including this God-given assignment: "and through him to reconcile to himself all things, whether things on earth or things in heaven, by making peace through his blood, shed on the cross" (Colossians 1:20). Therefore, your purpose in life is to find that portion of creation over which God has given you dominion and to rule over it in the will of God. Do you know your purpose, or are you just working to make money? Are you extending God's compassion and authority in your purpose, or are you simply paying the bills? Do you want to know your purpose, or are you happy with the way things are in your work life?

July 3

Dealing with Godless Fools

Today's reading: Psalms 11-15

"The fool says in his heart, 'There is no God.' They are corrupt, their deeds are vile; there is no one who does good" - Psalm 14:1.

A correct understanding of God is required for any and all righteousness. Without that, God identifies the godless as fools and their ability to do good is minimized. Therefore, the best way to turn around evil and wickedness is to convert the evil doer into a God-fearer. That makes world evangelism the top priority for anyone who wants to make a difference in the world. You can pursue evangelism by going and doing, or by supporting those who are gifted and willing to go, including a local church who preaches the gospel and makes evangelism a priority. Remember, no one is beyond God's reach, and the Apostle Paul is a good example of that:

> Even though I was once a blasphemer and a persecutor and a violent man, I was shown mercy because I acted in ignorance and unbelief. The grace of our Lord was poured out on me abundantly, along with the faith and love that are in Christ Jesus (1 Timothy 1:13-14).

Are you committed to the work of evangelism? How so? How can you increase your role in reducing the number of godless fools in the world?

July 4

Your Stuff

Today's reading: Psalms 16-20

"I say to the Lord, 'You are my Lord;

apart from you I have no good thing'" - Psalm 16:2.

In today's verse, David made a clear statement of commitment and devotion to the Lord. Perhaps it's a good thing that David did not live in our materialistic age, where the emphasis is to own cars and more cars, clothes and trendier clothes, games and more complex games, homes and bigger homes. When you invest so much into the things along with their care and maintenance, those things can begin to own you instead of you owning them. Paul wrote about contentment to the Philippians:

> I am not saying this because I am in need, for I have learned to be content whatever the circumstances. I know what it is to be in need, and I know what it is to have plenty. I have learned the secret of being content in any and every situation, whether well fed or hungry, whether living in plenty or in want. I can do all this through him who gives me strength (Philippians 4:11-13).

Are you hoarding things? Are you struggling with some of your stuff having a hold on you? Is that interfering with your peace in the Lord? Is it time to divest yourself of some of your possessions, going through your drawers, closet, garage, attic, library or other storage unit to eliminate some of your clutter?

JULY 5

FEAR NO EVIL

Today's reading: Psalms 21-25

"Even though I walk through the darkest valley, I will fear no evil, for you are with me; your rod and your staff, they comfort me" - Psalm 23:4.

David faced the temptation to fear, but he avoided it by determining *not* to be afraid no matter how foreboding the situation was. Instead, he chose to focus on the fact that the Lord was with him to comfort him in his troubles. Fear is the great enemy of your faith, and even if the Lord speaks to you (as some have said, "If only I had a word from the Lord"), you will still fear some evil coming upon you unless you decide not to. When the women went to the tomb to anoint Jesus, they found an angel who told them "not to fear." Yet even with that exhortation, Matthew wrote, "So the women hurried away from the tomb, afraid yet filled with joy" (Matthew 28:8). Are you afraid? Has God revealed His will to do and told you not to fear, yet you still find fear gripping your heart and restricting your actions? Do you see that you must act in the midst of fear and not wait for the fear to subside or go away?

July 6

Handling Fear

Today's reading: Psalms 26-30

"The Lord is my light and my salvation— whom shall I fear? The Lord is the stronghold of my life—of whom shall I be afraid?" - Psalm 27:1.

The Bible in general and the book of Psalms in particular speak about fear a great deal, since it is so common and prevalent among all human emotions. Fear neither be ignored, nor can it be allowed to rule by saying, "I'm only human." Recently I received an email update from Seth Godin that spoke about fear. Here is what he wrote:

> If you can say this out loud, when you've been holding back, avoiding your confrontation with the truth, you will free yourself to do something important. Saying it takes away the power of the fear. On the other hand, if you say it 8 times or 11 times or every time, you're using the label to reinforce your fear, creating an easy escape hatch to avoid doing something important.

> Saying it amplifies the fear. The brave thing is to find the unspeakable fear and speak it. And to stop rehearsing the easy fears that have become habits.

Are you hiding or masquerading your fear, thus denying its existence or hold on you? Are you reinforcing your fear by speaking it often? In today's verse the psalmist acknowledged his potential for fear but by asking himself questions that did not allow the fears to take root or grow.

July 7

Doctor Jesus

Today's reading: Psalms 31-35

"Then I acknowledged my sin to you and did not cover up my iniquity. I said, 'I will confess my transgressions to the Lord.' And you forgave the guilt of my sin" - Psalm 32:5.

God is faithful and ready to forgive sin, if the sinner asks for forgiveness. When sinners hide or deny guilt, they have no need for forgiveness and will continue in their sinful ways. As we have seen throughout this devotional, God requires honesty, not for His benefit since He already knows the truth, but for yours. What's more, those who consider themselves righteous do not need Jesus' help, as indicated by the Pharisees' attitude:

> While Jesus was having dinner at Levi's house, many tax collectors and sinners were eating with him and his disciples, for there were many who followed him. When the teachers of the law who were Pharisees saw him eating with the sinners and tax collectors, they asked his disciples: "Why does he eat with tax collectors and sinners?" It is not the healthy who need a doctor, but the sick. I have not come to call the righteous, but sinners (Mark 2:17).

Do you need Doctor Jesus to heal your sinful heart and ways?

Are you aware of your sin? Or are you denying it due to pride or fear? Is it time to confess some sins to God?

July 8

Your Heart Matters

Today's reading: Psalms 36-40

"Take delight in the Lord, and he will give you the desires of your heart" - Psalm 37:4.

There is much confusion and distrust about the issue of the heart. Many have been taught and believe that the heart is evil, will always be evil and is *never* to be trusted. That makes their faith a "head" faith – lacking emotion and passion, but strong on doctrine and, if not careful, legalism. What's more, those same people have been taught to distrust their own thought process. Paul wrote these words: "And the peace of God, which transcends all understanding, will guard your hearts and your minds in Christ Jesus" (Philippians 4:7). The problem to this approach is this: Does the Spirit's presence in your life ever make a difference in your heart and mind? If the heart is so evil, then how can today's verse from Psalm 37 be true? Could it be true because there are desires that God put in your heart, and following your heart is not dangerous but absolutely essential to finding and doing God's will? Therefore, the real question today is: What's in your heart, and why are you so afraid of following it?

July 9

Jesus' Help

Today's reading: Psalms 41-45

"You are God my stronghold. Why have you rejected me? Why must I go about mourning, oppressed by the enemy?" - Psalm 43:2.

While the psalms accurately described what the writers were experiencing, there is an aspect of Psalms that pertained to Jesus and the suffering and rejection He encountered during His mission to earth. Jesus embodied the message of Psalms, and endured God's judgment to set you free from that judgment. The writer of Hebrews explained the rationale behind Jesus' humanity, so I will let those words explain what I never could:

> For this reason he had to be made like them, fully human in every way, in order that he might become a merciful and faithful high priest in service to God, and that he might make atonement for the sins of the people. Because he himself suffered when he was tempted, he is able to help those who are being tempted (Hebrews 2:17-18).

Do you go to Jesus for help, believing He can relate to your situation because He Himself was flesh and blood, just like you? Do you understand that Jesus is your Helper not just because He is God, but also because He is your brother?

July 10

Wealth Prep

Today's reading: Psalm 46-50

"People who have wealth but lack understanding are like the beasts that perish" - Psalm 49:20.

Many people dream of winning the lottery and therefore play it every day, providing governments, companies and illegal entities a lot of money. Yet few who play are prepared for the pressures that come with money and don't understand how difficult it can be to serve the Lord and also have and maintain riches. Jesus spoke about this issue on many occasions, saying things like this: "Truly I tell you, it is hard for someone who is rich to enter the kingdom of heaven" (Matthew 19:23) and "But woe to you who are **rich**, for you have already received your comfort" (Luke 6:24). The understanding that today's verse refers to is that God gives wealth but expects the wealthy to use their money to relieve the plight of the poor as God's and their heart direct. Do you dream of lottery riches? Or are you working hard to amass a fortune from business? If you are doing either, then gird yourself with a proper perspective on wealth and God's desire to place your money under His direction and Lordship before you have it.

JULY 11

GOD'S BUSINESS

Today's reading: Psalms 51-55

"Restore to me the joy of Your salvation and sustain me with a willing spirit. Then I will teach transgressors Your ways, and sinners will be converted to You" - Psalm 51:12-13.

Psalm 51 is David's prayer of repentance, probably after his sordid relationship with Bathsheba and the circumstances surrounding their son's birth and death. When David sinned, he did not run *from* God but *to* Him. He did not go into hiding, but instead made a commitment to the Lord to reach out and teach others about the Lord and His ways, but only after God touched and restored David in his inner man. You should note that David was not just interested in himself, but also connected his restoration to God's best interests, which were and are to reach others for Him. In a sense, Paul saw this same dynamic when he admitted his sin, but then saw that God had touched him to go reach others:

> Here is a trustworthy saying that deserves full acceptance: Christ Jesus came into the world to save sinners—of whom I am the worst. But for that very reason I was shown mercy so that in me, the worst of sinners, Christ Jesus might display his immense patience as an example for those who would believe in

him and receive eternal life (1 Timothy 1:15-16).

Are you reaching out to other sinners? Do you see that part of your healing and restoration is so you can make God's business your business?

July 12

Listening for God

Today's reading: Psalms 56-60

"Save us and help us with your right hand, that those you love may be delivered. God has spoken from his sanctuary: 'In triumph I will parcel out Shechem and measure off the Valley of Sukkoth. Gilead is mine, and Manasseh is mine; Ephraim is my helmet, Judah is my scepter. Moab is my washbasin, on Edom I toss my sandal; over Philistia I shout in triumph'" - Psalm 60:5-8.

David was in deep distress (again) and was crying out to God for help in today's verses. In the midst of his seeking, God spoke to him and let David know that He, God, was in control of everything. While David was praying, God spoke, David heard what He said and wrote it down. Notice that the Lord did not speak about David's situation, but expanded David's vision to see more accurately and completely who God is and what He was doing in the earth. While David's circumstances did not immediately change, his perspective of his circumstances did. Paul was in Corinth and it did not seem to be going well, and then the Lord spoke to him and changed his viewpoint:

> One night the Lord spoke to Paul in a vision: "Do not be afraid; keep on speaking, do not be silent. For I am with you, and no one is going to attack and harm you, because I have many people in this city." So Paul stayed in Corinth for a year and a half, teaching them the word of God (Acts 18:9-11).

Are you praying and listening? Do you expect to hear from the Lord? Are you hearing and then resting in the perspective of your life God is giving you as you pray? *Lord, I realize I am talking more than listening when I pray, and I need to adjust that. I want and need to hear Your voice, and from this point, I will spend more time listening as You reveal Your will and heart to me.*

July 13

Word Ambush

Today's reading: Psalms 61-65

"Hide me from the conspiracy of the wicked, from the plots of evildoers. They sharpen their tongues like swords and aim cruel words like deadly arrows. They shoot from ambush at the innocent; they shoot suddenly, without fear" - Psalm 64:2-4.

David was a mighty warrior, but in this prayer, he prayed that God would hide him from those who spoke evil. He had bravely faced Goliath and embarked on other military engagements, but when it came to gossip, slander and criticism, David asked God to hide him rather than have to face those who uttered vicious and harmful words. This provides two lessons. The first is it shows the power of words and their ability to harm – they are like deadly arrows. Don't underestimate their power to cause you harm, even to depress you. So don't go out of your way to hear things that others have said about you that are negative. The second is the power of *your* words. If you have felt the sting of others' vitriol, then don't be the source of that same pain for others. Speak words that build up and encourage, or don't say anything at all. Do you expose yourself to the harmful words of others toward you? Why do you listen? Why do you seek to find them out? Are you guilty of launching deadly arrows towards others? Are you ambushing the innocent with your criticism and gossip?

July 14

Weakness

Today's reading: Psalms 66-70

"You, God, are awesome in your sanctuary; the God of Israel gives power and strength to his people" - Psalm 68:35.

Superhero movies abound and people flock to see them, identifying with these seemingly ordinary people who do extraordinary exploits. Books abound with stories of athletes and business leaders who excelled through exceptional effort and talent, and we refer to them as celebrities. Yet David made a statement as he closed Psalm 68 that it was God who gives His people power and strength. Therefore, it was not their own abilities that caused them to excel, but God's supernatural ability placed in them. Much has been made of Paul's discussion of his weakness and strength, and here is one verse from that discussion: "For to be sure, he was crucified in weakness, yet he lives by God's power. Likewise, we are weak in him, yet by God's power we will live with him in our dealing with you" (2 Corinthians 13:4). Paul fulfilled his Empire-wide apostolic tour not in the power of his spiritual gifts, which were quite significant, but in the knowledge of his weakness that he could not do God's will without God's supernatural strength and help. Are you involved in something that shows forth your human weakness while you function in your strengths? What can you say God has helped you do what only He could have done through you?

July 15

Career Counselor

Today's reading: Psalms 71-75

"No one from the east or the west or from the desert can exalt themselves. It is God who judges: He brings one down, he exalts another" - Psalm 75:6-7.

Promotion in your work, association, politics or career is not only a matter of education, experience, talent and preparation. While all those are important, the real issue in career growth is God's will for you and where He desires to place you. God does not promote people with potential, but rather people who have developed that potential. Yet even those who have developed their potential are not guaranteed success (as they deem success), because that is in God's hands. Joseph, Daniel, David, Deborah, Paul, and Joshua, just to name a few, became leaders by God' sovereign choice and not based on interviews, education or talent. Are you toiling hard for the next promotion? Are you offended when you are bypassed for the next pay or responsibility level? Are you disappointed that you were not hired - or that you were fired? Relax and stop fretting. The Lord is your agent and career counselor, and you will move on when He deems it the right time according to His will and plan.

JULY 16

GOD IS ABLE

Today's reading: Psalms 76-80

"They spoke against God; they said, 'Can God really spread a table in the wilderness? True, he struck the rock, and water gushed out, streams flowed abundantly, but can he also give us bread? Can he supply meat for his people?'" - Psalm 78:19-20.

When the Lord led Israel out of Egypt, He led them into the Sinai desert. They considered their surroundings and chose to panic, lashing out at the Lord, even though they had seen His power to provide when He sent forth water from a rock. They had to trust the Lord daily for their provision and they grumbled, opting not to believe Him able to provide bread and meat in spite of the water miracle. You can easily fall into the same trap, challenging the Lord's goodness today, even though He has acted on your behalf again and again in the yesterdays of your life. Jesus challenged His disciples to also remember God's ability to provide and have faith:

> "You of little faith, why are you talking among yourselves about having no bread? Do you still not understand? Don't you remember the five loaves for the five thousand, and how many basketfuls you gathered? Or the seven loaves for the four thousand, and how many basketfuls you gathered?" (Matthew 16:8-10).

Are you in a panic today because you don't see where tomorrow's provision is coming from? Has unbelief got you in a dither? Are you questioning God's ability to provide for you?

JULY 17

SEEK HIS KINGDOM

Today's reading: Psalms 81-85

"'For the Lord God is a sun and shield; the Lord bestows favor and honor; no good thing does he withhold from those whose walk is blameless" - Psalm 84:11.

Today's verse basically tells you that God is everything you need, every day and in every way. If you need light, He is the sun, heating and brightening your way. If you need protection from the sun, He is your shield. He grants honor for work done and favor in the eyes of those who can help you along the way. He does not withhold any good thing you need in your life and walk with him - *if* your walk is blameless (meaning you keep short accounts, asking forgiveness of God and others when you sin). Therefore, if you don't have something it is because God has decided you don't need it. Jesus stated it this way:

> So do not worry, saying, "What shall we eat?" or "What shall we drink?" or "What shall we wear?" For the pagans run after all these things, and your heav-

> enly Father knows that you need them. But seek first his kingdom and his righteousness, and all these things will be given to you as well (Matthew 6:31-33).

Can you make peace today with the fact that there some things you don't have only because God has chosen not to give them to you, and He has a good reason for doing so? Are you perhaps the thing standing between God and what you need?

JULY 18

HOLY GEOGRAPHY

Today's reading: Psalms 86-90

"Indeed, of Zion it will be said, 'This one and that one were born in her, and the Most High himself will establish her'" - Psalm 87:5.

In the Old Testament, Zion was the place where God resided in Israel's mind, for it was in Jerusalem and close to where the Temple stood. Even while they were in Babylonian exile, the Jews talked, sang, wrote, and dreamed about Zion. God's people were "born" there, for that is the place where they communed and met with God. There is still a romantic notion of God living in a place, and some are still captivated by the thought that there is geography special to God. There is not. Today, God doesn't reside in a place or territory, He lives in and with His people:

> I saw the Holy City, the new Jerusalem, coming down out of heaven from God, prepared as a bride beautifully dressed for her husband. And I heard a loud voice from the throne saying, "Look! God's dwelling place is now among the people, and he will dwell with them. They will be his people, and God himself will be with them and be their God" (Revelation 21:2-3).

Are you fascinated with holy geography or holy living? Are you infatuated with end time fables, or are you fixated on living out a holy life and helping spread the gospel to all nations and people groups?

July 19

A Refuge from the Storm

Today's reading: Psalm 91-95

"Whoever dwells in the shelter of the Most High will rest in the shadow of the Almighty" - Psalm 91:1.

When I was in a dangerous country on a ministry assignment, our team met every morning at 7 AM, and part of our regimen was reciting Psalm 91 in its entirety as a group. After that, we were more focused on God's promises of protection as we went about our business. God does not have a shelter nor does He cast a shadow. The psalmist was writing poetry and provided images to comfort the mind and soothe the soul of the reader. The psalmist was of course referring to God's presence with His people that should bring rest and freedom from anxiety. Jesus lived in this truth as evidenced by His calm in the midst of a storm: "One day Jesus said to his disciples, 'Let us go over to the other side of the lake.' So they got into a boat and set out. As they sailed, he fell asleep. A squall came down on the lake, so that the boat was being swamped, and they were in great danger" (Luke 8:22-24). Are you in a storm right now? Are you in a panic due to the size of the waves or water in the boat? Then it's time to read Psalm 91 daily or hourly to regain your faith focus that God is in control, even when the storm seems to be ready to take you down. *Lord, there is a storm raging in my life right now, and I have been in a panic. Today's encouragement really helps me to see that You are bigger and more powerful than any storm could ever be. I ask that You calm the waves that are terrifying me, and speak to the wind that tries to overpower me. I put my trust in You as together we weather this storm.*

July 20

Change

Today's reading: Psalms 96-100

"Sing to the Lord a new song; sing to the Lord, all the earth. Sing to the Lord, praise his name; proclaim his salvation day after day. Declare his glory among the nations, his marvelous deeds among all peoples" - Psalm 96:1-3.

For you to sing a new song to the Lord means that you must stop singing the old song. No, that is not an endorsement for contemporary music over hymns, but rather an indication that God desires to bring change into your life. As a believer, you should eat change for breakfast, so to speak, for the Spirit who lives in you is always moving and changing you and the things around you. Unfortunately, you may be standing in the way of that change due to your old nemesis: fear. You can fear the new thing so you oppose it for what you believe are spiritual reasons - not wanting to get ahead of or miss the Lord. Jesus Himself said in Revelation 21:5, "He who was seated on the throne said, 'I am making everything new!' Then he said, 'Write this down, for these words are trustworthy and true!'" What changes are you resisting that, if you embraced them, would allow you to sing a new song? What excuses are you using to resist the change?

July 21

Choosing Friends

Today's reading: Psalm 101-105

"My eyes will be on the faithful in the land, that they may dwell with me; the one whose walk is blameless will minister to me" - Psalm 101:6.

David declared that he was careful about choosing both his

friends, associates, and his spiritual leaders. He understood what Paul wrote much later: "Do not be misled: 'Bad company corrupts good character'" (1 Corinthians 15:33). Paul also wrote, "Do not be yoked together with unbelievers. For what do righteousness and wickedness have in common? Or what fellowship can light have with darkness?" (2 Corinthians 6:14). Paul clarified his instruction about contact with unbelievers when he wrote, "But now I am writing to you that you must not associate with anyone who claims to be a brother or sister but is sexually immoral or greedy, an idolater or slanderer, a drunkard or swindler. Do not even eat with such people" (1 Corinthians 5:11). Are your friends and associates claiming to be believers but behaving badly? Are you in church fellowship with folk who do not evidence Christian behavior and attitudes? Be honest: Is their behavior rubbing off on you and affecting your walk and devotion to the Lord? If it is, what are you prepared to do about it?

July 22

Friendship Betrayed

Today's reading: Psalms 106-110

"In return for my friendship they accuse me, and hatred for my friendship" - Psalm 109:4-5.

There is an aspect of Psalms that not only describes the experience of the psalmist, but also points ahead to the ministry and suffering of Jesus. Jesus lived the psalms, just like you do when you read them to identify with the human pathos they represent and narrate. In these verses, we learn that Jesus (along with David) was a friend to others, yet His friendship was rejected and was repaid with hatred and accusations. Jesus even chose Judas, whom He knew would betray Him. What did David (and Jesus) do in response to these hurtful acts? They prayed! They took their disappointment and pain and told their heavenly Father about it. What do you do when your goodness is rejected and met with an evil or callous response? Do you lash out at others? Do you become despondent or depressed? Do you become bitter or hold a grudge? Or do you take it to the Lord to ask Him to touch your pain and heal your heart? Do you hold back from any future friend-like investments in others?

JULY 23

WATER IN A DRY PLACE

Today's reading: Psalms 111-115

***"Tremble, earth, at the presence of the Lord, at the presence of the God of Jacob, who turned the rock into a pool, the hard rock into springs of water"* - Psalm 114:7-8.**

God led His people in to the wilderness, another word for the Sinai desert. The temperatures were scorching, the nights were bitter cold, there was no food, and of course there was no water. What's more, there were millions of people, plus all their herds of animals, and they wandered there for 40 years before they entered the Promised Land. Did any of them starve or die of thirst? Absolutely not! God was able to provide for them; in fact, He led them there to prove that He could provide under impossible conditions to build their faith. Instead, they hardened their hearts and did not have faith:

> For I do not want you to be ignorant of the fact, brothers and sisters, that our ancestors were all under the cloud and that they all passed through the sea. They were all baptized into Moses in the cloud and in the sea. They all ate the same spiritual food and drank the same spiritual drink; for they drank from the spiritual rock that accompanied them, and that rock was Christ. Nevertheless, God was not pleased with most of them; their bodies were scattered in the wilderness (1 Corinthians 10:1-5).

Are you like the Israelites in the desert, not trusting God even though He has shown Himself strong on your behalf again and again, providing something from nothing for you? Are you in a desert, while God sustains you? Do you resent the desert, or appreciate God's presence while you live there?

July 24

Leaders and Kings

Today's reading: Psalms 116-120

"It is better to take refuge in the Lord than to trust in princes" - Psalm 118:9.

God is a leadership God. He works through leaders, but the tendency of mankind has been to put expectations on their leaders that should only be put on the Lord. This has led time and again to the glorification and deification of leaders, and that always gets people in trouble – for leaders are mortal and will eventually pass from the scene, no matter how effective or evil they are. Israel craved a leader, a king like the rest of the nations had, and it got them into trouble when they put the leader before their allegiance to God. Samuel had this to say to Israel when the demanded a king: "But you have now rejected your God, who saves you out of all your disasters and calamities. And you have said, 'No, appoint a king over us'" (1 Samuel 10:19). As a follower, are you putting too much trust in leaders, expecting them to do what only the Lord can do for you? As a leader, are you demanding more loyalty and commitment than is appropriate? You should pray for your leaders, submit to your leaders, but reserve your ultimate trust and loyalty for the take you down. Lord, there is a storm raging in my life right now, and I have been in a panic. Today's encouragement really helps me to see that You are bigger and more powerful than any storm could ever be. I ask that You calm the waves that are terrifying me, and speak to the wind that tries to overpower me. I put my trust in You as together we weather this storm.

July 25

Whole Lotta Shakin' Going On

Today's reading: Psalms 121-125

"Those who trust in the Lord are like Mount Zion, which cannot be shaken but endures forever" - Psalm 125:1.

It is easy to misinterpret a Bible promise to mean something that it does not mean. In Isaiah, God makes the promise that no weapon formed against you shall prosper (see Isaiah 54:17). The verse doesn't mean the weapons won't be formed or won't try to be effective against you, it simply says they won't be successful. Jesus said the gates of hell would not prevail against the Church; He didn't say the gates would not *try* to prevail. In today's verse, it states that the people of God are like Mount Zion that won't be shaken and destroyed. It does not mean that shaking won't happen to remove everything in your life not consistent with the stability and purity of Mt. Zion. In Hebrews 12, the writer had this to say about shaking:

> At that time his voice shook the earth, but now he has promised, "Once more I will shake not only the earth but also the heavens." The words "once more" indicate the removing of what can be shaken—that is, created things—so that what cannot be shaken may remain. Therefore, since we are receiving a kingdom that cannot be shaken, let us be thankful, and so worship God acceptably with reverence and awe, for our "God is a consuming fire" (12:26-29).

Is there shaking going on in your life? Is your confidence shaken because there is shaking? Do you see that God is removing what can be shaken so that what cannot be shaken will prevail in your life, which is His will and purpose?

JULY 26

A KINGDOM WORKER

Today's reading: Psalms 126-130

"In vain you rise early and stay up late, toiling for food to eat—for he grants sleep to those he loves" - Psalm 127:2.

The concept of work is different for a believer than for someone who doesn't know the Lord. For the unbeliever, work is how he or she makes money. For believers, God has promised to provide, so they work to extend God's kingdom rule on the job. What does that mean? A believer works to witness and reveal God to fellow workers, clients and customers. They manifest God's love and righteousness where integrity, honesty, fairness, a work ethic and submission are concerned. Where possible, a Kingdom worker also exercises creativity and authority to bring new ideas and order to his or her sphere of work. Is there a difference between your work and the work of those around you who do not know the Lord? Is your attitude gentle and submissive, or strident and competitive? Do you see your work as your source of provision, or do you see God as the source? Do you understand that He is using your job to provide for you, but He doesn't need your job to provide? What difference should all these truths make in your job, attitude and faith expectations?

JULY 27

VINDICATION

Today's reading: Psalms 131-135

"For the Lord will vindicate his people and have compassion on his servants" - Psalm 135:14.

One of the most difficult aspects of life to surrender to the Lord is your reputation. When someone makes an accusation or charges you with an offense, everything in you wants to defend yourself and correct what people are thinking about you. Yet the Lord desires that you trust your reputation with Him, allowing Him to be your agent and handle your public image. He promises to vindicate you, but He will do it on His own terms and in His own time. You must keep in mind that He may not clear your name in a way that suits you, but rather causes you to trust Him even more for your career, public image and relationships. The Bible already advised you that God is the one who will avenge wrongs done to you in Hebrews 10:30: "For we know him who said, 'It is mine to avenge; I will repay.'" Have you been contemplating taking revenge on someone who has wronged you? Have you been distressed over a wrong done to you or about an accusation or charges made against you? Can you see that the Lord wants you to trust Him and not take matters or your defense into your own hands?

JULY 28

GETTING REAL WITH GOD

Today's reading: Psalms 136-140

"You have searched me, Lord, and you know me. You know when I sit and when I rise; you perceive my thoughts from afar" - Psalm 139:1-2.

God already knows your thoughts and your words before you speak them. That is in part why the psalms are so brutally honest, for the writers knew it was ridiculous to try and hide their true feelings. Therefore, when someone says, "I would never say that to the Lord," they are missing the point that, if they think it, it's as good as saying it, for God knows. You need to be honest with God in prayer, not for His sake, but for yours. God is not interested in formula praying or in you using King James' English when you address Him. You don't have to end your prayers "in Jesus' name" to get them heard and answered, but you do have to appear before God as you are and not as someone saying what you think God would want you to say. Are you being real with God in prayer? Do you pray transparent prayers, or are you trying to impress God or others with your prayer words? Do you see that God cannot change you into the person He wants you to be if you are pretending to already be that person?

JULY 29

HANDING CRITICISM (AND THE CRITIC)

Today's reading: Psalms 141-145

"Let a righteous man strike me—that is a kindness; let him rebuke me—that is oil on my head. My head will not refuse it, for my prayer will still be against the deeds of evildoers" - Psalm 141:5.

Receiving input from others, especially when it isn't requested and falls into the category of "constructive criticism," can be a challenging event. David vowed in today's verse that he would not reject the rebuke from others and would not be angry at the 'rebuker.' Instead, he made a commitment to keep his focus on the real enemies in his life. What's more, David described those confrontations with those who rebuked him as "kindness" and "oil for my head." The wisdom book of Proverbs had much to say about this life experience of receiving criticism: "Whoever remains stiff-necked after many rebukes will suddenly be destroyed—without remedy" (Proverbs 29:1) and "A rebuke impresses a discerning person more than a hundred lashes a fool" (Proverbs 17:10). How do you receive a rebuke from someone else? Do you get angry at them? Do you defend yourself, or do you see the process as potentially valuable as you learn about some negative or weak area in your life that can be corrected for God's glory?

JULY 30

YOUR EMOTIONAL HEALTH

Today's reading: Psalms 146-150

"He heals the brokenhearted and binds up their wounds" - Psalm 147:3.

The Lord is mindful of your emotional condition and can heal your hurts just like He can heal your physical problems. If the Lord is that interested in your emotional health, then you should be as well. That means you should take your feelings seriously, especially if you are depressed, angry, tense or fearful. All those emotional conditions can not only affect your energy levels, they can also impact your physical health. If you had a physical problem, you would hopefully consult a physician. In the same manner, if you have an emotional problem, you should consult a counselor or pastor with whom you can share your condition and get some help. This help is really God's way of healing your broken heart and binding up your emotional wounds. Are you paying attention to your emotional state? Are you trying to "tough it out" even though your heart is hurting? What is stopping you from getting some help? Is it pride? Finances? A bias against counseling or counselors? Do you really believe that emotional health is possible and a priority?

JULY 31

STUDYING GOD'S WORD

Today's reading: Psalm 119

***"Open my eyes that I may see wonderful things in your law"* - Psalm 119:18.**

Today's verse contains a good prayer for you to pray when you are studying God's word. You are studying God's word, aren't you? I am not talking about doing a quick reading every now and then, but actually delving into the sometimes intricate but always rewarding concepts and history contained within the text. This process requires something from you to be a rewarding experience: 1) time invested; 2) a teacher, whether in person or through commentaries and books; 3) prayer; 4) consistency; 5) a desire to know the Word; and 6) a study of related concepts like language, history, geography and other helpful subjects. How much time do you devote to the study and not just casual reading of God's word? Why so little? What lifestyle or attitude changes can you make that will allow you to devote more time to the most important book there is?

August 1

Only One God

Today's reading: Psalms 1-5

"Therefore, you kings, be wise; be warned, you rulers of the earth. Serve the Lord with fear and celebrate his rule with trembling" - Psalm 2:10-11.

Modern theologians declare that there are many ways to God. As long as someone is sincere, their thinking goes, then God will understand, and they can have access to God on their own terms. Yet somehow, that doesn't even make logical sense, for if one says "This is good" and another says, "This is bad," then both cannot be correct – it must either be good or bad, it cannot be both. If some believe "Jesus is Lord" and others believe "Jesus is not Lord," then both cannot be correct, no matter how sincere they are. In today's passage, the Lord warned the kings of the earth, not just the kings of Israel, to serve the Lord, as He had told His people in Exodus, "I am the Lord your God, who brought you out of Egypt, out of the land of slavery. You shall have no other gods before me" (Exodus 20:2-3). Therefore, it is important to worship and reverence God for who He is and not for who you want Him to be. Are you fashioning a mental image or interpretation of God that is not consistent with who He is? Do you hold to the belief that there are many ways to God, that accuracy where the path to God is concerned is not important, but only sincere intent? What are you doing to ensure that you are serving God as He is and not as you want Him to be?

August 2
Suffering

Today's reading: Psalms 6-10

"My soul is in deep anguish. How long, Lord, how long?" - Psalm 6:3.

The psalmists all dealt with a common human experience, and that is suffering. Suffering is pain caused by broken relationships, misunderstandings, violence, persecutions and failures - all the human predicaments that lead to mental and physical turmoil and heartache. In today's verse, David inquired of the Lord as to how long his suffering was going to last. God often answered David's questions, but God seldom if ever answers this question that David and you have asked. If you knew "how long" your agony was going to last, you would do everything you could to end or avoid it, thus missing an important personal development experience. Therefore, you must trust God that it won't last a day longer than it needs to. Peter gave his readers a unique perspective on suffering in his first letter:

> Therefore, since Christ suffered in his body, arm yourselves also with the same attitude, because whoever suffers in the body is done with sin. As a result, they do not live the rest of their earthly lives for evil human desires, but rather for the will of God (1 Peter 4:1-2).

Have you armed yourself with the attitude of Christ, that suffering is beneficial and necessary? Do you see that your suffering sets you free from yourself so you can focus on the needs of others and do God's will? How will this change how you think of your suffering?

August 3

Helping the Poor

Today's reading" Psalms 11-15

"You evildoers frustrate the plans of the poor, but the Lord is their refuge" - Psalm 14:6.

God's heart is for the poor, who are the victims in a fallen world where injustice and oppression are the norm. The Bible is full of directives on how to treat, view, and care for the poor, but today's verse indicates that *evildoers* don't understand God's care or concern. Therefore, the poor have no alternative but to rely on the Lord as their refuge. When they do, those who try to take advantage of the poor will find God the poor's help in time of trouble – and the Enemy of their enemies. What's more, today's verse indicates that the poor don't want or need just a handout, but do need to play in a role and have a say in developing plans to escape their poverty. In Proverbs, the wisdom writer warned, "One who oppresses the poor to increase his wealth and one who gives gifts to the rich—both come to poverty" (22:19). Are you on the side of the poor? Do you help them through your church, in politics, in education or in business as they attempt to alleviate their own poverty? What more can you do to empathize and get in touch with their condition, and then act accordingly?

August 4

Source of Strength

Today's reading: Psalms 16-20

"Some trust in chariots and some in horses, but we trust in the name of the Lord our God" - Psalm 20:7.

David was a warrior king, renowned for his military prowess. Yet he learned not to trust in his own strength, experience, or gifting, but rather to trust in the name of the Lord. On once occasion, the Philistines attacked and David asked the Lord what he should do. The Lord replied, "Go, for I will surely deliver the Philistines into your hands" (2 Samuel 5:19b). The Philistines would not go away even after their defeat, and David could have assumed he was to attack them again in the same way as before. Instead, he trusted the Lord and asked again. This time the Lord advised,

> "Do not go straight up, but circle around behind them and attack them in front of the poplar trees. As soon as you hear the sound of marching in the tops of the poplar trees, move quickly, because that will mean the Lord has gone out in front of you to strike the Philistine army" (2 Samuel 5:23-24).

Are you relying on your own strength or God's? Are you seeking the Lord, even though you "know" how to do that for which you are asking guidance?

August 5

The Covenant

Today's reading: Psalm 21-25

"The Lord confides in those who fear him; he makes his covenant known to them" - Psalm 25:14.

God wants to share His "secrets" with you, revealing to you who He is and what He is doing in the earth. He especially wants to reveal to you His covenant ways, showing you the riches of the benefits for you a participant in His new covenant. One aspect of the covenant is described in Deuteronomy, and it has to do with wealth and the need to be faithful to the Lord:

> You may say to yourself, "My power and the strength of my hands have produced this wealth for me." But

> remember the Lord your God, for it is he who gives you the ability to produce wealth, and so confirms his covenant, which he swore to your ancestors, as it is today. If you ever forget the Lord your God and follow other gods and worship and bow down to them, I testify against you today that you will surely be destroyed (Deuteronomy 8:17-19).

Do you understand that God is a covenant-making and covenant-keeping God? Do you further understand the terms of the covenant or agreement you have made with Him? Are you taking full advantage of the covenant blessings that are yours as a partaker of the covenant?

August 6

Jesus in Your Storm

Today's reading: Psalms 26-30

"The voice of the Lord is over the waters; the God of glory thunders, the Lord thunders over the mighty waters. The voice of the Lord is powerful; the voice of the Lord is majestic. The voice of the Lord breaks the cedars; the Lord breaks in pieces the cedars of Lebanon" - Psalm 29:3-5.

The Lord is all powerful over nature and, if He is powerful over nature, He can and is also over mankind. These verses cause one to reflect not only on the Flood, over which the Lord presided with complete authority, but also on the incidents on the Sea of Galilee where the Lord demonstrated again and again that He was in control of His own creation:

> After he had dismissed them, he went up on a mountainside by himself to pray. Later that night, he was there alone, and the boat was already a considerable distance from land, buffeted by the waves because the wind was against it. Shortly before dawn Jesus went

> out to them, walking on the lake. When the disciples saw him walking on the lake, they were terrified. "It's a ghost," they said, and cried out in fear. But Jesus immediately said to them: "Take courage! It is I. Don't be afraid" (Mark 4:24-27).

Is there a storm in your life, and are you afraid? Then picture Jesus walking in the midst of your tempest, calm and in complete control. Then hear Him saying to you what He said to the disciples, "Fear not!" After that, decide to put your trust in His power that is so beautifully described in today's passage.

August 7

Guidance

Today's reading: Psalm 31-35

"Since you are my rock and my fortress, for the sake of your name lead and guide me" - Psalm 31:3.

David was in trouble (again) and cried out to the Lord in one long prayer contained in Psalm 31. In the midst of his pain, he prayed that God would lead and guide him. God must make His will clear to you if He expects you to fulfill it, and He is a great communicator who has any number of ways of getting through to you. The problem is that fear or unbelief can cloud your sight and block your ability to hear. The writer of Hebrews warned against this tendency in Hebrews 3:

> See to it, brothers and sisters, that none of you has a sinful, unbelieving heart that turns away from the living God. But encourage one another daily, as long as it is called "Today," so that none of you may be hardened by sin's deceitfulness. We have come to share in Christ, if indeed we hold our original conviction firmly to the very end. As has just been said: "Today, if you hear his voice, do not harden your hearts as you did in the rebellion" (3:12-15).

Has there been something on your heart to do for years, but you keep putting if off? Do you have a recurring thought but dismiss it as your own voice instead of God's? Where is fear causing you to misinterpret or block out God's voice that you have prayed would come and guide you?

August 8

A Surrendered Heart

Today's reading: Psalms 36-40

"Sacrifice and offering you did not desire—but my ears you have opened—burnt offerings and sin offerings you did not require. Then I said, 'Here I am, I have come—it is written about me in the scroll. I desire to do your will, my God; your law is within my heart'" - Psalm 40:6-8.

The sacrifice mentioned in today's passage is not doing something you don't want to do or giving something you don't want to give. It refers to the animal and plant offerings made as part of the worship experience of an Old Testament. You can feel spiritual when you go to church, of when you do make a "sacrifice" – something that you designate as holy that is for God's use or purpose. Yet the psalmist was clear that isn't what God desires. He wants *all* of you and not some part of who you are or what you have. He doesn't require external pious acts, but rather a heart condition of surrender that leads to willing, righteous acts. When that is present, the dynamic explained in Isaiah 50:4 is also present: "The Sovereign Lord has given me a well-instructed tongue, to know the word that sustains the weary. He wakens me morning by morning, wakens my ear to listen like one being instructed." Do you delight in religious acts that are under your control - doing them when you want as you want? Or is your goal a surrendered heart that leads to daily instruction of what to do today based on what you hear from the Lord? *Lord, I like the concept of waking up every morning to hear Your voice. From this time forward, that will be my goal. I will listen for Your instructions for the day ahead of me. What's more, I will journal what I hear so I don't lose track of it as I engage my day.*

August 9

Resisting Joy

Today's reading: Psalms 41-45

"You love righteousness and hate wickedness; therefore God, your God, has set you above your companions by anointing you with the oil of joy" - Psalm 45:7.

This verse was highlighted in the June 18 entry since it is quoted in Hebrews 1:9; here it is in its original context in the Psalms. God anoints you with joy to help you know what you are supposed to do for Him, and then to give you the strength to do it. Yet many of us have been taught not to trust joy because it is an emotion and is subject to sinful and selfish manifestations. Yet, why would God create you with joy to perform some deed, and then not allow you the outlet to express and savor that joy? Joy is not only your strength (see Nehemiah 8:10), it is also the means by which you can pick up your cross and follow Him, as Jesus taught through His own life:

> Therefore, since we are surrounded by such a great cloud of witnesses, let us throw off everything that hinders and the sin that so easily entangles. And let us run with perseverance the race marked out for us, fixing our eyes on Jesus, the pioneer and perfecter of faith. For the joy set before him he endured the cross, scorning its shame, and sat down at the right hand of the throne of God. Consider him who endured such opposition from sinners, so that you will not grow weary and lose heart (Hebrews 12:1-3).

Are you expressing your joy or are you ambivalent about its role in your life? What would you do with your life if you followed your joy?

August 10

Keeping Track

Today's reading: Psalms 46-50

"You hate my instruction and cast my words behind you" - Psalm 50:17.

The rebuke in today's verse was aimed at people who lived by and studied God's word. Yet God laid the charge against them that they hated His instruction and somehow cast His words aside, or literally "behind them." This may portray an image of someone taking something tangible, like a book, and tossing it away with disdain. Yet all someone has to do to cast God's word aside is to leave it where it was received and walk away. Each step takes that person farther away, reducing his or her chance of obeying that word. Are you guilty of this? If you don't journal, there is a good chance you are guilty, otherwise you will forget or disregard what God has taught you, "walking away" from it in your pursuit of career, hobbies, family matters or education. Thus, the word is left behind as you walk on. Why don't you keep a journal? What are you recording in your journal? Do you expect God to teach you things? Do you accept those things in faith and seek to act on them? If you do journal, do you read through your entries to ensure you have retained and carried out God's instruction?

August 11

A Contrite Heart

Today's reading: Psalms 51-55

"My sacrifice, O God, is a broken spirit; a broken and contrite heart you, God, will not despise" - Psalm 51:17.

As we saw earlier this month, God is not interested in religious acts that signify external compliance with His will. He is interested in your heart, for if He has your heart's allegiance, then the external acts will flow from within and be acceptable in His sight. This contrite, broken heart is not just to be present when you do wrong, but you should work to maintain that heart condition at all times, which is called humility, a sense of your own weakness and dependence on the Lord, and contrition. The prophet identified the benefit of a contrite heart in 2 Chronicles 16:9: "For the eyes of the Lord range throughout the earth to strengthen those whose hearts are fully committed to him." Jesus addressed the church at Ephesus about their heart and behavior when He said, "Yet I hold this against you: You have forsaken the love you had at first. Consider how far you have fallen! Repent and do the things you did at first. If you do not repent, I will come to you and remove your lampstand from its place" (Revelation 2:4-5). Would you describe your heart condition as broken and contrite? Do you see yourself as God sees you, or are you evaluating your heart based on your own perspective? How would you approach God today if you had a broken, contrite heart? What would you say?

August 12

In the World, Not of It

Today's reading: Psalms 56-60

"I am in the midst of lions; I am forced to dwell among ravenous beasts—men whose teeth are spears and arrows, whose tongues are sharp swords" - Psalm 57:4.

Many of the psalms express the psalmists' struggles to live a righteous life in the midst of evil people. These writers knew they could not withdraw from the world, but had to live for God in the midst of it, while trusting the Lord for protection and vindication of their faith lifestyle. Yet often God's people have taken themselves out of the world, sometimes by being in church often (if not always), and at times by cloistering themselves away so as not to have contact with this rough-and-tumble world. Jesus addressed this tension when He said,

> I have given them your word and the world has hated them, for they are not of the world any more than I am of the world. My prayer is not that you take them out of the world but that you protect them from the evil one. They are not of the world, even as I am not of it. Sanctify them by the truth; your word is truth (John 17:14-17).

How are you doing as you live in this world as a pilgrim? Have you withdrawn into your own world? Have you isolated yourself, or do you trust God for protection while you serve as His agent of reconciliation and hope? Can you see that God loves this world and wants you to love it while not being of it?

AUGUST 13

GOD'S CREATION

Today's reading: Psalms 61-65

***"You care for the land and water it; you enrich it abundantly.The streams of God are filled with water to provide the people with grain, for so you have ordained it. You drench its furrows and level its ridges; you soften it with showers and bless its crops. You crown the year with your bounty, and your carts overflow with abundance"* - Psalm 65:9-11.**

God is in love with His creation, and He tends to it personally and with great care. In today's passage, the psalmist celebrates the abundance of crops that come from God's role as divine farmer. What's more, the psalms contain an ongoing focus on and fascination with God and His creation, referring regularly to mountains, rivers, streams, thunder, lightning, grass, seas and animals. Then Jesus came and continued this focus, using nature and everyday life as the foundation for His teaching. If God is so connected to His creation, then you should be as well. This would involve taking time to appreciate and acknowledge God's role in creation as He obviously intended mankind to do:

> Now the Lord God had planted a garden in the east, in Eden; and there he put the man he had formed. The Lord God made all kinds of trees grow out of the ground—trees that were pleasing to the eye and good for food. In the middle of the garden were the tree of life and the tree of the knowledge of good and evil (Genesis 2:8-9).

What can you do to learn more about the Lord as you study His creation? What can you do to incorporate those lessons with others, even if it's just your family? What can you do to better care for God's creation?

August 14
Body Duty

Today's reading: Psalms 66-70

"Lord, the Lord Almighty, may those who hope in you not be disgraced because of me; God of Israel, may those who seek you not be put to shame because of me" - Psalm 69:6.

The psalmist was once again in trouble, this time he had water up to his neck and it was rising! While David was praying and crying out for help, he had an interesting request. He was not simply asking that he be delivered. He asked that he be spared for the sake of his fellow believers. You are connected to other people if you put your hope in the Lord. That makes you part of a body and therefore not free to do what you want, for you are joined to them. When one part is in pain, it affects all, and the same is true if one part is doing well. You may not like being a part of a body, you may not like what the body is doing, but you cannot escape the fact that you are part, and when one part is disgraced, it has implications for all. Paul developed the metaphor of the believers being part of a body and explained,

> But God has put the body together, giving greater honor to the parts that lacked it, so that there should be no division in the body, but that its parts should have equal concern for each other. If one part suffers, every part suffers with it; if one part is honored, every part rejoices with it (1 Corinthians 12:24b-26).

Are you cognizant of your place in the body of Christ? Do you see your responsibility to contribute to body health and well-being? How are you fulfilling that duty?

August 15

One Something

Today's reading: Psalms 71-75

"*We are given no signs from God; no prophets are left, and none of us knows how long this will be*" - Psalm 74:9.

One time I was in a tough place financially, and the phone rang for someone to schedule me to consult for them three months later. I was discouraged before the phone rang and was greatly encouraged after the call. Then I thought, "Hey, there won't be any money from that call for three months. Why do I feel so much better?" Then I reasoned, "If I could feel so much better after the call, how can I feel that way before the call?" When you are in a difficult season, the toughest part can be not knowing how long the season will last. Therefore, it is important to encourage yourself today by thinking, "I am just a phone call, unexpected event, chance meeting, sales call, test score, or doctor's visit away from my breakthrough" and then to live and behave like that breakthrough has *already* taken place. David did this before he went into a battle to recover his loved ones: "But David encouraged himself in the Lord his God" (1 Samuel 30:6b KJV). Do you need to encourage yourself today rather than wait for others to do it? Can you encourage yourself with the thought that you are only "one something" away from victory, while not knowing when that one something will occur? *Lord, it's difficult to live in faith at the moment when nothing seems to be happening. Yet You are the God of the turnaround, and You can change my situation overnight with just one act of Your mighty hand. Therefore, I have decided to enjoy today in anticipation of what You will do.*

AUGUST 16

ATTITUDE TOWARD LEADERS

Today's reading: Psalms 76-80

"You led your people like a flock by the hand of Moses and Aaron" - Psalm 77:20.

God was the One leading in the wilderness, but He did so through His appointed leaders, Moses and Aaron. God is still a leadership God, working through those whom He gives insight and courage to be out in front of the people. At the same time, Moses and Aaron were not perfect men, and the people often suffered because of them. You must have realistic expectations where leaders are concerned; they cannot be God for you – making your decisions and exerting authority God never intended them to have. Yet God expects you to submit to authority because He has established the authority. Peter wrote these words to servants, and you would do well to extract a lesson from what he was teaching:

> Slaves, in reverent fear of God submit yourselves to your masters, not only to those who are good and considerate, but also to those who are harsh. For it is commendable if someone bears up under the pain of unjust suffering because they are conscious of God (1 Peter 2:19-20).

What is your attitude toward your leaders? Do you respect authority, not because it is perfect, but because it is the will of

God? Do you expect too much from authority while you submit, requiring their perfection or their ability to hear God on your behalf?

AUGUST 17

GOD SPEAKS

Today's reading: Psalms 81-85

"I removed the burden from their shoulders; their hands were set free from the basket. In your distress you called and I rescued you, I answered you out of a thundercloud; I tested you at the waters of Meribah" - Psalm 81:6-7.

Notice the psalmist was writing in these verses, but he was not speaking. It was the Lord speaking His words through the writer – in the first person. This is another indication that God speaks to His people through His written Word, and you would do well to treat those words not as just another book, but as the special instruments they are. This high view of Scripture was endorsed and taught by Peter himself, who wrote:

> We also have the prophetic message as something completely reliable, and you will do well to pay attention to it, as to a light shining in a dark place, until the day dawns and the morning star rises in your hearts. Above all, you must understand that no prophecy of Scripture came about by the prophet's own interpretation of things. For prophecy never had its origin in the human will, but prophets, though human, spoke from God as they were carried along by the Holy Spirit (2 Peter 1:19-21).

Are you approaching the Scriptures like God is speaking to you? If you do, how often do you give Him a chance to talk to you through your reading? Do you rush through, or do you linger and savor God's words to you? When you "hear" something, do you act on it?

August 18

Procrastination

Today's reading: Psalms 86-90

"A thousand years in your sight are like a day that has just gone by, or like a watch in the night" - Psalm 90:4.

This verse should cause you to think of its equivalent in the New Testament: "But do not forget this one thing, dear friends: With the Lord a day is like a thousand years, and a thousand years are like a day" (2 Peter 3:8). If you do the math, if a day is like 1,000 years, then an hour is like 46 years, and a minute is like nine months with the Lord. Therefore, if the Lord promises to be there in just a minute, you know His concept of time may not be like yours! Yet, the opposite is also true: nine months in the Lord can go by as quickly as a minute. The thing you have been putting off, dare I say procrastinating over because you thought it was going to take too long, can happen much more quickly than you thought, if you learn how to have faith for time. What is real cause of your procrastination? Is it really lack of time, or are you using that as a cover-up excuse? What project have you been putting off because you assumed you did not have the time? What more could you do, not if you got more organized, but if you began to put off fear that you have so little time and believed you had all the time in the world?

August 19

Living in Fear

Today's reading: Psalms 91-95

"A thousand may fall at your side, ten thousand at your right hand, but it will not come near you" - Psalm 91:7.

Today's verse is great to recite, but difficult to apply. It's easy to say that no harm will befall you until there is harm all around you. Then you have a chance to live in the promise of this verse or panic. This verse is not a license for recklessness, but it has enabled many believers to combat fear and put themselves in harm's way to serve and help others in need. This promise pertains to cancer, heart disease, poverty, germs, plagues, and other maladies and curses of life, which the Lord Jesus died to abolish. An accompanying promise to today's is found in Isaiah 53:5: "But he was pierced for our transgressions, he was crushed for our iniquities; the punishment that brought us peace was on him, and by his wounds we are healed." Do you live in fear of calamity? Do you worry about what *may* happen and then structure your life to avoid those remote possibilities? What don't you do because of fear - not travel, avoid crowds, obsess over what you eat? What do you do because of fear - gulp massive quantities of vitamins, store food and weapons, or read fear mongering, end-time novels?

August 20

Hearing God's Voice

Today's reading: Psalms 96-100

"Moses and Aaron were among his priests, Samuel was among those who called on his name; they called on the Lord and he answered them. He spoke to them from the pillar of cloud; they kept his statutes and the decrees he gave them" - Psalm 99:6-7.

Moses, Aaron, and Samuel called on the Lord and He answered them. God is always answering, but we are not always listening. When we hear, sometimes we mistake His voice for something or someone else. Take for example the story in John 12 when Jesus said, "Father, glorify your name!" (John 12:29b). In response to Jesus' prayer, this is what happened: "Then a voice came from heaven, 'I have glorified it, and will glorify it again.' The crowd that was there and heard it said it had thundered; others said an angel had spoken to him. Jesus said, 'This voice was for your benefit, not mine'" (John 12:30). The people who heard the voice did not recognize it because they were not really expecting to hear His voice. Therefore, if you say, "If only God would speak to me" about this or that, there is no guarantee you will hear God's answer unless you really want to hear it! Where are you having trouble hearing God's voice because of your inner turmoil or doubt? Do you really expect to hear? Are you tuning all your attention to hear, or are you holding back?

AUGUST 21

GOD IS ORDERING YOUR STEPS

Today's reading: Psalms 101-105

"He called down famine on the land and destroyed all their supplies of food; and he sent a man before them—Joseph, sold as a slave" - Psalm 105:16-17.

When it is said that God rules in the affairs of men, the story of Joseph is a classic example of that truth. In these verses, the psalmist gives his view of that historical event and God's role in it. God created and used a famine to get people moving where He wanted them to be – specifically Joseph to Egypt, followed later by his family. God then sent Joseph, his father's favorite, to Egypt. Joseph was not sent as an emissary, however, but as a slave, betrayed and sold by his brothers. Why would God do something that seems so difficult and harsh? Perhaps because there is no way Joseph or his family ever would have gone to Egypt without the "help" of some circumstances that guided their every step, even though they were not conscious of God's guiding hand. Later, Joseph was able to summarize his life experience by saying to his brothers, "You intended to harm me, but God intended it for good to accomplish what is now being done, the saving of many lives" (Genesis 50:20). Can you trust God that He is ordering your steps to get you where He wants you to be, regardless of whether or not He has explained or you understand right now? Can you trust that God is using the circumstances in your life to prepare you for His purpose?

August 22

Grumbling

Today's reading: Psalms 106-110

"Then they despised the pleasant land; they did not believe his promise. They grumbled in their tents and did not obey the Lord" - Psalm 106:24-25.

The Israelites were a nasty, unruly lot as they left Egypt and made their way to the Promised Land. Even though God had showed Himself strong on their behalf and parted the Red Sea, they were obstinate and gave Moses a hard time, which angered the Lord. One of the behaviors that characterized them during their Wilderness experience was grumbling, which is a form of complaining about their lives, conditions, and provisions. They did this grumbling in their family tents, thus contaminating one another, creating a downward negative spiral that led them to disobedience and rebellion. Paul addressed the practice of grumbling in one of his epistles: "Do everything without grumbling or arguing, so that you may become blameless and pure, "children of God without fault in a warped and crooked generation. Then you will shine among them like stars in the sky" (Philippians 2:14-15). Have you fallen into the habit of grumbling? Do you complain about your life situation or the particulars therein? Do you gripe at home with loved ones, thus poisoning their perspective and teaching them to do likewise? Do you see the benefit of being positive and not dwelling on or rehearsing the negative?

August 23
Don't Grow Weary

Today's reading: Psalms 111-115

"The Lord remembers us and will bless us: He will bless his people Israel, he will bless the house of Aaron, he will bless those who fear the Lord— small and great alike" - Psalm 115:12-13.

The Lord never forgets what you did for Him or for His people. It may seem like He has forgotten, but He has a sharp pencil and a big book, He writes everything down, and in time repays and rewards. Paul wrote it best when he advised the Galatians:

> Do not be deceived: God cannot be mocked. A man reaps what he sows. Whoever sows to please their flesh, from the flesh will reap destruction; whoever sows to please the Spirit, from the Spirit will reap eternal life. Let us not become weary in doing good, for at the proper time we will reap a harvest if we do not give up. Therefore, as we have opportunity, let us do good to all people, especially to those who belong to the family of believers (Galatians 6:7-10).

Have you grown tired of sowing? Does it seem like God has forgotten your good deeds? Where do you need to renew your hope in giving or serving, reminding yourself that God is watching and will not forget your cause or your faithfulness?

August 24
Simple Things

Today's reading: Psalms 116-120

"Praise the Lord, all you nations; extol him, all you peoples. For great is his love toward us, and the

faithfulness of the Lord endures forever. Praise the Lord" - Psalm 117:1-2.

Today's two verses are the only verses in the entire psalm, making it the shortest psalm of all 150. It is not particularly profound, nor does it reveal some truth that cannot be found someplace else. Yet, it has a place in the inspired words of God, indicating God's approval and priority. How often have you not said or done something because it seemed so obvious or simple? You kept your words or idea to yourself because you did not want to come off as simple, shallow, or even stupid. Today's psalm gives you a model to follow that no matter how something seems to you, it may have value to other people and to God! What's more, these verses summarize a simple yet appropriate behavior that is acceptable in every and any season – and that is the praise of the Lord your God because of His great love. Have you been too quiet because you have been judging either your unspoken words or undone acts of kindness or service? How can you become less critical of your own righteous impulses, no matter how simple they may be? Can you praise the Lord today for who He is and His great love, even if you are in a difficult place?

August 25

God over Nature

Today's reading: Psalms 121-125

"Our help comes from the Lord, who made heaven and earth" - Psalm 124:8.

The psalmists repeatedly referred back to God's natural acts of creation to describe and frame God's majesty and power. Thus, they regularly mention the Flood, the Genesis story, and the parting of the Red Sea as Israel left Egypt as examples of God's ability to help His people, regardless of how daunting the circumstances seemed to be. Perhaps that is why Jesus on several occasions had encounters with nature that proved His divinity and His authority over the forces of nature that were overwhelming to the disciples, but were well within Jesus' power to control, as told in John 6:16-21:

> When evening came, his disciples went down to the lake, where they got into a boat and set off across the lake for Capernaum. By now it was dark, and Jesus had not yet joined them. A strong wind was blowing and the waters grew rough. When they had rowed about three or four miles, they saw Jesus approaching the boat, walking on the water; and they were frightened. But he said to them, "It is I; don't be afraid." Then they were willing to take him into the boat, and immediately the boat reached the shore where they were heading.

Are you afraid of the forces aligned against you? Do you need a reminder of God's power over your situation that seems to you to be out of control? Do you need to call on the God of the storm to get into your boat today?

August 26

Restoration

Today's reading: Psalms 126-130

"When the Lord restored the fortunes of Zion, we were like those who dreamed. Our mouths were filled with laughter, our tongues with songs of joy. Then it was said among the nations, 'The Lord has done great things for them'"
- Psalm 126:1-2.

A few of the psalms were written in the sixth century B.C., and all of them were edited and took the shape we know today when Israel was in exile in Babylon. They were pining away in a foreign land for their beloved Jerusalem and all that it represented. Then the Lord began to bring them back and it was almost too good to be true, but it was true. You may have lost something, either through your own misdeeds or an act of God that defies explanation. Today's passage reminds you that when the Lord restores what you lost, it will be a joyous and happy occasion. God is truly a God of restoration, as was also pointed out again in Joel 2:25-26:

> "I will repay you for the years the locusts have eaten—the great locust and the young locust, the other locusts and the locust swarm—my great army that I sent among you. You will have plenty to eat, until you are full, and you will praise the name of the Lord your God, who has worked wonders for you; never again will my people be shamed."

Do you need to be reminded today that your God is a God of restoration? Can you maintain hope that what you have lost can and will be restored? Can you thank God today for your restoration before you see it?

August 27

Dangers of Idolatry

Today's reading: Psalms 131-135

"The idols of the nations are silver and gold, made by human hands. They have mouths, but cannot speak, eyes, but cannot see. They have ears, but cannot hear, nor is there breath in their mouths. Those who make them will be like them, and so will all who trust in them"
- Psalm 135:15-18.

One of the many problems with idolatry is that it dehumanizes the worshiper. According to today's passage, those who worship idols become like those idols. They cannot speak, see, or hear spiritual things apart from those that idolatry imparts to them. Idols can be either external or internal, physical or mental, animate or inanimate. Paul wrote to the Corinthians and advised them how to deal with idolatry:

> What harmony is there between Christ and Belial? Or what does a believer have in common with an unbeliever? What agreement is there between the temple of God and idols? For we are the temple of the living God. As God has said: "I will live with them and walk among them, and I will be their God, and they will be my people." Therefore, "Come out from them and be separate," says the Lord. "Touch no unclean thing, and I will receive you" (2 Corinthians 6:15-17).

Check your heart to see if anything or anyone has taken a place in your life that is hindering your walk with the Lord and your ability to comprehend your real spirituality in Christ.

August 28
Craziness

Today's reading - Psalms 136-140

"How can we sing the songs of the Lord while in a foreign land?" - Psalm 137:4.

A few of the psalms were composed while the author was in exile in Babylon during the sixth century B.C. In today's verse, the author was asking how he could be creative when the situation in his life and nation were so painfully chaotic. Yet, he was being creative as he wrote Psalm 137, even though the conditions were not ideal. Sometimes you can use the craziness in or around your life as a legitimate excuse not to produce or create; at other times, you can actually create the craziness as a cover for the fear that you will not be able to create. Rather than face failure, you will create a situation that prevents you from even starting. There was a man who told Jesus that he wanted to follow Him, but first had to go home and wait for his father to die (which could have taken decades). Here is Jesus' response: "Another disciple said to him, 'Lord, first let me go and bury my father.' But Jesus told him,

'Follow me, and let the dead bury their own dead'" (Matthew 8:21-22). Jesus was saying to stop looking for excuses and follow through. Where are conditions preventing you from being productive or creative? Did you create that situation as an escape from responsibility? Can you still be creative even if you are in a tough spot if you stop making excuses?

AUGUST 29

THE KINGDOM OF GOD

Today's reading: Psalms 141-145

"Your kingdom is an everlasting kingdom, and your dominion endures through all generations" - Psalm 145:13.

Jesus came preaching the kingdom of God. Another phrase for the Kingdom is God's government, which means Jesus taught that people everywhere must come under God's rule or authority. Every kingdom has a king and a set of rules by which the people are governed. Therefore, God's will for you is not to make you a member of a church but a subject of His kingdom under the rule of King Jesus! When you are under that rule, you will extend God's kingdom wherever He chooses to send you – school, work, church, neighborhood – by obeying His laws and inviting others to come into the Kingdom through faith in Christ: "He sent them out to proclaim the kingdom of God and to heal the sick" (Luke 9:2). Are you spreading the good news of the Kingdom, or preaching religion and membership in a church or denomination? Do you see that when people come into the Kingdom, they will become part of a church because it is the will of the King? If they become members of a church and don't see themselves as subjects of the Kingdom, then they will settle for a religious experience, and will seek to do the will of man instead of the will of God.

August 30
Humility

Today's reading: Psalms 146-150

"The Lord sustains the humble but casts the wicked to the ground" - Psalm 147:6.

God loves and cares for the humble, the people who are not proud and who recognize their need for the Lord. The humble do not take matters into their own hands, but rather trust Him to provide for, protect, and defend them. Humility is an attitude, and Mary, Jesus' mother, spoke of its importance. Later, Jesus addressed the implications of those who have or do not have this attitude. First, look at what Mary said: "He has brought down rulers from their thrones but has lifted up the humble" (Luke 1:52). Then here is what Jesus had to say: "For all those who exalt themselves will be humbled, and those who humble themselves will be exalted" (Luke 14:11). The important thing to remember is that you maintain this attitude and determine whether you fit into the proud or humble category. Do you need to adjust your attitude today? Do you need to humble yourself before the Lord, or someone else? Is there an area of your life where arrogance and rudeness prevail? If the answer is "yes," then you need to correct that or else the Lord will.

August 31
The Word of God

Today's reading: Psalm 119

"I have hidden your word in my heart that I might not sin against you" - Psalm 119:11.

The Bible is not to be studied as any other book, for it is a living book that will guide your life and inform your decisions. In Jesus' day, there were men called the Sadducees, who did not believe in the resurrection, angels, demons, or an afterlife. Yet they revered the books of Moses and were the ruling class of Israel's priesthood. They had probably memorized much of the Old Testament, and had firm theological beliefs and were convinced they were "right." Therefore, when they came to test Jesus with questions about the resurrection and afterlife, they were confident they could confuse Him and prove the rightness of their interpretations Jesus started His response to them by saying, "Are you not in error because you do not know the Scriptures or the power of God?" (Mark 12:24). Jesus told the Bible experts they did not know the Bible! Why do you study God's word? To gain knowledge or to learn how to live? Do you argue Scripture with others, trying to prove the rightness of your position instead of using it to gain the rightness of heart that God requires? As today's verse advises, do you store verses and concepts in your heart that you may live a righteous life?

September 1
Silence

Today's reading: Psalms 1-5

"Tremble and do not sin; when you are on your beds, search your hearts and be silent" - Psalm 4:4.

Today's' verse does not contain the words of David, but rather the words of God. David prayed and God answered with His response, advising not only David but also His people to be silent and search their hearts. Yet in this busy world, it is difficult to take some time to think, reflect, and allow God to speak to you. In fact, you can become addicted to the activity, frantically racing from event to event because you are afraid of what the silence will bring. Will you hear from the Lord? Will you be missing out on something else more important? Will the silence reveal some major deficiency in your life or walk? Jesus understood the importance of silence as Luke reported: "But Jesus often withdrew to lonely places and prayed" (Luke 5:16). When is the last time you took some time off to be alone and think or pray? Why don't you do more of that? Are you afraid? What are you afraid of? *Lord, I am too busy. My busy-ness keeps me from engaging You on a personal basis. I have substituted church attendance and listening to others talk about You for actually listening to You for myself and that's wrong. Forgive me!*

September 2

Under Attack

Today's reading: Psalms 6-10

"My shield is God Most High, who saves the upright in heart" - Psalm 7:10.

You don't need a shield unless something is being thrown or launched at you, and you need something to deflect the missile. David was declaring that God was his shield because David was under attack and only God could protect and save him. You are under the same kind of attack, and it's because of your stand for and in the Lord. (If you are not under attack, save this for future reference, because you will be.) Paul went on to describe what you are to do to protect yourself from these attacks:

> Put on the full armor of God, so that you can take your stand against the devil's schemes. For our struggle is not against flesh and blood, but against the rulers, against the authorities, against the powers of this dark world and against the spiritual forces of evil in the heavenly realms (Ephesians 6:11-12).

Have you accepted the reality that you are in a war not of your own making, but of your own choosing? Do you realize that you have accepted Christ and therefore His enemies are your enemies? Do you comprehend that some of your problems cannot be framed or solved unless you approach them as spiritual and part of the warfare against God's saints?

September 3

God's Slowness

Today's reading: Psalm 11-15

"The Lord is in his holy temple; the Lord is on his heavenly throne. He observes everyone on earth; his eyes examine them. The Lord examines the righteous, but the wicked, those who love violence, he hates with a passion" - Psalm 11:4-5.

Because God is silent at times, it is easy to think that He doesn't care or isn't paying attention – but He does and He is. David wrote in today's passage that He is watching and examining everyone, and has a particular disdain for those who love violence. In fact, David wrote that God "hates" the wicked and violent. That sounds harsh to us because hatred as a human emotion is connected to sin and is to be avoided. Yet God is incapable of sin, so David is indicating that God has no tolerance for those who oppress others, even if it seems like He is being tolerant. Peter described the reason that God is slow to act: "The Lord is not slow in keeping his promise, as some understand slowness. Instead he is patient with you, not wanting anyone to perish, but everyone to come to repentance" (2 Peter 3:9). Have you interpreted God's slowness to act to mean He either accepts your behavior or doesn't care? Do you see that God leaves room so that you can repent, for when He judges your behavior, you cannot say He did not allow plenty of time for repentance? Of what attitude or behavior do you need to repent before its too late?

September 4

Happy with Life

Today's reading: Psalms 16-20

"Lord, you alone are my portion and my cup; you make my lot secure. The boundary lines have fallen for me in

pleasant places; surely I have a delightful inheritance" - Psalm 16:5-6.

David was saying that in the midst of all his success, possessions, positions, and authority, God was His greatest and the most important presence in his life. It was God's presence that led to the success, possessions, position, and work that David was enjoyed, and David was overflowing with gratitude and praise. David's son later wrote about having joy in your life's work and lot when he wrote:

> This is what I have observed to be good: that it is appropriate for a person to eat, to drink and to find satisfaction in their toilsome labor under the sun during the few days of life God has given them—for this is their lot. Moreover, when God gives someone wealth and possessions, and the ability to enjoy them, to accept their lot and be happy in their toil—this is a gift of God. They seldom reflect on the days of their life, because God keeps them occupied with gladness of heart (Ecclesiastes 5:18-20).

Are you happy with your lot in life? Are you thankful for the work you have to do, the relationships you have, and the relationship with God the Father through Christ? Do you survey the boundary lines of your inheritance that comes from the Lord and delight in your lot? Are you pleased with the body of work you have produced?

September 5

Faith Victories

Today's reading: Psalms 21-25

"The king rejoices in your strength, Lord. How great is his joy in the victories you give!" - Psalm 21:1.

God gave David strength and it gave David great joy. Yet this strength was for a purpose, and that was to win battles and achieve great things that gave God glory. David then shared in that glory, and it led David to praise and worship. God is not empowering you to make you feel good or to help you out from time to time. God desires that you have victory in every area of life: finances, relationships, purpose, goals, victory over sin, and spreading the gospel. Ultimately, Jesus died to give you victory over the last enemy and that enemy is death. John wrote about victory in his first epistle, when he said:

> In fact, this is love for God: to keep his commands. And his commands are not burdensome, for everyone born of God overcomes the world. This is the victory that has overcome the world, even our faith. Who is it that overcomes the world? Only the one who believes that Jesus is the Son of God (1 John 5:3-5).

Are you living an overcoming life? Are you experiencing victory in important areas of work and ministry? Is your faith making a difference in your day-to-day existence? Can you list the faith victories you have recently experienced?

September 6
Dark Nights

Today's reading: Psalms 26-30

"For his anger lasts only a moment, but his favor lasts a lifetime; weeping may stay for the night, but rejoicing comes in the morning" - Psalm 30:5.

There are seasons of life when things don't go well. People betray you, businesses fail, sickness attacks, families struggle, or ministries go through hard times. When any of that happens, it can seem like the pain will never end, but the good news is that it does. What's more, those dark nights are often followed by seasons of joy, restoration, and happiness. The challenge is that you don't know how long the dark night will last before the morning of rejoicing comes. You can only encourage yourself with the faith knowledge that the good times will return. Job experienced this turnaround as we read in Job 42:10-12:

> After Job had prayed for his friends, the Lord restored his fortunes and gave him twice as much as he had before. All his brothers and sisters and everyone who had known him before came and ate with him in his house. They comforted and consoled him over all the trouble the Lord had brought on him, and each one gave him a piece of silver and a gold ring.

Are you in a dark night? Can you thank God for the joyful morning long before it comes? Can you remain steady in your faith walk, even when it's so dark that you cannot see your hand in front of your face?

September 7

A Spacious Place

Today's reading: Psalms 31-35

"I will be glad and rejoice in your love, for you saw my affliction and knew the anguish of my soul. You have not given me into the hands of the enemy but have set my feet in a spacious place" - Psalm 31:7-8.

David was in trouble again, but he took comfort in the fact that God saw and knew about it. David was surrounded by his enemies, but God put him in a spacious place. In other words, David had options that would allow him to escape or defeat his enemies, because the Lord was with him. God knows what you are going through and sees your affliction. Therefore, you can rejoice in the fact that He has your back. When Gehazi, Elisha's servant, saw that they were surrounded, he panicked, but read what happened next:

> When the servant of the man of God got up and went

> out early the next morning, an army with horses and chariots had surrounded the city. "Oh no, my lord! What shall we do?" the servant asked. "Don't be afraid," the prophet answered. "Those who are with us are more than those who are with them." And Elisha prayed, "Open his eyes, Lord, so that he may see." Then the Lord opened the servant's eyes, and he looked and saw the hills full of horses and chariots of fire all around Elisha (2 Kings 6:15-17).

Do you feel like you are surrounded and overwhelmed? Are you in anguish over your circumstances? Then pray Elisha's prayer that God may open your eyes to see the spacious place in which He has placed you!

SEPTEMBER 8

MIND YOUR BUSINESS

Today's reading: Psalm 36-40

"Be still before the Lord and wait patiently for him; do not fret when people succeed in their ways, when they carry out their wicked schemes" - Psalm 37:7.

Today's verse contains three commands for you to follow. The first is to "be still before the Lord." Just the other day, you hopefully read an entry in this book named *Silence*, which urged you to spend some quiet time away from the noise of cell phones and computers. The next command is to "wait patiently" for Him. This does not mean you live a passive life, but rather that you recognize things that only God can do, and trust Him to do those while you do what it is that only you can do. Then the final command is "not to fret." You can waste much emotional energy when you worry, fuss or get agitated over things that are not your business in the first place. Peter tried to meddle in and fret over another person's destiny and this is how Jesus responded: "When Peter saw him [John], he asked, 'Lord, what about him?'

Jesus answered, 'If I want him to remain alive until I return, what is that to you? You must follow me'" (John 21:21-22). Are you fretting over the affairs of someone else? Are you allowing that to keep you from being still and staying focused on your business and walk with the Lord? Why do you think you are so driven to get upset over things that are not really yours to fret over?

September 9

Help the Weak

Today's reading: Psalms 41-45

"Blessed are those who have regard for the weak; the Lord delivers them in times of trouble. The Lord protects and preserves them—they are counted among the blessed in the land—he does not give them over to the desire of their foes. The Lord sustains them on their sickbed and restores them from their bed of illness" - Psalm 41:1-3.

David outlined a series of blessings not for those who fast and pray, or who do great exploits for God, or who preach great sermons. David saw how God blessed those who helped the weak among them, who were mindful of other people's situations to be empathetic and helpful. Paying attention to others, even when your needs are greater than theirs, is the heart of Christian behavior, because Jesus commanded His people to "love one another." Paul described this love more completely when he wrote:

> Love is patient, love is kind. It does not envy, it does not boast, it is not proud. It does not dishonor others, it is not self-seeking, it is not easily angered, it keeps no record of wrongs. Love does not delight in evil but rejoices with the truth. It always protects, always trusts, always hopes, always perseveres. Love never fails (1 Corinthians 13:4-8a).

Are you consumed with your own needs or those of others? What practical things have you done lately to help those who are weak, especially those not part of your family? What steps can you take to be even more aware and sensitive to the needs of the needy? *Father, I want to do all I can for the poor and weak, things that will please You as I am helping others. Open my eyes to see the needs all around me, and then help me overcome my hesitancy and fear that keeps me from saying or doing what is in my power to do to assist them.*

September 10

Fulfill Your Vows

Today's reading: Psalms 46-50

"Sacrifice thank offerings to God, fulfill your vows to the Most High, and call on me in the day of trouble; I will deliver you, and you will honor me" - Psalm 50:14-15.

It is important that you treat God as you would any business partner. When you make a promise, you should keep it, and not break your word to Him just because you can't see Him or because He is gracious. If you vowed to be more generous, keep your word. If you vowed to pray more, then pray. If you vowed to be a better spouse, parent, student, child, or worker, then work to fulfill what you promised to do or become. If you do that, then the promise in today's passage is that God will answer you when you are in trouble. If you ignore your vows, then He will ignore you. Jesus encountered people who made promises, and then were unable to follow through:

> As they were walking along the road, a man said to him, "I will follow you wherever you go." Jesus replied, "Foxes have dens and birds have nests, but the Son of Man has no place to lay his head." He said to another man, "Follow me." But he replied, "Lord, first let me go and bury my father" (Luke 9:57-59).

Have you made a vow to God? Are you fulfilling it? If not, what are you going to do about it?

SEPTEMBER 11

CONSTANT BATTLES

Today's reading: Psalms 51-55

"He rescues me unharmed from the battle waged against me, even though many oppose me" - Psalm 55:18.

Both Psalms and Revelation inform the believer that warfare is the constant companion of those who put their faith in God. In Psalms, the battle is physical, for David was always under attack from his enemies, which were sometimes from his own family! In Revelation, the battle is spiritual, and the forces that align themselves against God attack God's people with ruthless regularity. The message in both books is clear: God is your source of strength, deliverance, and victory, and is your only help or hope of salvation in the midst of your powerful enemies. How will you be victorious in this battle? John wrote this:

> Now have come the salvation and the power and the kingdom of our God, and the authority of his Messiah. For the accuser of our brothers and sisters, who accuses them before our God day and night, has been hurled down. They triumphed over him by the blood of the Lamb and by the word of their testimony; they did not love their lives so much as to shrink from death. Therefore, rejoice, you heavens and you who dwell in them! But woe to the earth and the sea, because the devil has gone down to you! He is filled with fury, because he knows that his time is short (Revelation 12:10-12).

Are you surprised at the level of warfare you are in? Are you fighting the good fight to overcome with the weapons of your testimony and faith in Christ? *Lord, I confess I am surprised at the warfare involved in gaining spiritual victories. I know my victory is secure in Christ, but I must be more aggressive to achieve the overcoming life You want me to have. Teach me to engage the spiritual battle without being overwhelmed. In other words, Lord, help me to know what only I can do and leave the rest for You.*

SEPTEMBER 12

YOUR SOURCE OF HELP

Today's reading: Psalms 56-60

"Give us aid against the enemy, for human help is worthless" - Psalm 60:11.

Ultimately, even if human help is involved in your deliverance, it is God who instigated or empowered the human help to be effective. You should be grateful to those who assist you, but your best and most profuse thanks should be to God. This is especially true of the company who pays you, for while God is using them, God is the one who is providing. Your company doesn't pay your bills, God pays your bills. What's more, He uses your company but He doesn't need your company. In Elijah's case, God used nature to provide for the man of God:

> "You will drink from the brook, and I have directed the ravens to supply you with food there." So he did what the Lord had told him. He went to the Kerith Ravine, east of the Jordan, and stayed there. The ravens brought him bread and meat in the morning and bread and meat in the evening, and he drank from the brook (1 Kings 17:4-6).

Do you understand that God is your source and your career counselor? Do you know that He can provide for you through your job or outside your job? Do you express thanks to God for your provision, even if your company name is on the check?

SEPTEMBER 13

BREAKING DOWN BARRIERS

Today's reading: Psalms 61-65

"Surely the lowborn are but a breath, the highborn are but a lie. If weighed on a balance, they are nothing; together

they are only a breath" - Psalm 62:9.

Almost all cultures tend to place those who have much above those who have not. The rich receive privileges, special laws and honor, while the poor receive whatever benefits their governments decide to give them. Yet wealth is a meaningless differentiation among human beings, for the wealth seems to be distributed not according to the value of someone's work or humanity, but is based on arbitrary decisions of what cultures deem important and unimportant. If you do a search in Proverbs of the words *rich* and *poor*, eleven verses will come up, one of which is "Rich and poor have this in common: The Lord is the Maker of them all" (Proverbs 22:2). Have you created artificial boundaries between yourself and those on the opposite end of your economic spectrum? Do you idolize the rich or despise the poor? If poor, do you have any rich friends? If rich, do you fellowship and have relationships with the poor? Paul wrote that "there is neither Jew nor Gentile, neither slave nor free, nor is there male and female, for you are all one in Christ Jesus" (Galatians 3:28). The gospel came not just to break down racial, gender, and national barriers, it also came to demolish class and economic barriers, so get busy crossing from where you are to minister to those who are not like you, regardless of whether live in a mansion or a shack.

September 14
Your Story

Today's reading: Psalms 66-70

"He turned the sea into dry land, they passed through the waters on foot—come, let us rejoice in him" - Psalm 66:6.

The psalmists were constantly rehearsing and restating their history, both as individuals and as members of the people of God. They did this to help themselves in their current crisis, reminding themselves that God had been faithful in the past and He would be again. They needed that reassurance because they were in the midst of difficult circumstances. You also need to learn to rely on your story of God's faithful track record with you in times of trouble. It may not even hurt to write down your story, including all the blessings and all the recoveries you have made in the Lord – the latter being difficult times you survived by God's grace. You can also include in this list the benefits God has bestowed on His people, things like forgiveness of sins, salvation, healing, health, His presence, fellowship with other saints, and the like. Do you need to review your story? Do you rejoice in what God has done for you, even if today is not a season with a reason to rejoice for you? Can you rehearse your past story in such a way that it encourages you today?

September 15

His Story

Today's reading: Psalms 71-75

"The day is yours, and yours also the night; you established the sun and moon. It was you who set all the boundaries of the earth; you made both summer and winter"
- Psalm 74:16-17.

Yesterday you saw how important it is to recite your story of how God has worked on your behalf. You do that to remind yourself of His power and love when you most need it. Today, you see the psalmist going beyond his story to draw on God's story of creation as a source of teaching and inspiration. God's power is displayed in more ways than His love and acts on your behalf. God did His own thing in creation to establish His glory and give testimony to His faithful acts of creation. Today's passage describes the order that God set in His creation, and the psalmist went on to warn his foes that this same God is working on the psalmist's behalf. Paul spoke to this issue as well when he wrote to the Romans:

> The wrath of God is being revealed from heaven against all the godlessness and wickedness of people, who suppress the truth by their wickedness, since what may be known about God is plain to them, because God has made it plain to them. For since the creation of the world God's invisible qualities—his eternal power and divine nature—have been clearly seen, being understood from what has been made, so that people are without excuse (Romans 1:18-20).

Can you add God's creative genius to your list of things that encourage you in times of trouble? Do you acknowledge and appreciate God's creative prowess when you behold nature and its orderly structure? Do you take hope that the same God who created heaven and earth is on your side?

September 16

Leaders and Followers

Today's reading: Psalms 76-80

"He chose David his servant and took him from the sheep pens; from tending the sheep he brought him to be the shepherd of his people Jacob, of Israel his inheritance" - Psalm 77:70-71.

In today's verse, the psalmist indicated that God was leading His people through His designated leader David. God works through leaders, and since all leaders are imperfect people, you can say that a perfect God uses imperfect people to get His work done. While leaders are flawed, God does hold them to a higher standard of ethics, behavior, and attitude, and also expects His people to recognize His choice of leaders. He further expects the followers to maintain their end of the bargain by maintaining a respectful and submissive attitude toward their leaders. The writer of Hebrews explained the responsibilities of followers in this way: "Have confidence in your leaders and submit to their authority, because they keep watch over you as those who must give an account. Do this so that their work will be a joy, not a burden, for that would be of no benefit to you" (Hebrews 13:17). What is your attitude toward the leaders in your life? Is it a joyful experience for them to lead you? If you are a leader, are you leading as God would want you to lead? How can you improve?

September 17

Times of Testing

Today's reading: Psalms 81-85

"In your distress you called and I rescued you, I answered you out of a thundercloud; I tested you at the waters of Meribah" - Psalm 81:7.

What is your concept of a test? If you are like most people, you think of a piece of paper in front of you as an examination to determine how much you know or retained of a school subject. Yet when the Bible mentions a test, it is talking about something totally different. The test God brings is similar to what they did to metals in ancient times. They would submit the metal to intense heat to see if there were impurities or what they called dross in the metal. If the heat revealed no dross, it was considered high quality. Your tests don't come so God can trick you or found out how much you know (He already knows that). God sends a test to show how far you have come and how effective His work in you has been, as He explained in Deuteronomy 8:2-3:

> Remember how the Lord your God led you all the way in the wilderness these forty years, to humble and test you in order to know what was in your heart, whether or not you would keep his commands. He humbled you, causing you to hunger and then feeding you with manna, which neither you nor your ancestors had known, to teach you that man does not live on bread alone but on every word that comes from the mouth of the Lord.

Are you going through a time of testing? Can you see the positive aspect of that process? Do you realize God may be "showing off" His work in you to the people around you as well as to spiritual powers you cannot see?

SEPTEMBER 18

BEHIND THE SCENES

Today's reading: Psalms 86-90

"Guard my life, for I am faithful to you; save your servant who trusts in you. You are my God; have mercy on me, Lord, for I call to you all day long" - Psalm 86:2.

Sometimes you may think God did not answer your prayer, but you must consider the possibility that things would have been worse or different than they are if you had *not* prayed. There are times it may appear God is not acting on your behalf, but you can never say that with absolute certainty. You never know what God has done and is doing that you cannot see or realize. What accidents did He prevent from occurring? What evil assignments against you did He overrule or thwart? What curses did He cancel? What consequences of your sin did He mercifully absolve? In Peter's case, we learn that Satan wanted to destroy him, but Jesus prayed that God would limit Satan's work and use it for God's glory when it was all over: "Simon, Simon, Satan has asked to sift all of you as wheat. But I have prayed for you, Simon, that your faith may not fail. And when you have turned back, strengthen your brothers" (Luke 22:31-32). Can you thank God in faith for what He is doing behind the scenes that you cannot see or hear? *I am sure, Lord, that You are working behind the scenes to protect and help me. I thank You for all You have done of which I am not aware. I pray for myself now that You would continue to protect me from my enemies, and also protect me from myself, from the hidden sins and negative attitudes that undermine Your work in my life. Don't stop helping me, Lord!*

September 19
Your Fruit

Today's reading: Psalm 91-95

"They will still bear fruit in old age, they will stay fresh and green, proclaiming, 'The Lord is upright; he is my Rock, and there is no wickedness in him'" - Psalm 92:15-16.

Age is not necessarily a factor in your ability to serve the Lord. In today's passage, the psalmist declared that those who love and follow God will *still* bear fruit in old age. This indicates they were bearing fruit while they were younger, so they will *still* bear fruit in their latter years. What is your fruit? How do you define it? What does it look like? Jesus empowered you to bear fruit and expects you to bear it as indicated by this promise:

> Very truly I tell you, whoever believes in me will do the works I have been doing, and they will do even greater things than these, because I am going to the Father. And I will do whatever you ask in my name, so that the Father may be glorified in the Son. You may ask me for anything in my name, and I will do it (John 14:12-14).

What works are you doing because Jesus went to the Father? What answers do you see when you pray? Does that promise from Jesus only pertain to acts He did like raising the dead and healing the lame, or does it also pertain to you writing books, learning languages, starting ministries, and helping the poor on a regular basis? Are you using your age – "I'm too old, I'm too young" - as an excuse to not bear fruit?

September 20
A New Song

Today's reading: Psalms 96-100

"Sing to the Lord a new song, for he has done marvelous

things; his right hand and his holy arm have worked salvation for him. The Lord has made his salvation known and revealed his righteousness to the nations" - Psalm 98:1-2.

The psalmists listed many appropriate responses to God's mercy and salvation, and in today's passage the act of singing was not just mentioned but commanded. Everyone is commanded to sing a new song to the Lord, and that can take place either in a corporate church setting or as a private act of worship. Yet one should not take priority over the other, so you must find a balance of personal worship as well as adding your voice to others in a public worship setting. I have watched people over the years come to church, stare at the hymnal or screen, and not open their lips to sing! Paul taught the Ephesians about this very thing:

> Do not get drunk on wine, which leads to debauchery. Instead, be filled with the Spirit, speaking to one another with psalms, hymns, and songs from the Spirit. Sing and make music from your heart to the Lord, always giving thanks to God the Father for everything, in the name of our Lord Jesus Christ (Ephesians 5:18-20).

Do you sing and take an active part in public worship? Do you give an exuberant response to your sports team and then withhold the same from God? How often do you sing a new song of praise to God?

September 21
The Light

Today's reading: Psalms 101-105

"The Lord wraps himself in light as with a garment; he stretches out the heavens like a tent and lays the beams of his upper chambers on their waters. He makes the clouds his chariot and rides on the wings of the wind. He makes winds his messengers, flames of fire his servants" - Psalm 104:2-4.

First, notice how beautifully these verses are written. They create a vivid picture of a powerful God who uses nature, which of course is His creation, as part of His transportation system. For humans, nature can be an awesome experience, but for God, it is His playground. Second, the psalmist mentions light, and light is a favorite word or theme in John's gospel, starting in the first chapter: "In him was life, and that life was the light of all mankind. The light shines in the darkness, and the darkness has not overcome it" (John 1:4-5). Yet, it wasn't just that John wrote about the light to describe Jesus, but Jesus also said it about Himself: "When Jesus spoke again to the people, he said, 'I am the light of the world. Whoever follows me will never walk in darkness, but will have the light of life'" (John 8:12). Therefore, light for guidance and understanding should never be a problem for you if you follow the Lord and keep your ways in the light. Are you walking in the light? Do you expect to find God's will easily, or do you think God is playing hide-and-seek with you, playing hard-to-get?

September 22

Acting Out Envy

Today's reading: Psalms 106-110

"In the camp they grew envious of Moses and of Aaron, who was consecrated to the Lord" - Psalm 106:16.

Envy is a sneaky disease, for you can look at someone's success, goods, relationships. reputation, money, job, ministry or looks, and secretly want what they have. In fact, you can get downright angry and agitated that you don't have what they have. That can lead to 1) bitterness; 2) an effort to get things similar to what they have; 3) an effort to actually take what they have; 4) a campaign to minimize what they have through sarcasm or character assassination; or 5) all of the above. In other words, envy is a dangerous attitude that must be dealt with ruthless abandon.

The story of Cain and Abel is rooted in envy and we read the tragic results in Genesis 4:

> Now Abel kept flocks, and Cain worked the soil. In the course of time Cain brought some of the fruits of the soil as an offering to the Lord. And Abel also brought an offering—fat portions from some of the firstborn of his flock. The Lord looked with favor on Abel and his offering, but on Cain and his offering he did not look with favor. So Cain was very angry, and his face was downcast. Then the Lord said to Cain, "Why are you angry? Why is your face downcast? If you do what is right, will you not be accepted? But if you do not do what is right, sin is crouching at your door; it desires to have you, but you must rule over it." Now Cain said to his brother Abel, "Let's go out to the field." While they were in the field, Cain attacked his brother Abel and killed him (4:2b-8).

Are you envious of someone else? What is that doing to your thoughts and actions? How do you feel toward the person whom you envy? What are you going to do if you are envious?

September 23

Leader's Blessing

Today's reading: Psalms 111-115

"The Lord remembers us and will bless us: He will bless his people Israel, he will bless the house of Aaron, he will bless those who fear the Lord—small and great alike" - Psalm 115:12-13.

You get the idea from these verses that the Lord is in the blessing business, for the psalmist indicated that God's heart was to bless all of Israel. It is interesting that He singles out the house of Aaron, which is seldom mentioned as a house, since they were the priests of the priests – the nephews of Moses who were the high priests in Israel. It's almost like God is saying in singling them out, "I see your service and there is a blessing for you as you serve me and the people." Paul indicated that anyone who desires to lead God's' people desires a good thing: "Here is a trustworthy saying: Whoever aspires to be an overseer desires a noble task" (1 Timothy 3:1). Can we deduce from this that there is a special or unique blessing for those who choose to willingly and eagerly serve as leaders?

September 24

The Cost of Fear

Today's reading: Psalms 116-120

"The Lord is with me; I will not be afraid. What can mere mortals do to me?" - Psalm 118:5.

This verse is a bold acclamation of fearlessness that is a worthy goal in life but one that can be difficult to obtain. Why is that? It is because we are Adam and Eve's children, and we were born in fear. It clings to us like lint on a dark wool blanket. What's more, we are so grooved with fear, and so accustomed to its presence, that we are unable to confront it. There is helpful fear, for you should be afraid of stealing from your company or of putting your hand down a snake hole. Yet, the fear of what others think, of criticism, of losing their approval, of rejection, and of not being part of the group can keep you from saying or doing what God wants. Even the parents of the man born blind whom Jesus healed succumbed to this fear and could not rejoice in their son's healing:

> "We know he is our son," the parents answered, "and we know he was born blind. But how he can see now, or who opened his eyes, we don't know. Ask him. He is of age; he will speak for himself." His parents said this because they were afraid of the Jewish leaders, who already had decided that anyone who acknowledged

> that Jesus was the Messiah would be put out of the synagogue. That was why his parents said, "He is of age; ask him" (John 9:20-23).

Of whom are you afraid? What is that fear costing you and keeping you from doing? What are you prepared to do about it?

September 25

Ongoing Salvation

Today's reading: Psalms 121-125

"We have escaped like a bird from the fowler's snare; the snare has been broken, and we have escaped" - Psalm 124:7-8.

I am sure God has saved you, your family, or your organization from something. Perhaps it was financial debt or lack, or a dysfunctional relationship, or a cruel supervisor, or some other dilemma that was inescapable, except by and through God's power and help. The psalmist in these verses likened his escape to a bird that is caught in a trap but somehow managed to escape its doom. That is why you can truly declare that you are saved – saved from eternal separation from God as well as the woe of life. Therefore, salvation is not a one-time experience; it is a way of life. Therefore, when you thank God for your salvation, you should be mindful that your Savior is saving you every day, over and over again. Paul wrote to the Thessalonians about being saved: "But we ought always to thank God for you, brothers and sisters loved by the Lord, because God chose you as firstfruits to be saved through the sanctifying work of the Spirit and through belief in the truth" (2 Thessalonians 2:13). Do you see the scope of your salvation? Do you understand that this is an ongoing salvation, for you were saved and are being saved on a daily basis? Are you mindful of God's saving power to protect you on a daily basis? Can you think Him today for His salvation?

September 26

Be a Blesser

Today's reading: Psalms 126-130

"May the Lord bless you from Zion; may you see the prosperity of Jerusalem all the days of your life. May you live to see your children's children—peace be on Israel" - Psalm 128:5-6.

Today's verses are a good prayer you can offer for others, and they are also a blessing that the psalmist was bestowing on his fellow believers. You were meant to participate in God's blessing-distribution business, giving those blessings freely and without bias or discrimination. In order to bless someone in a way that they can participate in the blessing, you must utter that blessing within their earshot so that they can, well, be blessed and uplifted as they hear your kind words. The good news is that blessings cost you nothing and you never run out – as long as your heart is to uplift and edify others. Peter spoke about your role as a blesser, even when others don't bless you, when he wrote: "Do not repay evil with evil or insult with insult. On the contrary, repay evil with blessing, because to this you were called so that you may inherit a blessing" (1 Peter 3:9). Are you living up to your full potential as a blesser of others? What is holding you back? Why are you so hesitant to utter words of life to others, when they are free and within your total control to do so?

September 27

Other Gods

Today's reading: Psalm 131-135

"I know that the Lord is great, that our Lord is greater than all gods" - Psalm 135:5.

The Bible is clear that there are no other gods besides Jehovah, but that doesn't mean people don't try to make them up or create them. Those so-called "gods" may seem to have some power, like the sun god or the moon god, but of course the only power they have is the purpose for which God created them. Yet the foolish and sinful heart of man ascribes a divine nature to those created things and identifies them as gods. Idols are not limited to nature, but can be anything to which a person attaches worshipful attention and energy, like careers, family, religious doctrine, money and reputation. The Lord brought Ezekiel in a vision to the Temple where he saw idolatry in the church or the leaders of God's people: "He then brought me into the inner court of the house of the Lord, and there at the entrance to the temple, between the portico and the altar, were about twenty-five men. With their backs toward the temple of the Lord and their faces toward the east, they were bowing down to the sun in the east" (Ezekiel 8:16). Is your heart divided? Do you worship anything or anyone other than the living God? Don't answer too quickly, but ask God to show you any unholy alliance or attachment you have with any created thing that rightfully belongs to the Creator.

September 28

Your Personality

Today's reading: Psalms 136-140

"I praise you because I am fearfully and wonderfully made; your works are wonderful, I know that full well" - Psalm 139:14.

Most people realize the truth of this verse where their physical makeup is concerned. How the body parts function together is truly amazing and is cause for awe-inspired worship. Yet many would not feel the same about their personality, believing they are seriously flawed and too marred for God to use them until He performed major internal surgery. Your personality, while affected by sin, is as much a creation of God as your internal organs and bodily functions. What aspect of your personality are you convinced is not from the Lord, like your impatience or your lack of mercy? Can you see that God can use your impatience to help fight child abuse or some other dysfunction where patience is *not* a virtue? Can you see that God can use your lack of mercy, which He orchestrated, to deliver a tough-to-say word to someone who needs to hear it? Can you see that God can use your short attention span to get things started that others with more diligence can finish? The point is that what you are considering a shortcoming may not be one at all, which means you can thank God for it rather than unsuccessfully waiting for Him to change what He created for His purposes in the first place.

September 29
Your Diet

Today's reading: Psalms 141-145

"Do not let my heart be drawn to what is evil so that I take part in wicked deeds along with those who are evildoers; do not let me eat their delicacies" - Psalm 141:4.

David often prayed for himself throughout the psalms. While you pray for others on your prayer list, it is a good idea to include yourself. If you don't know what to pray, then pray the prayers the psalmists prayed for themselves. Today's verse contains two "do not let me" prayers, both seeking a heart that would stay true to the Lord and avoid evil. The way to do this is to watch what you "eat" – what you allow into your heart through your ears and eyes. This theme of "eating well" is continued in Proverbs, where it says, "Since they would not accept my advice and spurned my rebuke, they will eat the fruit of their ways and be filled with the fruit of their schemes. For the waywardness of the simple will kill them, and the complacency of fools will destroy them" (Proverbs 1:30-32). What diet does your heart have?

Does it permit gossip and foolishness through reality television shows to enter? Do you read the Word or dime novels? Do you spend time with those who can encourage your heart or weigh it down? Do you study the lives of great people or fools? Do you listen to great music or trash? What else are you "eating"? Is it junk food or wholesome fare?

September 30

Do Like Jesus

Today's reading: Psalms 146-150

"He upholds the cause of the oppressed and gives food to the hungry. The Lord sets prisoners free, the Lord gives sight to the blind, the Lord lifts up those who are bowed down, the Lord loves the righteous. The Lord watches over the foreigner and sustains the fatherless and the widow, but he frustrates the ways of the wicked" - Psalm 146:7-9.

David described some of God's activities and they should sound familiar, for this is a similar list that is outlined in Isaiah and quoted by Jesus in Luke:

> He went to Nazareth, where he had been brought up, and on the Sabbath day he went into the synagogue, as was his custom. He stood up to read, and the scroll of the prophet Isaiah was handed to him. Unrolling it, he found the place where it is written: "The Spirit of the Lord is on me, because he has anointed me to proclaim good news to the poor. He has sent me to proclaim freedom for the prisoners and recovery of sight for the blind, to set the oppressed free, to proclaim the year of the Lord's favor." Then he rolled up the scroll, gave it back to the attendant and sat down. The eyes of everyone in the synagogue were fastened on him. He began by saying to them, "Today this scripture is fulfilled in your hearing" (Luke 4:16-21).

Jesus was doing the things that David attributed to God, so that is another indication of Jesus' divinity. Jesus expects you and I to do the same things He was doing as we represent Him on earth. How many of the list mentioned in today's passage are you doing (giving food, set prisoners free, give sight to the blind)? Which things are part of your strengths or gift package? How can you do more of what Jesus did?

October 1

For the Lord

Today's reading: Psalms 1-5

"Know that the Lord has set apart his faithful servant for himself; the Lord hears when I call to him" - Psalm 4:3.

God has called you to a life of service during which you will direct your purpose and use your gifts to help other people in many ways. Yet no matter how often or how much you serve others, God must remain the focus of your service. What you do, you do for Him, so that when people are ungrateful, unresponsive, or unapproachable, you will not become disillusioned or discouraged. This principle was reinforced throughout the Old Testament in the symbol of the burnt offering, which was not consumed by the priest, but was to be burned completely (without the blood and fat) as an offering only to the Lord: "You are to wash the internal organs and the legs with water, and the priest is to bring all of them and burn them on the altar. It is a burnt offering, a food offering, an aroma pleasing to the Lord" (Leviticus 1:13). Do your feelings get hurt when people don't recognize or appreciate you? Are you doing what you do ultimately for the Lord? Do you mind being a burnt offering, consumed in the fire of God's service and presence, as a sacrifice to Him in your service to others? *Lord, there are some people that I need to forgive today, people who have injured me and probably aren't even aware they have done so. They have not recognized my kindness to them, and I took it personally. I forgive them and I commit to continue to do good because you require it, not so others will recognize it.*

October 2

Be Childlike

Today's reading: Psalms 6-10

"Through the praise of children and infants you have established a stronghold against your enemies, to silence the foe and the avenger" - Psalm 8:2.

God often confounds the strong not through other strong people, but through those who are least likely. This theme ran through Jesus' ministry as He taught that you must be like a child to enter into the things of God: "And he said: 'Truly I tell you, unless you change and become like little children, you will never enter the kingdom of heaven'" (Matthew 18:3). What does this mean exactly? Children are dependent and trust easily. They are joyful and let their joy overflow to others. Children know how to work at play, their favorite activity. They are open to new things and they are teachable. Paul took this theme and explained it more fully:

> God chose the weak things of the world to shame the strong. God chose the lowly things of this world and the despised things—and the things that are not—to nullify the things that are, so that no one may boast before him. It is because of him that you are in Christ Jesus, who has become for us wisdom from God—that is, our righteousness, holiness and redemption. Therefore, as it is written: "Let the one who boasts boast in the Lord" (1 Corinthians 1:27b-31).

Where do you need to be more childlike where the things of God are concerned? Where have you become too grown up and sophisticated toward spiritual things? Do you trust your Father like a child, or have you seized control of your life and shut Him out?

October 3
Keep Your Word

Today's reading: Psalms 11-15

"Lord, who may dwell in your sacred tent? Who may live on your holy mountain?. . . . . . who keeps an oath even when it hurts, and does not change their mind" (Psalm 15:1, 4b).

Psalm 15 gives a few behavioral tendencies that the Lord expects from His people. The psalm starts with two questions, and then goes on to answer them with specific practices. In verse four, the behavior to focus on today is keeping your word and not being fickle. The violation of this principle is rampant among believers. When you say, "I will pray for you," and then don't, you have broken your word. When you say, "I'll be there," and you're not, you have broken your word. When you say, "I will call you and we'll get together," and you don't, you have broken your word. When you say, "I'm going to pray more," and you don't, you have broken your word. When you say, "I will be part of that group or team," and then don't show up, you have violated the principle David described in verse four. It would be better for you to say nothing than to give your word and not follow through. Are you in the habit of doing this? Where do you need to go back and apologize for your lack of follow through? Do you even see this as an issue or is it not that important? From this point forward, try not to say so much and then just go do it, rather than promise and disappear.

October 4
Fight for Victory

Today's reading: Psalms 16-20

"For who is God besides the Lord? And who is the Rock except our God? It is God who arms me with strength and

keeps my way secure" - Psalm 18:31-32.

It is interesting that David was the focus and author for much of the book of Psalms, and while he was a king, poet, song writer and shepherd, he was also a warrior. Much of what he wrote had to do with war, and much of the book of Revelation also contains the war theme. If David was a warrior and Jesus is depicted as a warrior, then the warrior must be part of your identity, too! God wants to teach you to fight for your inheritance, for the fighting will enhance your appreciation for your victory and will give you incentive to keep your winnings and not give them away cheaply. Paul wrote his beloved disciple Timothy and mentioned the warrior aspect of faith to him when he said,

> Timothy, my son, I am giving you this command in keeping with the prophecies once made about you, so that by recalling them you may fight the battle well, holding on to faith and a good conscience, which some have rejected and so have suffered shipwreck with regard to the faith (1 Timothy 1:18-19).

Is God arming you with strength? If so, for what purpose? Where do you need to fight for your victory in Christ? For family? Career? Finances? Ministry? Overcoming a prevailing sin?

October 5

Little by Little

Today's reading: Psalms 21-25

***"Through the victories you gave, his glory is great; you have bestowed on him splendor and majesty"* - Psalm 21:5.**

Yesterday we looked at your need to fight for the blessings God has in store for you. Today, we see the rest of the story, and that is that God gives you the victory in Christ. After the battle, God shares some of His glory with His servants who engage in the fight and see it through to the end. In Exodus, God shared His strategy for His people taking the land He had promised:

> I will send my terror ahead of you and throw into confusion every nation you encounter. I will make all your enemies turn their backs and run. I will send the hornet ahead of you to drive the Hivites, Canaanites and Hittites out of your way. But I will not drive them out in a single year, because the land would become desolate and the wild animals too numerous for you. Little by little I will drive them out before you, until you have increased enough to take possession of the land (Exodus 23:27-30).

Are you experiencing victory in your life? Is it going more slowly than you would like? Could it be that God is doing it little by little for the reasons mentioned in the Exodus passage? Can you thank God for the ultimate victory He promised, even if you can't see it in its totality today?

OCTOBER 6

CONFIDENT IN TROUBLE

Today's reading: Psalms 26-30

"Though an army besiege me, my heart will not fear; though war break out against me, even then I will be confident" - Psalm 27:3.

It is an important discipline to remain strong and confident when things are going against you. In today's verse, David made two astounding statements worthy of your attention and emulation. First, he had chosen *not* to be afraid even if any army besieged him. When the finances, relationships or work goes against you, can you say the same thing? Or do you worry about things, thinking, "Have I done something wrong? Have I missed the Lord? Will this situation end badly for me?" All those questions and others like them are fear questions. Second, David said he would maintain his confidence even if war broke out against him. Can you exhibit that same confidence when you are under attack, confidence not in your own ability but in the Lord? Elizabeth said something to Mary that you need to hear today: "Blessed is she who has believed that the Lord would fulfill his promises to her!" (Luke 1:45). Can you believe God's promises toward you even when there is a war raging against you? Can you keep your confidence in the Lord in the worst of times?

October 7

Your Hiding Place

Today's reading: Psalms 31-35

"You are my hiding place; you will protect me from trouble and surround me with songs of deliverance" - Psalm 32:7.

Did you ever have a hiding place when you were a child? Or maybe you have one now – a place where no one knows you or would think to look for you. David had a hiding place, and it was in the Lord! David was confident that God could veil his presence and keep safe from his enemies. For many years, David was on the run from murderous Saul who wanted to keep David from inheriting his throne, but God hid David and did not deliver David into Saul's hand. What's more, David undoubtedly wrote and sang songs speaking of God's protection from trouble, testifying to God's deliverance while his enemies were still all around his hiding place! Peter experienced this kind of deliverance when the angel escorted him out of prison and no one even knew he was going:

> Then the angel said to him, "Put on your clothes and sandals." And Peter did so. "Wrap your cloak around you and follow me," the angel told him. Peter followed him out of the prison, but he had no idea that what the angel was doing was really happening; he thought he was seeing a vision. They passed the first and second guards and came to the iron gate leading to the city.

> It opened for them by itself, and they went through it. When they had walked the length of one street, suddenly the angel left him (Acts 12:8-10).

Is God your hiding place? Have you learned to trust in His ability to protect and even hide you from trouble? Can you sing a song of deliverance before your safety or deliverance is secured as you put your trust in Him?

October 8

Quenching Your Thirst

Today's reading: Psalms 36-40

"For with you is the fountain of life; in your light we see light" - Psalm 36:9.

Throughout the gospels, Jesus referred to thirst as a spiritual condition, and the psalmist did the same in today's verse. The writer also introduced the concept of God bringing light to any life or situation, and Jesus expanded the concept when He said, "I am the way and the truth and the life. No one comes to the Father except through me" (John 14:6). Then Jesus brought in the water metaphor when He spoke with the woman at the well:

> Jesus answered her, "If you knew the gift of God and who it is that asks you for a drink, you would have asked him and he would have given you living water." "Sir," the woman said, "you have nothing to draw with and the well is deep. Where can you get this living water? Are you greater than our father Jacob, who gave us the well and drank from it himself, as did also his sons and his livestock?" (John 4:10-12).

Are you thirsty and trying to quench your thirst by way of your career, cars, education, travels, or relationships? Are you searching for light or answers in other philosophies outside the Lord and His word? What can you do to drink from the right source where your life, work and ministry are concerned?

October 9
Waves of Trouble

Today's reading: Psalms 41-45

"Deep calls to deep in the roar of your waterfalls; all your waves and breakers have swept over me" - Psalm 42:7.

The psalmist was describing his current situation, and the only thing he could compare it to was the roaring of a waterfall and the pounding of waves over his being. In other words, God was sending more his way than he thought he could handle, perhaps more than he ever expected. When God tests you, He often sends situations that seem overwhelming, but He does it for two reasons. One is to show the depth of His work in you, for if you reflect, you probably could not have handled what you are going through five or ten years back. The second is to prove to you His ability to save you to the uttermost from the uncertainties and perilous nature of life this side of the Lord's return. Paul experienced an example of this waterfall of trouble when he wrote Timothy to say, "Alexander the metalworker did me a great deal of harm. The Lord will repay him for what he has done" (2 Timothy 4:14). Are you experiencing the overwhelming waves and waterfall of tribulation? Does it seem like you will drown? There may be some consolation in knowing that God is still with you and you will have a testimony of His faithfulness whenever the waves stop pounding your soul.

October 10
Be Quiet

Today's reading: Psalms 46-50

"He says, 'Be still, and know that I am God; I will be exalted

among the nations, I will be exalted in the earth'" - Psalm 46:10.

There is a lot of noise all around you every day. When there isn't noise, you may create it by putting on some music, turning on the television, or going to the mall. Yet to hear the voice of the Lord or just to get in touch with your own thoughts and feelings, you must create some quiet space where you open yourself to the life of your inner being. That can be scary, for what if the Lord speaks to you? What if you have to confront your own guilt, fear or insecurity? The psalmist directed you to be still so that you can get a better perspective of who God is in all His glory and power. When you do that, your current situation, which may be a challenge for you, will fade into the awareness of God's awesome power that will ultimately be expressed in the Second Coming of Jesus. Take some time today and every day this week just to compose yourself, pen and journal close by, and then quiet your heart and mind to listen to God and sharpen your focus on His majesty, greatness and purpose for you and for all His creation.

October 11
Riches

Today's reading: Psalms 51-55

"Look what happens to mighty warriors who do not trust in God. They trust their wealth instead and grow more and more bold in their wickedness" - Psalm 52:7.

Wealth and riches are deceptive, causing you to put your trust in them and not in the Lord. The challenge is that you may not see yourself as wealthy, but when you compare yourself to the rest of the world, you may very well be! And that may cause you to put your trust in your credit cards, you earning ability, the marketability of your college degree, your savings, or your retirement fund, instead of the Lord. Jesus warned us about the dangers of money when He said, "No one can serve two masters. For you will hate one and love the other; you will be devoted to one and despise the other. You cannot serve both God and money" (Luke 16:13). Where has the power of money crept into your thinking and life philosophy, like the gold ring in *The Lord of the Rings*? How do you think you can guard against this insidious disease? Do you think that generous giving may be one way? What other ways can you think of?

October 12

Clever Lies

Today's reading: Psalms 56-60

"I trust in God, so why should I be afraid? What can mere mortals do to me?" - Psalm 56:11.

Today we return to another familiar theme in Psalms, and that is fear. We have not paid much attention to the thematic titles that some of the psalms have, but the heading for Psalm 56 states that David wrote this, "regarding the time the Philistines seized him in Gath." It was in this instance that David attempted to escape from Saul not by trusting in the Lord, but through the use of clever lies:

> David heard these comments and was very afraid of what King Achish of Gath might do to him. So he pretended to be insane, scratching on doors and drooling down his beard. Finally, King Achish said to his men, "Must you bring me a madman? We already have enough of them around here! Why should I let someone like this be my guest?" (1 Samuel 21:12-15).

When you are "cornered," do you resort to your own plans to escape? Have you employed clever lies and deception to protect yourself instead of trusting Him? Are there any of those lies that you need to correct with the truth and set the record straight with other people and with God?

October 13

Thirst for God

Today's reading: Psalms 61-65

"O God, you are my God; I earnestly search for you. My soul thirsts for you; my whole body longs for you in this parched and weary land where there is no water" - Psalm 63:1.

David was in the desert and he was probably thirsty. Yet he indicated his spiritual thirst was as great if not greater than his physical thirst. David went on to say, "You satisfy me more than the richest feast. I will praise you with songs of joy" (Psalm 63:5). Are you spiritually thirsty? If so, what are you doing to quench and satisfy that thirst? Bible reading is one way to accomplish that. Another is prayer, and another is not just reading the Word, but engaging in a systematic study that could lead to a certificate or degree. One thing about thirst is that you may quench it once, but it can reoccur the next day, so it's a never-ending process to keep it under control. That is not a weakness, but a blessing, for Jesus said, "God blesses those who hunger and thirst for justice [righteousness], for they will be satisfied" (Matthew 6:5). Are you thirsty? If not, what are you using to treat that thirst apart from the Lord? Do you think there is a way to increase your thirst for God? What may those things be?

October 14

Remember

Today's reading: Psalms 66-70

"When you, God, went out before your people, when you marched through the wilderness, the earth shook, the heavens poured down rain, before God, the One of Sinai, before God, the God of Israel" - Psalm 68:7-8.

David obviously wrote when he was in trouble, which was pretty much all of the time, and his writing must have helped him process his situation and regain his perspective. His complaints or laments almost always ended in praise, and he was especially effective at remembering, as a way to encourage himself in his troubles, all that God had done, not just for him, but for all the people of Israel. In today's passage, David went all the way back to the story of the Exodus and reiterated how God worked on Israel's behalf during that period of history. Jesus also emphasized the need to remember and established a rite to be practiced for the rest of time to commemorate what He did for His people: "And he took bread, gave thanks and broke it, and gave it to them, saying, 'This is my body given for you; do this in remembrance of me'" (Luke 22:19). Do you take time to remember what God has done not just for you but for all His people, of whom you are a part? Are you in a church where you celebrate the Lord's table regularly? Do you take time to read in the Bible the things God did for His people in the past and count them as if He did them for you? Why not take some time right now to reflect on God's goodness?

October 15

Bitter Trouble

Today's reading: Psalms 71-75

"Though you have made me see troubles, many and bitter, you will restore my life again; from the depths of the earth you will again bring me up" - Psalm 71:20.

Once again we turn to the topic of suffering and trouble, a common theme throughout both the book of Psalms and this devotional. The title of Psalm 71 does not indicate that David wrote it, but it certainly sounds like him as we have seen other verses that he wrote that are similar to today's. The psalmist had great hope that God would restore his fortunes and took consolation in that fact. Paul also carried this same hope through his own trials and tribulations when he wrote,

> Therefore, among God's churches we boast about your perseverance and faith in all the persecutions and trials you are enduring. All this is evidence that God's judgment is right, and as a result you will be counted worthy of the kingdom of God, for which you are suffering. God is just: He will pay back trouble to those who trouble you (2 Thessalonians 1:4-6).

Are you experiencing many bitter troubles? Can you keep your eye on the future, and thank God for when they will end and things will be back to "normal"? Can you even trust that God will "take care of" those who have made trouble for you?

October 16

The Sincerity Trap

Today's reading: Psalms 76-80

"Make vows to the Lord your God and fulfill them; let all the neighboring lands bring gifts to the One to be feared" - Psalm 76:11.

Believers are people of the Word, so obviously words are important to them. They listen to words, encourage others with words, pray with words, and study ancient words to gather more insight into what the Word may mean. That means when someone promises something using words, that someone may believe, if they were sincere, that commitment is as good as doing it, regardless of whether or not that someone follows through. According to that thinking, a statement, "I'll pray for you" or "I'll be there to help" or "I will give $15 every month to missions" is something one says but there is no need to actually *do* it if one is sincere when it was said. That of course is wrong thinking, and today's verse urges you to "make vows and fulfill them." Where have you fallen into the "sincerity trap," substituting and emphasizing intent rather than action? Where have you spoken a vow and not followed through? How can you make up for that flaw that is nothing short of deceptive and a lie? *Once again, I am confronted by my actions not being consistent with my words. Help me, Lord, to be a person that keeps my words few and my follow up true.*

October 17

Holy Discipline

Today's reading: Psalms 81-85

"But my people would not listen to me; Israel would not submit to me. So I gave them over to their stubborn hearts to follow their own devices" - Psalm 81:11-12.

God's discipline is seldom easy or pleasant, but it is much better than being left alone to suffer the consequences and reap the fruit of your own actions, attitudes, or thinking. When God confronts you with some truth about you and helps you escape that unpleasant reality, it is because He loves you. When He leaves you alone, which may seem preferable, then you are really in trouble, with no one to help or deliver you from yourself. The writer of Hebrews explained,

> Moreover, we have all had human fathers who disciplined us and we respected them for it. How much more should we submit to the Father of spirits and live! They disciplined us for a little while as they thought best; but God disciplines us for our good, in order that we may share in his holiness (Hebrews 12:9-10).

Are you being disciplined? Do you secretly wish that God would leave you alone, or that He is being too harsh, maybe even unfair? If so, then reconsider your thinking today and welcome God's "interference" in your life, seeing it as an act of love and not that of an arbitrary parent.

October 18
The Nations

Today's reading: Psalms 86-90

"Glorious things are said of you, city of God: 'I will record Rahab and Babylon among those who acknowledge me—Philistia too, and Tyre, along with Cush—and will say, 'This one was born in Zion'" - Psalm 87:3-4.

It is common in the Psalms for the Lord Himself to speak in the midst of what the psalmist was writing, as happened in today's passage. The psalmist was writing about the "city of God," when the Lord entered in to say that at some time in the future, other nations would be residents in God's city and not just Israel. This was fulfilled in Christ, who came to Israel but commanded His disciples to go to the ends of the earth to share the good news of the gospel, which they eventually gave their lives to do. The most notable of those early missionaries was Paul, who eagerly went to the nations to fulfill what was written in Psalm 87: "Through him we received grace and apostleship to call all the Gentiles to the obedience that comes from faith for his name's sake" (Romans 1:5). Do you have a heart to see the people of the nations come to Jesus? Do you pray toward that end? Give money to help the cause? Is there a particular nation that is on your heart? Why not take time today to pray for that nation or people group? You may even wish to get a map and lay your hands on that area where they live and ask God to fulfill the promise of Psalm 87 among them.

October 19
Assumptions

Today's reading: Psalms 91-95

"They say, 'The Lord does not see; the God of Jacob takes no notice'" - Psalm 94:7.

When God is silent, people come to one of two conclusions or assumptions, both of which are erroneous and potentially dangerous. The first is that He doesn't see what's going on, which is ludicrous. The other is that He agrees with what's going on, which may or may not be true. The Lord Himself addressed the second conclusion in Psalm 50:21: "When you did these things and I kept silent, you thought I was exactly like you. But I now arraign you and set my accusations before you." The first conclusion is addressed by Paul: "Or do you show contempt for the riches of his kindness, forbearance and patience, not realizing that God's kindness is intended to lead you to repentance?" (Romans 2:4). Have you been misinterpreting God's silence? Do you mistake His hesitancy to judge your attitude or behavior for His approval of who you are or what you do? Do you assume that God thinks like you and has the same "opinions"? Ask the Lord to point out to you where you may be reaching one of these wrong conclusions and then make the necessary course corrections.

October 20

Joy Commanded

Today's reading: Psalms 96-100

"Let all creation rejoice before the Lord, for he comes, he comes to judge the earth. He will judge the world in righteousness and the peoples in his faithfulness" - Psalm 96:13.

The key word in today's verse is *joy*, and it seems out of place, for this verse talks about the Lord coming to judge the earth and the world. While He judges the world with a stern standard, however, He also judges His people with faithfulness, and that is good news worth joyfully celebrating. It is of note that the Lord commanded His people to rejoice when they came into His presence for the annual festivals as reported in Deuteronomy 16:14-15:

> Be joyful at your festival—you, your sons and daugh-

> ters, your male and female servants, and the Levites, the foreigners, the fatherless and the widows who live in your towns. For seven days celebrate the festival to the Lord your God at the place the Lord will choose. For the Lord your God will bless you in all your harvest and in all the work of your hands, and your joy will be complete.

Is your joy complete? Do you come into God's presence with gladness or sadness of heart? Do you see that joy is a command? That means it is within your power to control, especially when you approach God and His relationship with you. What can do to turn on the joy spigot today to let your joy flow freely?

October 21

Rebuilding

Today's reading: Psalms 101-105

"For the Lord will rebuild Zion and appear in his glory. He will respond to the prayer of the destitute; he will not despise their plea" - Psalm 102:16-17.

Perhaps you are facing a situation in your life that was damaged or destroyed through sin, negligence or through the uncertainties of life. Maybe your business failed, or a relationship ended that you valued. You could have had a ministry setback or an investment go wrong into which you made a significant deposit. It's even possible that your own sin brought harm to those closest to you. Today's passage speaks to God's role as a Rebuilder, who will respond to your plea for help and partner with you to restore that which was lost, stolen or broken. Even Samson, who made such a mess of his life, was granted a second chance after his hair was cut and his strength lost: "But the hair on his head began to grow again after it had been shaved. . . Then Samson prayed to the Lord, 'Sovereign Lord, remember me. Please, God, strengthen me just once more, and let me with one blow get revenge on the Philistines for my two eyes'" (Judges 16:22, 28). God heard Samson and his strength and purpose were restored. Are you facing a rebuilding job in some area of your life? Then embrace the task with enthusiasm and ask the God who has restored what was lost for so many to help you restore your lost world. It's never too too late. *God, I accept the opportunity to restore what I forfeited in my life through my own negligence. Thank You for the second chance!*

October 22

Fruitful Fields

Today's reading: Psalms 106-110

"He turned rivers into a desert, flowing springs into thirsty ground, and fruitful land into a salt waste, because of the wickedness of those who lived there" - Psalm 107-33-34.

God has created all things to bear fruit as we read in Genesis, fruit that was according to "their kind" (see Genesis 1:22, 24, 28). In fact, today's passage tells us that God has to intervene to stop the fruitfulness process, and He intervenes when there is wickedness – some criteria that is not being met for the fruit to come forth. Therefore, if you are not bearing fruit, something has happened to stop your productivity that God has programmed you to bear. Jesus referred to the fruit-bearing process in John 15: 5-8:

> I am the vine; you are the branches. If you remain in me and I in you, you will bear much fruit; apart from me you can do nothing. If you do not remain in me, you are like a branch that is thrown away and withers; such branches are picked up, thrown into the fire and burned. If you remain in me and my words remain in you, ask whatever you wish, and it will be done for you. This is to my Father's glory, that you bear much fruit, showing yourselves to be my disciples.

In what area of life do you bear much fruit? Can you describe your fruit? What does it look like? If you are not bearing fruit, where have you cut yourself off from Jesus who is your source of productivity? You can examine what has led to this lack, but in most cases, it is fear that has caused your vine to shrivel and led to your barren fields.

October 23

Optimist or Pessimist?

Today's reading: Psalms 111-115

"Surely the righteous will never be shaken; they will be remembered forever. They will have no fear of bad news; their hearts are steadfast, trusting in the Lord" - Psalm 112:6-7.

When you put your trust in the Lord, you should have an optimism for life that is based on God's faithfulness and steadfastness. It is not an optimism that emanates from your trust in the economy, your company, or the reliability of other people. It is a confidence in the Lord Himself. The opposite of optimism is pessimism, and that brings an outlook on life that expects the worst instead of the best. The problem is that optimists and pessimists have a tendency to fulfill their own expectations, so that expecting the worst often helps deliver it. Today's passage speaks to fact that the righteous will not fear bad news. That doesn't mean bad news will never come; it simply means you are not looking for it with every unexpected phone call, message that the boss wants to meet with you, or expectation that someone you like or even love is going to reject you. Paul was confident and optimistic as he explained in 2 Corinthians 3:4-5: "Such confidence we have through Christ before God. Not that we are competent in ourselves to claim anything for ourselves, but our competence comes from God." Have you trained yourself to be pessimistic, to expect the worst so you won't be disappointed? Do you see that it is possible that when you expect the worst, you create the environment for the worst to happen? Can you also see that you learned to be pessimistic, and that means you can learn to be optimistic?

October 24
Get Ready

Today's reading: Psalms 116-120

"When hard pressed, I cried to the Lord; he brought me into a spacious place" - Psalm 118:4.

The psalmist was in a difficult place, perhaps hemmed in by negative circumstances, enemies or his own limitations. He cried to the Lord and God not only heard him but also removed the limitations and put him in a place where he could grow. God is able to change your fortunes overnight, as the Lord spoke that He would do in Isaiah:

> Sing, barren woman, you who never bore a child; burst into song, shout for joy, you who were never in labor; because more are the children of the desolate woman than of her who has a husband,' says the Lord. 'Enlarge the place of your tent, stretch your tent curtains wide, do not hold back; lengthen your cords, strengthen your stakes (Isaiah 54:1-2).

Where have you felt limited and restricted? Can you see that God is going to bless and prosper you, and that you need to get ready today for the blessings that will come, before they actually appear? Can you thank God for your breakthrough today, even though it is on its way and hasn't arrived yet? Think of it as a big shipment of furniture that is on its way to you, and you need to start making room and rearranging things now before it arrives. Get ready, for your blessing time is on its way – in fact, it's already here.

October 25

Persecution

Today's reading: Psalms 121-125

"Have mercy on us, Lord, have mercy on us, for we have endured no end of contempt. We have endured no end of ridicule from the arrogant, of contempt from the proud" - Psalm 123:3-4.

The theme of persecution runs through the book of Psalms, as it does throughout the New Testament, especially in the book of Revelation. God's people can never make peace with this world, for this world's values are totally opposed to the values and principles of God's kingdom. Some withdraw from the world because of the tension, yet some try to fit into and become friends with the world's ways. James warned against the latter strategy when he wrote,

> You adulterous people, don't you know that friendship with the world means enmity against God? Therefore, anyone who chooses to be a friend of the world becomes an enemy of God. Or do you think Scripture says without reason that he jealously longs for the spirit he has caused to dwell in us? (James 4:4-5).

Where have you cuddled up and gotten cozy with the world? Where are you trying to avoid inevitable persecution from or a confrontation with the world system? In what situation have you hoped what Paul wrote would not be true: "In fact, everyone who wants to live a godly life in Christ Jesus will be persecuted" (2 Timothy 3:12)?

October 26

Victory in Oppression

Today's reading: Psalms 126-130

"'They have greatly oppressed me from my youth,' let Israel

say; 'they have greatly oppressed me from my youth, but they have not gained the victory over me'" - Psalm 129:1-2.

Keep in mind that the psalms were edited into their current order -- and a few of them were written – when Israel was in Babylonian exile. There they were subjected to ridicule and idolatrous customs. Yet the Babylonians could not break their spirit. Perhaps you are in a bad ministry or job situation with a cruel overseer, or facing oppression from some other source. How can you keep that from gaining the victory over you? First, extend forgiveness, even if it means forgiving your oppressor(s) on a daily basis! Second, keep your commitment to obey the Lord strong; don't blame or be angry with Him over your situation. Third, have hope and remember your past, and live in the reality that God is with you and will one day make things right. Fourth, keep in mind that God is an avenger, and He will one day give to your oppressors as they deserve. Fifth, pray for mercy for your oppressor(s) so that you can also receive mercy from God. Finally, read Daniel's story in Daniel 1-6 to learn from how he handled his own Babylonian exile, for there you will see that while he was a prisoner, he always had the victory, even over his conquerors.

October 27

Signs Are for Unbelievers

Today's reading - Psalms 131-135

"He struck down the firstborn of Egypt, the firstborn of people and animals. He sent his signs and wonders into your midst, Egypt, against Pharaoh and all his servants" - Psalm 135:8-9.

Right before Israel left Egypt for good, the Lord unleashed the last of the plagues, which was the death of each firstborn creature in the land (except for those in Israel, of course). This finally convinced the Egyptians to release the Israelites so they could journey toward their Promised Land, but the plague did not convince the Egyptians to serve the Lord. That is a curious thing, for God proved His existence and power to them, but they did not believe. Many people have said, maybe even you, that if you had some kind of sign, then you would believe God was speaking to you. That is probably not accurate In most cases, God performs signs for the unbeliever to prove that He is real or that He is speaking to them. Yet, they can be so steeped in unbelief that they miss the message altogether! The same can happen to you. It is not faith that demands or looks for a sign, but unbelief, and still the sign is no guarantee that you will respond in faith. Where in your life are you waiting for sign that, even if it came, may not move you to action? Can you see that the problem is not God's lack of confirmation, but your fear and lack of trust? Perhaps today you stop holding God's purpose for your life hostage, demanding a sign in return for its release?

October 28

Your Creativity

Today's reading: Psalms 136-140

"Give thanks to the Lord, for he is good. His love endures forever" - Psalm 136:1.

Psalm 136 was obviously a song used during corporate Temple worship. The leader would probably sing a line and the people would respond with their own line throughout the entire psalm. Someone had to compose this psalm, expressing his creativity as He was led by the Spirit of God. You also have creativity that God wants you to express just like Adam did when he named the animals:

> Now the Lord God had formed out of the ground all the wild animals and all the birds in the sky. He brought

> them to the man to see what he would name them; and whatever the man called each living creature, that was its name. So the man gave names to all the livestock, the birds in the sky and all the wild animals (Genesis 2:19-20).

God did not whisper those names to Adam, nor did He "lay them on his heart or mind." God directed Adam's work, but Adam produced those names as an expression of his God-given creativity. Are you expressing your creativity, whether it is to write, sing, paint, rhyme, sculpt, or dance? Is your creativity expression some other activity not mentioned in that list? Do you see whatever that creativity is as a divine assignment? How can you develop and release it more regularly and effectively?

October 29

Surrounded

Today's reading: Psalms 141-145

"Keep me safe from the traps set by evildoers, from the snares they have laid for me. Let the wicked fall into their own nets, while I pass by in safety" - Psalm 141:9-10.

It is common practice to thank the Lord for the things you know He has done for you, things like heal your diseases, provide financially, forgive your sins, and on and on. That being true, do you thank the Lord for the things He has done of which you are not aware? The psalmist in today's passage prayed for those unseen instances when he needed God's help, didn't realize what was going on, and moved on safe from harm. The Lord promised to go before you but also to be your guard to protect you from what you cannot see: "But you will not leave in haste or go in flight; for the Lord will go before you, the God of Israel will be your rear guard" (Isaiah 52:12), as He had done for Israel during the Exodus: "Then the angel of God, who had been traveling in front of Israel's army, withdrew and went behind them. The pillar of cloud also moved from in front and stood behind them" (Exodus 14:19). Spend some time today thanking God for the things from which He has saved you and of which you are not aware. Pray David's prayer found in today's passage, asking that God will surround you to protect you from both the traps of life and those set by your enemies.

October 30

Praise Him

Today's reading: Psalms 146-150

"Praise him with the sounding of the trumpet, praise him with the harp and lyre, praise him with timbrel and dancing, praise him with the strings and pipe, praise him with the clash of cymbals, praise him with resounding cymbals" - Psalm 150:3-5.

The book of Psalms ends with an entry that is entirely devoted to praising the Lord. After all the topics that included questions, agony, joy, questions, answers, issues, and other challenges of life, the psalmist ends it as is fitting: with a call to worship! Like the psalmist, your life is full of surprises, pain, happiness, good and bad relationships, bad and good bosses, children who please or disappoint you, financial gain and loss, and circumstances for which there is no answer or solution. What do you do with all that? You focus on the One who changes not and you praise Him – not to get what you want as a manipulative practice, but as an expression of love and adoration for the one being in your life who is consistent, faithful and loving. When Daniel tried to figure out what all his visions meant, he wrote this: "I, Daniel, was worn out. I lay exhausted for several days. Then I got up and went about the king's business. I was appalled by the vision; it was beyond understanding" (Daniel 8:27). Daniel could not understand, so he learned to live with his limitations and went back to work. Are you trying to figure out the why's of life? Perhaps it's time to stop, live with it, and praise the Lord. *Lord, help me to know my limitations. There are some things I want to understand but cannot, so I need to accept that and focus on those things that I can comprehend.*

October 31

Fellowship with Believers

Today's reading: Psalm 119

"I am a friend to all who fear you, to all who follow your precepts" - Psalm 119:63.

The psalmist declared that his loyalties were with God's people, and not just those who claimed to be believers, but those who followed God's precepts as outlined in His word. This concept was radically applied in the days immediately following Jesus' Ascension, as reported by Luke:

> They devoted themselves to the apostles' teaching and to fellowship, to the breaking of bread and to prayer. Everyone was filled with awe at the many wonders and signs performed by the apostles. All the believers were together and had everything in common. They sold property and possessions to give to anyone who had need. Every day they continued to meet together in the temple courts. They broke bread in their homes and ate together with glad and sincere hearts, praising God and enjoying the favor of all the people. And the Lord added to their number daily those who were being saved (Acts 2:42-47).

Do you have friends from your church world? Do you have the singular focus we read about in today's verse that is on the Lord and His people? Do you have regular fellowship with committed believers? Are you hospitable and generous toward other followers of Jesus? What changes do you need to make in your life to make the same proclamation found in today's passage?

November 1

Bad Partnerships

Today's reading - Psalms 1-5

"Not a word from their mouth can be trusted; their heart is filled with malice. Their throat is an open grave; with their tongues they tell lies" - Psalm 5:9.

It has been a constant struggle for God's people to realize that they cannot expect Christian behavior from non-Christians. Yet, they continue to go into business, marry, and enter into agreements with those whose values are not biblical, and suffer the consequences. While this can happen even when agreements with believers are entered into, it is much more likely when the partner is an unbeliever. Paul was clear in his warning against such alliances:

> Do not be yoked together with unbelievers. For what do righteousness and wickedness have in common? Or what fellowship can light have with darkness? What harmony is there between Christ and Belial? Or what does a believer have in common with an unbeliever? What agreement is there between the temple of God and idols? For we are the temple of the living God (2 Corinthians 6:14-16).

Where have you expected good results from a bad partnership? What can you do to limit the damage or get out of the relationship altogether? Where do you need to repent that you relied on your own understanding, which was limited, instead of God's infinite and endless wisdom?

November 2

Where's God?

Today's reading: Psalms 6-10

"Why, Lord, do you stand far off? Why do you hide yourself

in times of trouble?" - Psalm 10:1.

We return to the common psalms theme: trouble and God's role in it. Obviously, the psalmist had expectations that were not being met, for he thought the Lord would intervene to either prevent or relieve his troubles. It seems the Lord did neither, leading to the psalmist's question and frustration. Yet God has His own plan and purpose for in your trouble, and He does not always respond to your cries for help as you wish. Jesus made a prediction in John 16:33 that speaks to the nature of the problem: "I have told you these things, so that in me you may have peace. In this world you will have trouble. But take heart! I have overcome the world." Jesus did not promise freedom from trouble, but His victory in the trouble – and that victory may not come the way you thought it would Are you wondering what exactly God is up to in your life? Is He not responding as you hoped, wished or asked for? Can you accept by faith that He is present and working, even though you cannot see, hear or touch Him?

November 3
Poor Causes

Today's reading: Psalms 11-15

"Lord, who may dwell in your sacred tent? Who may live on your holy mountain? . . . who lends money to the poor without interest; who does not accept a bribe against the innocent" - Psalm 15:1, 5.

Psalm 15 provides a list of those who meet the criteria of the questions posed in verse one. In today's verse, you see that those who use their money not for personal gain but to help others, especially the powerless, are counted among God's special people. Yet, it is not just money to help the poor that separates them in God's eyes. God also honors them when they do not side against the poor for some personal gain, advantage, or privilege. At this time of year, it is customary to reflect on what can be done for the poor, but this should be a year-round consideration, not just for what you can give but also for how you can take sides on an issue that will benefit the poor in education, government policy, or housing. Jesus is the ultimate role model when it comes to ministry to the poor, as Paul explained in 2 Corinthians 8:9: "For you know the grace of our Lord Jesus Christ, that though he was rich, yet for your sake he became poor, so that you through his poverty might become rich." Are you eager to help the poor, or is it just talk? Do you constantly spend on yourself with nothing left over for the poor? What more can you do not just to give money but also to support the cause of the poor?

November 4

Can

Today's reading: Psalms 16-20

"With your help I can advance against a troop; with my God I can scale a wall" - Psalm 18:29.

David didn't just talk about advancing or scaling a wall in battle. He did not just brag about his potential in the Lord, but rather He did what he talked about doing. When you say that you *can* do something, it doesn't mean you will do it. If you say, for example, "I *can* be a nice person," it doesn't necessarily translate into you being a nice person. *Can* is a word that states potential, but it remains potential until you act to fulfill and express that potential. Jesus said, "With man this is impossible, but not with God; all things are possible with God" (Mark 10:27). Where are you under-living your life, content to discuss all the possibilities in Christ, but also content to do nothing with them? Do you realize that for God to do the impossible, He must use you or someone who is willing to not only believe and talk about His power, but who also actually acts so that God's power can be deployed? Against what troop does God want you to advance, or which wall does He want you to scale? When you identify it, then start advancing and scaling today!

November 5
Loneliness

Today's reading: Psalms 21-25

"Turn to me and be gracious to me, for I am lonely and afflicted" - Psalm 25:16.

It is not a problem for many to be alone, but when they feel lonely, it can be a debilitating, depressing state of affairs. The interesting thing is that you can feel lonely even when you are in the midst of people, and this can stem from a variety of reasons. Friends and family are the antidote to loneliness, but you cannot have these relationships only for what you can get, but rather for what you can give, if you serious about overcoming loneliness. Proverbs 18:24 gives some advice for how to obtain friends: "A man who has friends must himself be friendly, but there is a friend *who* sticks closer than a brother" (NKJV). This indicates that you cannot sit back and demand that life give you friends; you must be friendly to attract those friends. Then you must be loyal to your friends in times of their trouble. Both scenarios require you to give, rather than moan or complain when others don't "give" whatever it is that you feel you need. Are you battling a sense of loneliness? What can you do to proactively break out of this predicament? Whose pain can you help carry while in the midst of your own pain? Whose friend can you be today?

November 6
Family Matters

Today's reading: Psalms 26-30

"When my father and my mother forsake me, then the Lord will take care of me" - Psalm 27:10.

When Jesus came, He often had a polarizing effect, for some in a family believed in Him while others did not. That often set the family members at odds with one another, and Jesus did not apologize for that ramification of putting faith in Him. In fact, Jesus had this to say about family and following Him:

> Do not think that I came to bring peace on earth. I did not come to bring peace but a sword. For I have come to "set a man against his father, a daughter against her mother, and a daughter-in-law against her mother-in-law"; and "a man's enemies *will be* those of his *own* household." He who loves father or mother more than Me is not worthy of Me. And he who loves son or daughter more than Me is not worthy of Me. And he who does not take his cross and follow after Me is not worthy of Me. He who finds his life will lose it, and he who loses his life for My sake will find it (Matthew 10:35-39).

Jesus was saying that a decision to follow Him was the highest priority in life, even more important than family. Is Jesus more important to you than family? Are you following Him regardless of how your family feels about it? Or have you altered your walk with the Lord in order to please your family? Can you see that you have your priorities out of line if you have done so?

November 7

Horses and Bigger Barns

Today's reading: Psalms 31-35

"No king is saved by the size of his army; no warrior escapes by his great strength. A horse is a vain hope for deliverance; despite all its great strength it cannot save" - Psalm 33:16-17.

It is not known who wrote Psalm 33, but let's assume it was David. David was a king and warrior who probably knew how to use a horse in battle, and had a large army at his command. Yet he came to this conclusion: none of that mattered in battle if the Lord wasn't on his side. There are some who put their trust in their bank account, marketable job skills, a lot of powerful connections, or life experience, but none of that will help them in the day of trouble if the Lord is not on their side. What's more, at some point, their life will end and none of that will help them make their transition to eternity. Jesus told a story about a man who put his trust in his business acumen:

> Then he said, "This is what I'll do. I will tear down my barns and build bigger ones, and there I will store my surplus grain." And I'll say to myself, "You have plenty of grain laid up for many years. Take life easy; eat, drink and be merry." But God said to him, "You fool! This very night your life will be demanded from you. Then who will get what you have prepared for yourself?" This is how it will be with whoever stores up things for themselves but is not rich toward God (Luke 12:18-21).

Are you rich toward God or rich in the things of the world? Where have you put your trust - in your retirement fund, as the man did in the parable, or in God's ability to provide and protect?

November 8

Mind Your Business

Today's reading: Psalms 36-40

"Cease from anger and forsake wrath;
***Do not fret; it leads only to evildoing"* - Psalm 37:8.**

The context of this verse is anger that comes from observing the wicked and seeing how they seemingly prosper and enjoy a carefree life. The psalmist advises the person who is fretting over someone else's good fortune, especially someone who seems to be unworthy, to let it go! If you spend your time fretting over the inequities of life, you will become more and more consumed with the issue, and your anger will spill over into other areas of your life – making you a not-so-nice-or-happy person to be around. What's more, it's really not much of your business how God chooses to deal with anyone else. The disciples were angry when the Samaritans showed disrespect to Jesus, and this is how Jesus responded to their anger:

> As the time approached for him to be taken up to heaven, Jesus resolutely set out for Jerusalem. And he sent messengers on ahead, who went into a Samaritan village to get things ready for him; but the people there did not welcome him, because he was heading for Jerusalem. When the disciples James and John saw this, they asked, "Lord, do you want us to call fire down from heaven to destroy them?' But Jesus turned and rebuked them" (Luke 9:51-55).

Are you angry at someone else or some other people group? What is that anger doing to you? Would Jesus approve of your attitude? If not, what are you going to do about it?

November 9

Wishful Thinking

Today's reading: Psalms 41-45

"I know that you are pleased with me, for my enemy does not triumph over me. Because of my integrity you uphold me and set me in your presence forever" - Psalm 41:11-12.

It is easy to read into a verse what you think, hope, or even want it to mean. In today's passage, the psalmist wrote that his enemy did not defeat him because God was with him. You can interpret that to mean that your enemies will not only never triumph over you, but also that they will never *try* to triumph over you. If that is how you read this, then you are mistaken and are opening yourself to great disappointment and perhaps even disillusionment as you serve the Lord. Your enemies will most certainly try to overwhelm you, and your greatest enemy is Satan himself, as represented through his evil forces, principalities, and powers. Jesus said something similar to what the psalmist said when He told Peter, "And I tell you that you are Peter, and on this rock I will build my church, and the gates of Hades will not overcome it" (Matthew 16:18). Jesus did not say that evil gates would not *try* to overcome the Church; He simply said they would not be successful when they do try. Are you struggling with the fact that you and God's people are under intense attack? Did you fall victim to wishful thinking that this would not happen to you? Can you stand in the truth of the promise that they will not be successful, while fully embracing the truth that they will try again and again?

November 10

God's Silence

Today's reading: Psalms 46-50

"When you did these things and I kept silent, you thought I was exactly like you. But I now arraign you and set my accusations before you" - Psalm 50:21.

It is common for people to consider their opinions and doctrines to be the exact replica of what God thinks and the Bible presents. The problem is that they have have reached a dangerous conclusion, for God's silence may be simply a hardened heart on the listener's part that causes deafness to the voice of God. You may be thinking, "How can anyone not hear God when He speaks?" but there are several examples when that exact thing occurred. One example is found in Acts 9:7: Why didn't the companions of Saul who heard what he heard ever testify on his behalf or come to faith in Christ with him? They could not hear or see what God was doing since they too were on their way to persecute believers. And then there this example: "Then a voice came from heaven, 'I have glorified it, and will glorify it again.' The crowd that was there and heard it said it had thundered; others said an angel had spoken to him" (John 12:28-29). Where have you assumed that God's silence indicated His approval of your behavior or position? Are you ready to ask God today to show you where your attitudes, beliefs, and behaviors are not in alignment with His will, and are you also ready to change what He shows you? Can you see when you have said, "God, speak to me," that He may be speaking but you may not be hearing?

November 11

Honest Prayers

Today's reading: Psalms 51-55

"Let death take my enemies by surprise;
let them go down alive to the realm of the dead,
for evil finds lodging among them" - Psalm 55:15.

Some are surprised at the tone of David's prayers in the psalms, for he did not mince words. He called on God to take out his enemies in the harshest of terms. David's enemies, however, were not just criticizing David; they were trying to kill him. Most of us have never faced that kind of enemy, so we should not judge David for his prayers. What's more, David was not seeking his own revenge, but rather was trusting in the Lord to fight his battles. Finally, David was not glossing over what was in his heart, but was putting it all before God, allowing God to sort through his emotions and motives to adjust them as He saw fit. In fact, David was simply praying to God using God's own words:

> It is mine to avenge; I will repay. In due time their foot will slip; their day of disaster is near and their doom rushes upon them. The Lord will vindicate his people and relent concerning his servants when he sees their strength is gone and no one is left, slave or free (Deuteronomy 32:35).

Are you putting your heart into your prayers, not holding back your emotions and feelings? Do you acknowledge when you have less than "Christian" thoughts, realizing that God already knows them? Are you pretending to be someone you are not when you pray?

November 12

Mercy Dispenser

Today's reading: Psalms 56-60

"Have mercy on me, my God, have mercy on me, for in you I take refuge. I will take refuge in the shadow of your wings until the disaster has passed" - Psalm 57:1.

You can never underestimate your need for mercy. You are not saved by mercy and then required to keep your salvation through meticulous Law-keeping. Your life requires mercy just like it does oxygen, water, and food, for without mercy, you lose the most important aspect of life – your relationship with the Lord. Mercy is what brings you to God, and mercy is what maintains that relationship. Therefore, you should live a life of mercy, both receiving and giving it freely. Jesus taught a parable about a servant who had been forgiven a huge debt but then refused to have mercy on his fellow servant:

> Then the master called the servant in. "You wicked servant," he said, "I canceled all that debt of yours because you begged me to. Shouldn't you have had mercy on your fellow servant just as I had on you?" In anger his master handed him over to the jailers to be tortured, until he should pay back all he owed (Matthew 18:32-34).

Are you a dispenser of mercy? Do you remember that God has had mercy on you yesterday and today, and will do so tomorrow? Upon whom can you have mercy today, not because they deserve it, but because you have been the recipient of it?

NOVEMBER 13

JOY REQUIRED

Today's reading: Psalms 61-65

"The whole earth is filled with awe at your wonders; where morning dawns, where evening fades, you call forth songs of joy" - Psalm 65:8.

God expects His people to be joyful. This verse tells you that at the start and the end of each day, God looks for songs of joy from you. Regardless of whether or not your work is going well or your relationships are painful, God is worthy of joyful praise for who He is and what He does. This was such a serious requirement in God's eyes that the Lord issued this warning to Israel:

> Because you did not serve the LORD your God joyfully and gladly in the time of prosperity, therefore in hunger and thirst, in nakedness and dire poverty, you will serve the enemies the LORD sends against you. He will put an iron yoke on your neck until he has destroyed you (Deuteronomy 28:47-48).

How do you start your day? How do you end it? Do you take time to acknowledge that God is the Lord? Are you careful to come before Him at least some of the time with joy instead of constant complaining, lamenting or petitioning?

NOVEMBER 14

OLD TESTAMENT FOCUS

Today's reading - Psalms 66 70

"For I endure scorn for your sake, and shame covers my face. I am a foreigner to my own family, a stranger to my own mother's children; for zeal for your house consumes me, and the insults of those who insult you fall on me" - Psalm 69:7-9.

David wrote this psalm about his own situation, but as you can see, the description also fits the Lord Jesus and His ministry on earth. In fact, much of the Old Testament is a prelude to the coming of the Messiah, describing His character, nature, mission, and persecution. Once the Messiah came, we are able to look back into the Old Testament and see Jesus everywhere. For example, when Jesus cleansed the Temple, John told us that Jesus' disciples thought of today's passage: "To those who sold doves he said, 'Get these out of here! Stop turning my Father's house into a market!' His disciples remembered that it is written: 'Zeal for your house will consume me'" (John 2:17-18). The point is that Jesus is the focal point of all Scripture, and He is to be the focus for your life and worship as well. Anything that takes away from Jesus is to be avoided, and that includes the fear-mongering, misguided end-time prophets who seem to focus more on the Antichrist than the Christ. Is Jesus the centerpiece of your biblical studies? When you read the Old Testament, do you see and think of Jesus as His disciples did as described in John 2? Have you gone off on a tangent to study about trivial things other than what God the Father did in and through His Son and those implications for your life?

November 15

Your Testimony

Today's reading: Psalms 71-75

"My mouth will tell of your righteous deeds, of your saving acts all day long—though I know not how to relate them all. Even when I am old and gray, . . . do not forsake me, my God, till I declare your power to the next generation, your mighty acts to all who are to come. . . . My tongue will tell of your righteous acts all day long, for those who wanted to harm me have been put to shame and confusion" - Psalm 71:15, 18, 24.

In today's three verses, the psalmist made a strong commitment to produce a constant stream of testimonies to draw attention to what the Lord had done in his life. This required that he was aware of all that God was doing in his life and not take it for granted. He wanted to tell the next generation what God had done for him so that they would be encouraged and equipped for their own walk with the Lord. And finally, the psalmist recognized that God had thwarted his enemies who had evil intent toward him, and wanted to recognize God's role in his deliverance and protection. Jesus alluded to this need to proclaim God's goodness when He said, "What I tell you in the dark, speak in the daylight; what is whispered in your ear, proclaim from the roofs" (Matthew 10:27). What are you doing to give your own testimonies to God's faithful love in your life? Are you writing them down for others to read? Are you putting them into words when you talk to your family and friends? Do you stand up in church to testify when given the opportunity? What more can you do to formulate and broadcast your testimonies, even on a daily basis?

November 16

How Long?

Today's reading: Psalms 76-80

"How long, Lord? Will you be angry forever? How long will your jealousy burn like fire? Pour out your wrath on the nations that do not acknowledge you, on the kingdoms that do not call on your name; for they have devoured Jacob and devastated his homeland" - Psalm 79:5-7.

The psalmist was asking how long God would take sides against His people and not judge those who did not know or serve the Lord. God, however, is more interested in shaping His own into the people they need to be than in judging the nations, which will happen in due time. Peter referred to this same pattern when he wrote about God's attention being focused on God's people first and foremost:

> However, if you suffer as a Christian, do not be ashamed, but praise God that you bear that name. For it is time for judgment to begin with God's household; and if it begins with us, what will the outcome be for those who do not obey the gospel of God? And, "If it is hard for the righteous to be saved, what will become of the ungodly and the sinner?" (1 Peter 4:16-18).

Have you had those same thoughts expressed by the psalmist that are the equivalent of, "God, why don't you go and deal with someone else for a while?" If so, can you see that it is much better that God be involved in your life, even if it's to correct you, than it is for God to ignore you? What's more, God won't allow your discipline or hard times to last one day longer than they need to last, so thank Him for the discipline and rejoice, even though times may be tough.

November 17

It's Not About You

Today's reading: Psalms 81-85

"With cunning they conspire against your people; they plot against those you cherish. 'Come,' they say, 'let us destroy them as a nation, so that Israel's name is remembered no more.' With one mind they plot together; they form an alliance against you" - Psalm 83:3-5.

The Lord takes it personally when anyone persecutes His church and His people. When Saul was on the Damascus Road on his way to arrest and harass believers, the Lord Jesus appeared to Him and said, "I am Jesus, whom you are persecuting" (Acts 9:5). Therefore, when you are persecuted – and you will eventually suffer for His name sake – it's not about you, so don't take it personally. If you are suffering for your relationship with the Lord, the persecutors hate the Jesus in you, and not only you. That is why you should be able to witness to them and pray for them, because you realize their eternal destiny is at stake. The good news is that, along with persecution, there will be tremendous blessings as well:

> "Truly I tell you," Jesus replied, "no one who has left home or brothers or sisters or mother or father or children or fields for me and the gospel will fail to receive a hundred times as much in this present age: homes, brothers, sisters, mothers, children and fields—along with persecutions—and in the age to come eternal life" (Mark 10:29-30).

Are you praying for your persecutors? Are you thanking God for your blessings, or allowing your suffering to mar your perspective of the blessings you have in Christ?

November 18

Your Legacy

Today's reading: Psalm 86-90

"May the favor of the Lord our God rest on us; establish the work of our hands for us—yes, establish the work of our hands" - Psalm 90:17.

You don't only want God to bless your work, you also want Him to establish it – to give it a foundation and lasting power that it may maximize its impact on others for the Lord. This is commonly referred to as a legacy, some ongoing effect that your presence on earth has made. In the New Living Translation, the latter half of this verse is worded, "And make the work of our hands stand strong. Yes, make the work of our hands stand strong." Most people will not have a building or sports arena named after them, so it will be their memory that will last in the minds of those closest to them, especially their family – and that will be their lasting work. The writer of Proverbs put it in vivid terms: "The name of the righteous is used in blessings, but the name of the wicked will rot" (Proverbs 10:7). What is your lasting legacy? What work do you pray that God will establish and make strong? What memories are you creating in the minds of those who know you? What remarks will people make in your eulogy at your funeral? Whatever you want them to remember about you in the future is what you need be doing now.

November 19

Profound Thoughts

Today's reading: Psalms 91-95

"For you make me glad by your deeds, Lord; I sing for joy at what your hands have done. How great are your works, Lord, how profound your thoughts!" - Psalm 92:4-5.

The psalmist was obviously enamored with God and all that He did. The writer also stated that God's thoughts are profound. Have you ever considered that God's thoughts are profound? That means they are full of meaning, insight, and knowledge. Where are God's thoughts accessible? Of course, they are present in God's word, which is why you must not only read the Word, but also study it, as well as listen to it preached and taught by one of God's anointed servants. When Nehemiah rebuilt the city walls, he invited Ezra to come preach and teach about God's word, and the people spent six hours listening to Ezra read and comment:

> So on the first day of the seventh month Ezra the priest brought the Law before the assembly, which was made up of men and women and all who were able to understand. He read it aloud from daybreak till noon as he faced the square before the Water Gate in the presence of the men, women and others who could understand. And all the people listened attentively to the Book of the Law (Nehemiah 8:2-3).

How much time are you spending in God's Word, interacting with God's profound thoughts? Who is teaching you God's word? Who are you teaching?

November 20
Empty–Handed

Today's reading: Psalms 96-100

"Ascribe to the Lord the glory due his name; bring an offering and come into his courts" - Psalm 96:8.

When the Lord instituted the concept of an offering, it was not because He needed anything from mankind. It was simply to make mankind mindful that all he had came from the Lord. At the same time, the offerings were used to support and feed the priests who carried out their priestly duties according to the ordinances of the Lord. Nothing has changed today, for God still requires that you come to Him with offerings, which keep you grounded in the knowledge that it is not your efforts that feed you – it is the Lord who provides. Such was the importance of the offering to the Lord that these were His instructions for the Jewish festivals when men came to Jerusalem:

> "Three times a year all your men must appear before the Lord your God at the place he will choose: at the Festival of Unleavened Bread, the Festival of Weeks and the Festival of Tabernacles. No one should appear before the Lord empty-handed. Each of you must bring a gift in proportion to the way the Lord your God has blessed you" (Deuteronomy 16:16-17).

Do you appear before the Lord empty-handed? Do you give the Lord something of substance, or just a few pennies according to what you have left over? Do you see that your giving is an act of worship, and not an economic transaction?

November 21
Rhythm of Life

Today's reading: Psalms 101-105

"He made the moon to mark the seasons, and the sun

knows when to go down. You bring darkness, it becomes night, and all the beasts of the forest prowl. The lions roar for their prey and seek their food from God. The sun rises, and they steal away; they return and lie down in their dens. Then people go out to their work, to their labor until evening" - Psalm 104:19-23.

There is a rhythm of life, established by God through His wisdom and creativity. Psalm 104 focuses on God's creation, which includes not only the objects you see, but the patterns that men, animals, and planets follow. The psalmist is reminding the reader that if God is in control of all that, then He has no problem being in control of your life as well. Jesus repeated this lesson when He taught, "Are not five sparrows sold for two pennies? Yet not one of them is forgotten by God. Indeed, the very hairs of your head are all numbered. Don't be afraid; you are worth more than many sparrows" (Luke 12:5-6). Are you fretting over your financial or professional situation? Do you see the lesson in today's verses, and are you ready to apply them to your life where you are right now? Can you also see how silly it is to worry about whether or not God will provide for you?

November 22

The Unexpected

Today's reading: Psalms 106-110

"He turned the desert into pools of water and the parched ground into flowing springs; there he brought the hungry to live, and they founded a city where they could settle" - Psalm 107:35-36.

If you visit Israel today, you will visit the Jordan Valley, where the desert has been transformed into a lush agricultural area, the fruit of which is exported to cities all over Europe! That is exactly what the psalmist said God is able to do – take that which others say is useless and make it useful and productive. He can do the same in your life, business, or ministry so that your focus will not be on your own talent, intelligence or resources, but on Him and His goodness. This theme is found throughout the Bible and is summarized in Ezekiel 21:26: "This is what the Sovereign Lord says: 'Take off the turban, remove the crown. It will not be as it was: The lowly will be exalted and the exalted will be brought low.'" What opportunity have you passed up because it did not "look" good? What vision did God give you of prosperity, but you are ignoring it because right now it looks like poverty? Where is there a desert where God wants to do the unexpected and convert it to a garden and make you the beneficiary?

November 23

Trust Reminder

Today's reading: Psalms 111-115

"All you Israelites, trust in the Lord—he is their help and shield. House of Aaron, trust in the Lord—he is their help and shield. You who fear him, trust in the Lord—he is their help and shield" - Psalm 115:9-11.

These verses are in the midst of a series of psalms that encourage the reader to trust in the Lord, no matter what people say to discourage such thinking or what the circumstances look like. It is interesting that the theme of trusting the Lord comes up over and over again in the psalms. Of course, that means we need to be reminded over and over again of our need to trust in the Lord and not ourselves or others. In fact, even when God has proved Himself to us, we tend to stray and put our faith in other things, as did Israel:

> . . . in the wilderness. There you saw how the Lord your God carried you, as a father carries his son, all the way you went until you reached this place." In spite of this, you did not trust in the Lord your God, who went ahead of you on your journey, in fire by night and in a

> cloud by day, to search out places for you to camp and to show you the way you should go (Deuteronomy 1:31-33).

Are you in a panic right now, even though God has shown Himself strong on your behalf over and over again? Are you living in the worries of tomorrow, instead of the joy of today? Are you fretting over what might not happen next year, instead of thanking God for what you have today?

November 24
Goals

Today's reading: Psalms 116-120

"I was pushed back and about to fall, but the Lord helped me. The Lord is my strength and my defense; he has become my salvation" - Psalm 118:13-14.

David was not simply a defensive warrior, but he often went on the offensive and met with stiff resistance. Then there were times when his enemies tried to push him back, but he refused to yield any ground, and called on the Lord for help. The Apostle Paul was also a warrior, and he encountered the same opposition from external forces as well as internal forces like fear. How did Paul keep from retreating or falling back? He set goals and those kept him on the advance as he reported in one of his letters:

> Not that I have already obtained all this, or have already arrived at my goal, but I press on to take hold of that for which Christ Jesus took hold of me. Brothers and sisters, I do not consider myself yet to have taken hold of it. But one thing I do: Forgetting what is behind and straining toward what is ahead, I press on toward the goal to win the prize for which God has called me heavenward in Christ Jesus (Philippians 3:12-14).

Are you advancing and progressing in life, or are you stagnant or even losing ground? Do you have goals? Are they enough to press against what's resisting your progress so that you can move forward and grow? Write out two or three goals that will help you regain the momentum that the Lord would want you to experience.

NOVEMBER 25

JESUS' PRIORITY

Today's reading: Psalms 121-125

"For the sake of the house of the Lord our God, *I will seek your prosperity*" - Psalm 122:9.

Jesus gave His life not only to save souls, but also to place those souls in a Church that He was building. The Apostle Paul realized this truth, and gave his adult life to found, structure, and nurture churches all throughout the Roman Empire, not considering his work a success until he saw a church with elders founded where he had preached. A few of Paul's letters were to individuals like Timothy and Titus, but the majority of his letters were filled with instructions for the church that were to be read in the church assemblies. If Jesus and Paul gave His life to establish the Church, it was obviously His top priority, and you would do well to make it your top priority as well. Jesus told Peter,

> And I tell you that you are Peter, and on this rock I will build my church, and the gates of Hades will not overcome it. I will give you the keys of the kingdom of heaven; whatever you bind on earth will be bound in heaven, and whatever you loose on earth will be loosed in heaven (Matthew 16:18-19).

Are you doing what you can to assist Christ to build His church? Do you give to your church? Do you contribute your spiritual gifts to help edify and build up your church? What more can you do?

November 26

Faith to Replace

Today's reading: Psalms 126-130

"Restore our fortunes, Lord, like streams in the Negev" - Psalm 126:4.

It is common to experience loss in life due to its fragile nature. The good news is that God is with you in those times of loss, and He is able to restore what was lost in His own way that is also meaningful to you. For example, you can lose a business but start another one consulting with people about how not to lose a business! You can lose a relationship only to have the Lord replace that loss by giving you other relationships to take its place. God is a God of restoration, replacing what was lost as He promised His people:

> I will repay you for the years the locusts have eaten—the great locust and the young locust, the other locusts and the locust swarm—my great army that I sent among you. You will have plenty to eat, until you are full, and you will praise the name of the Lord your God, who has worked wonders for you; never again will my people be shamed (Joel 2:25-26).

Have you experienced some loss recently or in the past? Have you allowed yourself to mourn that loss? Is it time to stop mourning, and begin praying that God will "restore your fortunes"? Can you have faith and hope that God will replace what was lost, and perhaps even increase today what was lost yesterday?

November 27

Weaned or Unweaned?

Today's reading: Psalms 131-135

"But I have calmed and quieted myself,

**I am like a weaned child with its mother;
like a weaned child I am content" - Psalm 131:2.**

If you have ever been around older children who are still feeding on breast milk, you know it can be an awkward scenario when those children are hungry. When they are hungry, the child doesn't care where he or she is or who their mother is with, they will find their mother and look for lunch. David wrote that he was like a weaned child in God's presence, not straining or grasping to get something, but simply there to enjoy God's presence and His person. In other words, David did not pursue God for what God could give or what David needed. Jesus warned against seeking God only out of your need when after He had fed the 5,000, the people eagerly sought Him out:

> Very truly I tell you, you are looking for me, not because you saw the signs I performed but because you ate the loaves and had your fill. Do not work for food that spoils, but for food that endures to eternal life, which the Son of Man will give you. For on him God the Father has placed his seal of approval (John 6:26-27).

Are you like a weaned or un-weaned child with the Lord? Do you spend time with Him to enjoy His presence, or to make your list of demands and requests, only to move on after that when you get what you want? Why not take a few minutes today and simply read His word, talk to God, or listen for His voice not because you need anything, except to be close to your Lord, Friend, and Master?

NOVEMBER 28

THE GOD OF CREATION

Today's reading: Psalms 136-140

"Who by his understanding made the heavens, His love endures forever. who spread out the earth upon the waters, His love endures forever. who made the great lights—His

love endures forever" - Psalm 136:5-7.

A recurring reference in the entire Book of Psalms is the creation story from Genesis 1 and 2. Why is that? Keep in mind that many of the psalms were written when the author was in some kind of trouble. Then the psalms were edited and given their final order and format during the Babylonian Exile, when Israel was far from home, wondering when God was going to restore their Land and national identity. In the midst of personal and national trouble, the community of faith encouraged itself with the reminder of God's great power as evidenced in His creative acts to establish the universe. They correctly concluded that if God could make all they could see around them, then He was capable of acting on their behalf to change things for the better. Perhaps you need a similar dose of their thinking. Look around you today, and consider all the works of nature and creation. They were all made by the God you serve, the same God who loves you and has made wonderful promises to you, some of which may seem light years away at this point in your life. Can you encourage yourself today like the psalmist did? Can you make the transition from knowing that God *can* do anything to the confidence that God can do - and *will* do - anything for you?

November 29
Mind Battle

Today's reading: Psalms 141-145

"The enemy pursues me, he crushes me to the ground; he makes me dwell in the darkness like those long dead. So my spirit grows faint within me; my heart within me is dismayed. I remember the days of long ago; I meditate on all your works and consider what your hands have done. I spread out my hands to you; I thirst for you like a parched land" **- Psalm 143:3-6.**

You are probably surprised (not) that David was in trouble again, so he penned this psalm telling God of his troubles, and his desperate need for the Lord's presence and help. David was fighting battles against his enemies, but notice that that he was also battling an internal one, and that was his thoughts. He forced himself to focus his thoughts on God's works of old, including what God had done for David in the past. David also confessed that his greatest need was not for deliverance, but for God Himself! Your mind can be your greatest ally in times of trouble or your greatest enemy, for that is where you assess the threat and risk of your current situation. You can either give in to your fears, or combat them with massive doses of God's word, along with flashbacks and reruns of your past testimonies and victories. Don't be surprised at how long and difficult the process is to keep your mind at peace. Just fight the fight, and don't give in to despair, terror or worry.

November 30

Language of Praise

Today's reading: Psalms 146-150

"Praise God in his sanctuary; praise him in his mighty heavens. Praise him for his acts of power; praise him for his surpassing greatness" - Psalm 150:1-2.

The Book of Psalms ends with the simple admonition to praise the Lord, not just for what He does, His "acts of power," but for who He is, His "surpassing greatness." Where is the appropriate place to praise? It is not only in church or "his sanctuary," but also anyplace in His creation, His "mighty heavens." If you are going to praise the Lord in and out of church, you are going to need a language of praise, which can only be developed as you practice. What do you say to the Lord when you praise Him? Are you specific? Do you have your own language of praise that you use regularly? Do you praise the Lord and tell Him why you are praising Him? This is not for God's benefit, for He knows who

He is. It is for your benefit, so that you can be clear in your own mind and heart as to who God is compared to the other relationships and priorities in your life. The end of Jude's epistle is a good example of a language of praise, which you would do well to imitate:

> To him who is able to keep you from stumbling and to present you before his glorious presence without fault and with great joy—to the only God our Savior be glory, majesty, power and authority, through Jesus Christ our Lord, before all ages, now and forevermore! Amen (Jude 24-25).

December 1

Go to Bed

Today's reading: Psalms 1-5

"In peace I will lie down and sleep, for you alone, Lord, make me dwell in safety" - Psalm 4:8.

There is one sure sign that you trust the Lord and have put all of life's circumstances in His hands, and that is you are able to sleep. When you have, you do not lie in bed and reflect on all your problems, frantically trying to figure out what you are going to do. When you realize that everything is up to God, you go to bed for one reason, and that is to get some rest. It can be a difficult thing to achieve this kind of freedom, for no one enjoys not being in control of their lives at first. Once you have reached that point, however, it brings great peace, just like it did for Jesus:

> One day Jesus said to his disciples, "Let us go over to the other side of the lake." So they got into a boat and set out. As they sailed, he fell asleep. A squall came down on the lake, so that the boat was being swamped, and they were in great danger. The disciples went and woke him, saying, "Master, Master, we're going to drown!" He got up and rebuked the wind and the raging waters;

> the storm subsided, and all was calm (Luke 8:22-24).

Notice that Jesus was the One who initiated their trip, so He undoubtedly knew the storm was coming. He knows your imminent storms, too, but He has everything under control. He wants you to learn to put your trust in Him and not your own strength. Can you go to bed and sleep when your storms are raging? If not, then you have some work to do to shore up your trust in the Lord.

December 2

Enemies of the Cross

Today's reading - Psalms 6-10

"In his arrogance the wicked man hunts down the weak, who are caught in the schemes he devises. He boasts about the cravings of his heart; he blesses the greedy and reviles the Lord" - Psalm 10:2-3.

David wrote with elegance and flair, and his description of the wicked in Psalm 10 is no exception. He described their activities, and showed that arrogance and pride were their motivators as they persecuted and tormented the righteous. David pointed out that pride distorted their priorities, for they blessed the greedy and reviled the Lord! Unfortunately, it is possible for a believer to also have his or her values out of kilter, as Paul warned in Philippians 3:17-19:

> Join together in following my example, brothers and sisters, and just as you have us as a model, keep your eyes on those who live as we do. For, as I have often told you before and now tell you again even with tears, many live as enemies of the cross of Christ. Their destiny is destruction, their god is their stomach, and their glory is in their shame. Their mind is set on earthly things.

Paul was not describing unbelievers in those verses, but indicating that there are some believers who actually walk as enemies of the cross because their priorities are misaligned. Are your priorities those of the world or of Christ? Don't answer too quickly, but spend some time praying, asking God to show you if any of your priorities are indeed flawed, and listening for His response.

December 3

Poor Benefits

Today's reading - Psalms 11-15

"'Because the poor are plundered and the needy groan, I will now arise,' says the Lord. 'I will protect them from those who malign them'" - Psalm 12:5.

The poor are mentioned 21 times in the psalms, so it is safe to say they are a priority to the Lord. Therefore, they should be your priority as well. At this time of year, it is common to pay attention to the poor, for the holidays remind those who have to share with those who have not. Yet the poor should not only be a priority during the holidays, but a focal point for your giving all year round. There is tremendous spiritual benefit to helping the poor, as Jesus described when He rebuked the Pharisees for being outwardly righteous but inwardly full of darkness:

> You foolish people! Did not the one who made the outside make the inside also? But now as for what is inside you—*be generous to the poor, and everything will be clean for you.* Woe to you Pharisees, because you give God a tenth of your mint, rue and all other kinds of garden herbs, but you neglect justice and the love of God. You should have practiced the latter without leaving the former undone (Luke 11:40-42 emphasis added).

Jesus insinuated that when you are generous to the poor, it creates a clean heart in the giver, for it is an act the benefits of which can only come from God and not from the poor themselves. Are you generous to the poor? What can you do now and in the coming year to remember the poor on a regular basis?

December 4
You Done Good

Today's reading: Psalm 16-20

"The Lord has dealt with me according to my righteousness; according to the cleanness of my hands he has rewarded me. For I have kept the ways of the Lord; I am not guilty of turning from my God. All his laws are before me; I have not turned away from his decrees" - Psalm 18:20-22.

At first, David's claim in these verses seems a bit boastful, for David declared his own righteousness to be sound and without flaw. Yet, it was a true assessment when you consider the early days of his career, when he was obedient and humble. In fact, the title of this psalm says this: "He sang to the Lord the words of this song when the Lord delivered him from the hand of all his enemies and from the hand of Saul." Paul gave an interesting admonition in his letter to the Romans when he wrote, "For by the grace given me I say to every one of you: Do not think of yourself more highly than you ought, but rather think of yourself with sober judgment, in accordance with the faith God has distributed to each of you" (Romans 12:3). Paul's warning was not to think of yourself at all, but to think with appropriate, non-exaggerated judgment. Then Paul went on to speak of the fact that each member of the body has spiritual gifts, including you. You have probably chronicled your faults, but what are your strengths? What are your spiritual gifts that, when you employ them, there are good results with God's help? Where have your spiritual disciplines been what they should be? Where has God rewarded you for your faithfulness? Where have "you done good" in the Lord?

December 5

The New Covenant

Today's reading: Psalms 26-30

"The Lord confides in those who fear him; he makes his covenant known to them" - Psalm 25:14.

The Lord is a covenant-making and covenant-keeping God. He is the One who initiated the covenants, which have been defined as "a mutual agreement between two parties usually ratified in blood." The blood indicated the seriousness of the pact, which was a life and death bond between those who entered into it. When you are in covenant with God, He is obligated to fulfill the terms of the covenant, as are you. What are God's terms of the new covenant made in Christ? Jesus told us at the Last Supper when He said, "Then he took a cup, and when he had given thanks, he gave it to them, saying, 'Drink from it, all of you. This is my blood of the covenant, which is poured out for many for the forgiveness of sins'" (Matthew 26:27-28). God's role in the new covenant is to forgive sins. Your role is to acknowledge your sins, ask forgiveness through Christ, and accept God's forgiveness. Then you are to forgive others as God has forgiven you. Are you walking in the terms of the new covenant on a daily basis? Do you ask for forgiveness of your sins? Do you accept that forgiveness, forgiving yourself as the Father forgives you? Do you see that you cannot earn forgiveness, but God grants it freely as one of the stipulations of the new covenant made through Jesus' death on the cross?

December 6

KISS

Today's reading: Psalms 26-30

"One thing I ask from the Lord, this only do I seek: that I may dwell in the house of the Lord all the days of my life,

to gaze on the beauty of the LORD and to seek him in his temple" - Psalm 27:4.

David asked for one thing: to dwell close to God all the days of his life, never to feel or be separated. David's requests were streamlined and simple. He did not ask for many things that would gratify his desires and wants. He did not have a laundry list of wishes that He made known to God. David simplified his life by focusing on the most important thing, which was his relationship with the Lord. How about you? Are your desires that simple, or is your life complicated and full of drama because you want so many things, like career, relationships, possessions, success or fame? John's first epistle warned us to keep things simple, like David did:

> Do not love the world or anything in the world. If anyone loves the world, love for the Father is not in them. For everything in the world—the lust of the flesh, the lust of the eyes, and the pride of life—comes not from the Father but from the world. The world and its desires pass away, but whoever does the will of God lives forever (1 John 2:15-17).

Perhaps it's time to apply the words behind the acronym KISS, which stands for "Keep It Simple, Silly!" Where has the love of the things in this world made your life complex? Are you sharing your heart that belongs to the Lord with too many other things? What can you do to simplify?

DECEMBER 7

DO YOUR PART

Today's reading: Psalms 31-35

"I sought the LORD, and he answered me; he delivered me from all my fears. Those who look to him are radiant; their faces are never covered with shame. This poor man called, and the LORD heard him; he saved him out of all his

troubles. The angel of the Lord encamps around those who fear him and he delivers them" - Psalm 34:4-7.

When Adam and Eve hid from God after they sinned, it was because they were afraid. They also covered themselves with fig leaves because they were ashamed of their nakedness. Thus, fear and shame were the first consequences of the Fall, and Adam and Eve's children are still encumbered with those two problems. David's report in today's passage tells us that his relationship with the Lord relieved him of those two human experiences. In order for that to happen like it did for David, however, we see some key action verbs in these verses: *sought, looked to,* and *called.* Are you seeking the Lord until you get answers from Him? Are you looking to Him as your source of wisdom and strength? Do you call on the Lord not just when you are in trouble, but for all your life needs? And finally, do you fear the Lord, which is a healthy fear that keeps you from sin? The point of all this is that if you want to be free from the negative fear and shame that all Eve's children have, then you must engage concrete actions to make that happen. In other words, you do your part and God will do His.

December 8

No Shortcuts

Today's reading: Psalms 36-40

"I waited patiently for the Lord; he turned to me and heard my cry. Blessed is the one who trusts in the Lord, who does not look to the proud, to those who turn aside to false gods" - Psalm 40:1, 4.

The first thing to notice in these verses is that David had to wait patiently for the Lord. God does not operate according to your timetable. There is a song that says, "He may not come when you want Him, but He always comes on time." Even while he was waiting, however, David kept on crying out to the Lord for help.

The second thing to see is that while you are waiting, there can be a temptation to take a shortcut to look to the proud or for help from those who trust in false gods. Those who do not give in to that temptation are blessed because they maintain their trust in the Lord, even when the Lord doesn't seem to be moving in their direction. Moses was a good example of this kind of trust, as described by the writer of Hebrews:

> By faith Moses, when he had grown up, refused to be known as the son of Pharaoh's daughter. He chose to be mistreated along with the people of God rather than to enjoy the fleeting pleasures of sin. He regarded disgrace for the sake of Christ as of greater value than the treasures of Egypt, because he was looking ahead to his reward. By faith he left Egypt, not fearing the king's anger; he persevered because he saw him who is invisible (Hebrews 11:24-27).

Are you trusting in the Lord, all the while praying to Him for deliverance or direction? Are you resorting to shortcuts, as Moses could have done, or are you doing what he did, and that is trusting in the Lord with your whole heart? Do you see the One who is invisible and thus persevering in your faith?

December 9

Is God at Fault?

Today's reading - Psalms 41-45

"If we had forgotten the name of our God or spread out our hands to a foreign god, would not God have discovered it, since he knows the secrets of the heart? Yet for your sake we face death all day long; we are considered as sheep to be slaughtered. Awake, Lord! Why do you sleep? Rouse yourself! Do not reject us forever" - Psalm 44:20-23.

In today's passage, the psalmist was bemoaning the state of Israel, which had obviously fallen on hard times. The writer was stating his case that the nation had done nothing wrong, yet the Lord had given them over to their enemies. Does this happen in life? Do bad things seemingly happen to good people? Does God at times appear to be asleep, as the psalmist asked in verse 23? The answer to all those questions is "yes," and God seldom explains or justifies Himself when those things do happen. Yet those events are occasions when believers need to humble themselves and search their own heart according to the truth that Paul wrote: "This righteousness is given through faith in Jesus Christ to all who believe. There is no difference between Jew and Gentile, or all have sinned and fall short of the glory of God, and all are justified freely by his grace through the redemption that came by Christ Jesus" (Romans 3:22-24). Are you willing to examine your heart and be open to your own wrong when considering circumstances beyond any explanation? Are you also willing to put your trust in God's faithfulness when your situation would seem to call that faithfulness into question? Do you need to release any judgment you have made against the Lord?

December 10

Leaving an Inheritance

Today's reading: Psalms 46-50

"Why should I fear when evil days come, when wicked deceivers surround me—those who trust in their wealth and boast of their great riches? For all can see that the wise die, that the foolish and the senseless also perish, leaving their wealth to others. Their tombs will remain their houses forever, their dwellings for endless generations, though they had named lands after themselves" - Psalm 49:5-6, 10-11.

The psalmists were all excellent writers, inspired by the Spirit of God to pen words that were poignant, picturesque, and profound. Today's verses paint a picture of the wealthy who put their trust in their riches, only to see death like everyone else, consequently their money, property and possessions serving no purpose as their empty, worthless legacy is buried with them in their graves. The righteous has nothing to fear, even though those with money throw their weight around and intimidate others. Proverbs 13:22 states, "A good person leaves an inheritance for their children's children, but a sinner's wealth is stored up for the righteous." How do you define a successful life? What inheritance and legacy are you leaving for your children and grandchildren? Is it only land, stocks and money, or is it also a righteous life well-lived, a life that cared for the poor and downtrodden, that invested money and time in God's kingdom work? What do you need to do that you will receive the endorsement from God that everyone should want to hear, "Well done, good and faithful servant!"?

December 11

Confidence or Dread?

Today's reading: Psalms 51-55

"Do all these evildoers know nothing? They devour my people as though eating bread; they never call on God. But there they are, overwhelmed with dread, where there was nothing to dread. God scattered the bones of those who attacked you; you put them to shame, for God despised them" - Psalm 53:4-5.

David was once again calling out to the Lord because he was in trouble and the evildoers seemed to have the upper hand. Then he looked again and those same evildoers were overcome by God's superior power that He deployed on behalf of His people. One of the characteristics David noticed that his enemies were afraid, when there was nothing to be afraid of. This is reminiscent of what the wisdom writer wrote in Proverbs 28:1: "The wicked flee though no one pursues, but the righteous are as bold as a lion." Are you overwhelmed with dread when there is nothing to dread? Do you live in fear of a particular sickness or disease? Are you afraid of losing your job, or of being humiliated? Do you fear poverty? What is it that causes you to cower in fear instead of boldly proceeding with full confidence in God's ability to protect and preserve you? Have a talk with yourself today and then keep the conversation going, using Bible verses, past testimonies, and future goals that will enable you to move beyond dread to confidence as stated in Psalm 71:5: "For you have been my hope, Sovereign Lord, my confidence since my youth."

December 12

Missions Mind

Today's reading: Psalms 56-60

"I will praise you, Lord, among the nations; I will sing of you among the peoples. For great is your love, reaching to the heavens; your faithfulness reaches to the skies" - Psalm 57:9-10.

David's desire was to worship not only in Israel, but also among all the nations. This came from David's awareness that God was not just the God of his people, but God of all the people on earth, whether those people realized it or not. David saw it as his duty to make them aware of his and their God, thus making him a missionary of sorts. Jesus picked up on this theme when He came, trying to instill a missions' values into His disciples, who were slow to embrace that perspective, preferring instead to stay among the people with which they were familiar. It was the Apostle Paul who championed the cause of missions in the early church, and his zeal took him all over the Roman Empire to preach the gospel and plant churches. The Apostle Peter also understood God's desire for the nations when he said, "I now realize how true it is that God does not show favoritism but accepts from every nation the one who fears him and does what is right" (Acts 10:34-35). Do you have a missions' mind for the nations, or is it just for your own people and culture? Are you supporting others who have a missions' burden through prayer and giving? Are you open to some kind of foreign missions involvement for yourself, whatever that may look like?

December 13

Bread and Water

Today's reading: Psalms 61-65

"You, God, are my God, earnestly I seek you; I thirst for you, my whole being longs for you, in a dry and parched land where there is no water" - Psalm 63:1-3.

David was a poet who had a way with words. While God inspired the words, David used his gift, perfected his skill, and gave God something to use as David wrote the psalms. God does not use people with potential; He uses people who have taken the time and made the effort to develop their potential. In today's verses, David expressed his desperate need for God, likening his need to the quest of a thirsty person in a desert. Jesus likened Himself to bread from heaven and water for life, indicating that He was and is the answer for anyone's most basic need for life: "Everyone who drinks this water will be thirsty again, but whoever drinks the water I give them will never thirst. Indeed, the water I give them will become in them a spring of water welling up to eternal life" (John 4:13-14) and "Very truly I tell you, the one who believes has eternal life. I am the bread of life. Your ancestors ate the manna in the wilderness, yet they died. But here is the bread that comes down from heaven, which anyone may eat and not die" (John 6:47-49). Is that how you feel about your need for God? Is that a sometimes-thing, or an always-felt need? Is Jesus your daily bread and water? How do you express and meet your need for Him?

December 14
Blessed in Need

Today's reading: Psalms 66-70

"But as for me, I am poor and needy; come quickly to me, O God. You are my help and my deliverer; Lord, do not delay" - Psalm 70:5.

David acknowledged his poverty before God, and that meant he was in constant need of God's help, as we have seen throughout this study. There are many who reject the Lord and church attendance because they claim it is merely a crutch for the weak, and they are exactly right! This neediness is a good thing, for then it frees the needy person to cry out to God for help. Jesus Himself told you how good it is to be needy and to recognize it:

> Blessed are you who are poor, for yours is the kingdom of God. Blessed are you who hunger now, for you will be satisfied. Blessed are you who weep now, for you will laugh. Blessed are you when people hate you, when they exclude you and insult you and reject your name as evil, because of the Son of Man (Luke 6:20-22).

Are you needy and encountering opposition in your life? Then according to Jesus, you are blessed! Do you see yourself as blessed, or do you wallow in your neediness, desperately trying to find some way to become self-sufficient? Do you see that when you try to make your own way, you are resisting the situation that God has established so He can be your Helper and Deliverer? *I do see how I have tried to make my own way, Lord, and I am missing a wonderful opportunity to trust You. I am scared, however, that You won't come through or won't act in a timely manner, which is silly. I promise to let go and let You work on my behalf.*

December 15
Proof

Today's reading: Psalms 71-75

"Whom have I in heaven but you? And earth has nothing I desire besides you. My flesh and my heart may fail, but God is the strength of my heart and my portion forever" - Psalm 73:25-26.

The psalmist was declaring his absolute allegiance and devotion to the God of heaven, stating that he had no other heavenly interests apart from the Lord. The way you can prove your own devotion is not only to proclaim it, but also to prove it by obeying God's word, which are His instructions from heaven for how to live here on earth. Peter explained the role the Word is to play in your life when he wrote,

> His divine power has given us everything we need for a godly life through our knowledge of him who called us by his own glory and goodness. Through these he has given us his very great and precious promises, so that through them you may participate in the divine nature, having escaped the corruption in the world caused by evil desires (2 Peter 1:3-4).

Throughout this devotional, your reading and study of the Word have been emphasized over and over again. That's because the psalmists themselves stressed the importance of the Word. Does the Word have a central place in your life? What proof do you have that it does? As a new year approaches, what goals can you set that relate to your growth in the knowledge and application of God's word? *Lord, it is the time when I think about my goals for the next year. Today, I am thinking about goals where Your Word is concerned. Now is the time to grow in my knowledge of the Bible. My goal is to get into a study program that will help me learn more, not just for the sake of learning, but that I may know and do more of Your will for my life. That also may include me teaching others, and I welcome the opportunity to do that. Amen.*

DECEMBER 16

DEPRIVING OTHERS

Today's reading: Psalms 76-80

"We will not hide them from their descendants; we will tell the next generation the praiseworthy deeds of the LORD, his power, and the wonders he has done, and they in turn would tell their children. . . . Then they would put their trust in God and would not forget his deeds but would keep his commands" - Psalm 78:4, 7.

You have a testimony, probably many, of what the Lord has done for you, your family, your business, or your ministry. You are obligated to tell others your story for two reasons. The first is so God will receive glory from what He has done, causing people to say, "Praise the Lord," or "Thank You, Jesus!" The second is so people will be encouraged to put their trust in the Lord and keep His commands, as the psalmist wrote in today's passage. When you don't write, publish, broadcast, preach, speak, or converse about your testimony, you are depriving others of what they may need to move on in the Lord. When you belittle your testimony, thinking, "This isn't very significant," or when you engage in false humility, "I had better not draw attention to myself and just be quiet," you may seem like you are being spiritual, but you are not. You are being disobedient. When your heart pounds, your breathing rate increases, your fear level rises, and you focus on what may happen if you do share, *then* you should press through and definitely find a way to tell your story, whether it is a few sentences or 500 pages. Where have you been talking yourself out of declaring the wonders God has done for you? Do you see how you are depriving others of their hope and God of His glory? *I see that when I close my mouth, Lord, I am cheating others out of the help they can derive from how You have worked in my life. I have been afraid of what others would think or say, and I have underestimated what I have that can help others if I share it. Forgive me for being so self-conscious and help me to step out and find more opportunities to share in the days to come.*

December 17
The Church

Today's reading: Psalms 76-80

"Hear us, Shepherd of Israel, you who lead Joseph like a flock. You who sit enthroned between the cherubim, shine forth before Ephraim, Benjamin and Manasseh. Awaken your might; come and save us" - Psalm 80:1-2.

Most people apply the psalms to personal problems and read them for personal benefit, and there is nothing wrong with that. Yet some of the psalms were corporate in nature, and Psalm 80 is one of them. The psalmist was not praying "I" or "me" prayers but rather "us" and "we" prayers, for he was concerned about the state of the people of God. The writer knew that his destiny was tied in part to the destiny of the covenant community. This was not simply an ethnic concern, since all of them were Jews, but a concern for the state of the "church." You also should have a concern not just for your own welfare but also for that of the church, for which Jesus shed His blood for it to be established. Paul wrote about Jesus' love for the church in Ephesians 5:25-30:

> Husbands, love your wives, just as Christ loved the church and gave himself up for her to make her holy, cleansing her by the washing with water through the word, and to present her to himself as a radiant church, without stain or wrinkle or any other blemish, but holy and blameless. In this same way, husbands ought to love their wives as their own bodies. He who loves his wife loves himself. After all, no one ever hated their own body, but they feed and care for their body, just as Christ does the church—for we are members of his body.

Do you love the church? Are you part of one? Do you pray for its welfare? And how about your concern for the larger Church? Do you desire to see it doing well so that your fellow believers can prosper and that God can be magnified in the earth?

December 18

Life is Short

Today's reading: Psalms 86-90

"Remember how fleeting is my life. For what futility you have created all humanity! Who can live and not see death, or who can escape the power of the grave?" - Psalm 89:47-48.

The psalmist was pouring his heart out to the Lord, burdened by the pressures of life and God's seeming withdrawal of His presence from the writer's situation. The psalmist was reminding the Lord, and perhaps himself, that his life was short, and God must help him to get free from the trouble so he could pursue God and God's purpose without interference. Do you have that same mindset that leads to the same kind of prayers? Are you living like your life is short? Do you make the most of every day, and are you living in the urgency of this moment? Do you live like you are dying, which in a sense you are? Read these verses and then set goals for tomorrow and the coming year that are consistent with the truth of today's verses:

> However many years anyone may live, let them enjoy them all. But let them remember the days of darkness, for there will be many. Everything to come is meaningless. You who are young, be happy while you are young, and let your heart give you joy in the days of your youth. Follow the ways of your heart and whatever your eyes see, but know that for all these things God will bring you into judgment. So then, banish anxiety from your heart and cast off the troubles of your body, for youth and vigor are meaningless (Ecclesiastes 11:8-10).

December 19

Properly Placed Trust

Today's reading: Psalms 91-95

"Who will rise up for me against the wicked? Who will take a stand for me against evildoers? Unless the Lord had given me help, I would soon have dwelt in the silence of death" - Psalm 94:16-17.

The psalmist was in trouble and danger, and he asked a rhetorical question for which there was only one answer: The Lord was his only help. The writer raised a good point that was that no one can take the place of the Lord or be as faithful or loyal as He is. Men and women will often disappoint you, but the Lord will not. Paul, Jesus, David, Joseph, Daniel, and others had people fail and even betray them, which only made their commitment to God that much stronger because He was their only source of help and strength. Given this truth, God still requires you to give yourself to others in friendship and service, realizing that they may not reciprocate and will often disappoint you. Jesus is your example in this, for He certainly served people but kept His expectations in His Father: "But Jesus would not entrust himself to them, for he knew all people. He did not need any testimony about mankind, for he knew what was in each person" (John 2:24-25). Are you dealing with disappointment over a betrayal of friendship or unmet expectations where another person is concerned? Do you see that God may be showing you not to put unrealistic trust in others, but to place all your trust in Him?

December 20

Part of the Group

Today's reading: Psalms 96-100

"Know that the Lord is God. It is he who made us, and we are his; we are his people, the sheep of his pasture" - Psalm 100:3.

You are a "sheep," a follower of the Lord, no matter how mature you are or how many years you have walked with Him. Notice also that the psalmist was talking about multiple sheep, which constitute a flock. This means you are part of a larger group, which of course is known today as the church. All this requires humility – the understanding that you never arrive and that you are never to be alone, for you need the gifts, insight, and opportunities for love, personal growth and generosity that are afforded you in your group setting. Therefore, you are not only to focus on your personal well-being, but also of the health of your group or church. Paul wrote most of his letters to churches and not individuals, and had this to say about the church in his letter to Timothy:

> Although I hope to come to you soon, I am writing you these instructions so that, if I am delayed, you will know how people ought to conduct themselves in God's household, which is the church of the living God, the pillar and foundation of the truth (1 Timothy 3:14-15).

Are you part of a church group? Do you have its best interests at heart? Do you just show up from time-to-time, or do you invest time, money and your spiritual gifts to benefit others?

December 21

Your Thoughts

Today's reading: Psalms 101-104

"May my meditation be pleasing to him, as I rejoice in the Lord" - Psalm 104:34.

The psalmist prayed that his meditation would be pleasing to the Lord. That meant that the psalmist was not only careful to give God verbal praise, but he was also mindful of his thoughts, making sure that those were pleasing to the Lord as well. You have a running dialogue all day with yourself, and God is listening in while you talk Have you ever thought about God listening to your thoughts, and making sure that they are acceptable to the Lord? The objective is not to think one thing that is inappropriate but then say something appropriate. to cover that thought. Your goal should be that your thoughts *and* your speech are sources of pleasure for God. The psalmist gives a tip on how to keep your meditation acceptable, and that is to rejoice in the Lord, thus providing fertile ground for good meditation. Jesus showed that God is concerned with your thought life when he confronted the Pharisees: "Immediately Jesus knew in his spirit that this was what they were thinking in their hearts, and he said to them, 'Why are you thinking these things?'" (Mark 2:8). What is your thought life like? Do you even pay attention to your thoughts or realize how important they are? What can do today to maintain your joy so that your thoughts are as pure as God wants them to be?

December 22

Getting and Giving Mercy

Today's reading: Psalms 106-110

"Some became fools through their rebellious ways and suffered affliction because of their iniquities. They loathed all food and drew near the gates of death. Then they cried to the Lord in their trouble, and he saved them from their distress" - Psalm 107:17-19.

There are times when you mess up, and then reap the consequences of your actions financially, relationally, professionally, or spiritually. Those consequences can be serious, but the Lord is merciful and will listen to your cries for help, if you are not proud and choose to humble yourself to ask for forgiveness and assistance. You don't deserve His help, but that's where mercy comes in, for mercy is not getting what you deserve (and grace is getting what you don't deserve). Once you have received mercy, the best thing to do is to extend that same mercy to someone else, as Jesus made clear in His parable on forgiveness:

> Then the master called the servant in. "You wicked servant," he said, "I canceled all that debt of yours because you begged me to. Shouldn't you have had mercy on your fellow servant just as I had on you?" In anger his master handed him over to the jailers to be tortured, until he should pay back all he owed. This is how my heavenly Father will treat each of you unless you forgive your brother or sister from your heart (Matthew 18:32-35).

Do you need to humble yourself and ask for God's mercy for something you have done? Do you need to extend mercy to someone and forgive them for what they have done to you?

December 23

Seated on High

Today's reading: Psalms 111-115

"The Lord is exalted over all the nations, his glory above the heavens. Who is like the Lord our God, the One who sits enthroned on high, who stoops down to look on the heavens and the earth?" - Psalm 113:4-6.

The Lord is exalted high above all things, which means He oversees them, but does not need them. His people are also seated with Him in that lofty position, and Jesus summed up their situation and status well when He said, "My kingdom is not of this world. If it were, my servants would fight to prevent my arrest by the Jewish leaders. But now my kingdom is from another place" (John 18:36). That means God's people should be involved in politics, business, and social work, but they should not take their identify or give their allegiance to any of those. Paul described the posture of God's people when he wrote, "And God raised us up with Christ and seated us with him in the heavenly realms in Christ Jesus, in order that in the coming ages he might show the incomparable riches of his grace, expressed in his kindness to us in Christ Jesus" (Ephesians 2:6-7). Are you seated on high with a heavenly view of the things of earth, or are you immersed in this life to the extent that it robs you of your heavenly peace? Do you love this world so much that it waters down and affects your commitment to the Church?

December 24

Family Joy

Today's reading: Psalms 116-120

"Blessed is he who comes in the name of the Lord. From the house of the Lord we bless you. The Lord is God, and he has made his light shine on us. With boughs in hand, join in the festal procession up to the horns of the altar" - Psalm 118:26-27.

This is the time of year to celebrate and rejoice, for all heaven and nature sang to announce the birth of Christ. Rejoicing was a common element in almost all the Old Testament feasts and holy days. For example, here are the Lord's directions for families when they assembled together to celebrate:

> Use the silver to buy whatever you like: cattle, sheep, wine or other fermented drink, or anything you wish. Then you and your household shall eat there in the presence of the Lord your God and rejoice. And do not neglect the Levites living in your towns, for they have no allotment or inheritance of their own (Deuteronomy 14:26-27).

Notice that God commanded them to feast, and the feast included "wine or fermented drink." The most important thing was that the people were to rejoice in families, and also remember to share their joy and provision with the priests who were serving among them. Why do you think the Lord commanded His people to feast and rejoice? Are you rejoicing and feasting with God as your focus? Are you sharing with your spiritual leaders as you celebrate? Give some thought to the necessity of joy as part of your walk with the Lord as a family, and see what else you can do this holiday season to let the good times roll.

December 25

God's Favor

Today's reading: Psalms 121-125

"Lord, do good to those who are good, to those who are upright in heart. But those who turn to crooked ways the Lord will banish with the evildoers" - Psalm 125:4-5.

The words of the psalmist in these verses are vaguely reminiscent of the words the angels said to the shepherds on the night Jesus was born: "Glory to God in the highest heaven, and on earth peace to those on whom his favor rests" (Luke 2:14). The Lord's favor was on Mary and Joseph, the shepherds, and the Magi, who were all upright in heart, while God relegated evil Herod to irrelevance, after he tried everything possible to destroy Jesus, who he perceived (correctly) as a rival to his throne. Part of God's favor is His guidance, and on one hand, God showed each character in the Christmas story exactly what they were supposed to do through various messengers: the shepherd's angels, Caesar's decree for a census, Joseph's dreams, and the Magi's star. On the other hand, Herod rejected God's directive to worship Jesus, and instead tried to wipe Him out.? What does God's favor on your life mean to you? Are you obeying God's guidance through the means He has chosen to use? Take some time to read the Christmas story in Luke 2 and Matthew 1 and 2 today, looking for examples of God's favor that you can apply to your life right now. *Lord, I thank You for Jesus and the story of His birth. You loved mankind so much that You sent Your Son to reconcile us to You. I rejoice today in Your goodness and I pray that I may live the reality of the Christmas story not just today, but every day. Help me to take the joy I have today and live it throughout the year!*

December 26

Earned Joy

Today's reading: Psalms 126-130

"The Lord has done great things for us, and we are filled with joy" - Psalm 126:3.

The Christmas story is full of joy. Joseph and Mary were joyful that they had a son. The shepherds were joyful that the angels had announced the birth to them. The angels were joyful that God's purpose was being fulfilled through the events in Bethlehem. And the Magi were joyful, for after having traveled hundreds of miles, the star led them to the exact spot where Jesus was residing:

> After they had heard the king, they went on their way, and the star they had seen when it rose went ahead of them until it stopped over the place where the child was. When they saw the star, they were overjoyed. On coming to the house, they saw the child with his mother Mary, and they bowed down and worshiped him. Then they opened their treasures and presented him with gifts of gold, frankincense and myrrh (Matthew 2:9-11).

Can you see that the Magi paid a price to find Jesus, and so, in a sense, they earned their joy because they responded to the star in faith, and were rewarded? What star is God showing you that you need to follow? What will it be like when you find what the star is taking you to?

December 27
God with Us

Today's reading: Psalm 131-135

"He swore an oath to the Lord, he made a vow to the Mighty One of Jacob: 'I will not enter my house or go to my bed, I will allow no sleep to my eyes or slumber to my eyelids, till I find a place for the Lord, a dwelling for the Mighty One of Jacob'" - Psalm 132:2-5.

David swore an oath that he would build a house for God's presence, and that house, the Temple, has been the focus of Israel for the last 3,000 years! Yet David's preoccupation with a building is not God's highest priority, for God is more interested in living in His people's hearts than in a building. Today, God's people are still concerned, sometimes infatuated with "God's house," when it is only bricks-and-mortar, a functional place to house worship activities. Joseph had a dream that Mary was going to have a baby boy and that His name was to be Jesus, and Matthew explained why the significance of that name:

> "She will give birth to a son, and you are to give him the name Jesus, because he will save his people from their sins." All this took place to fulfill what the Lord had said through the prophet: "The virgin will conceive and give birth to a son, and they will call him Immanuel" (which means 'God with us')" (Matthew 1:21-23).

Does God actually live in a building, making it holy? Are you more concerned with church buildings, or God's presence in the hearts of His people, including your own? What are the implications that God is living inside you? *Lord, I carry You with me wherever I go! That is an awesome thought, but it also means You can't go where I don't take You. This coming year, I need to do a better job of introducing You into more of my work, family, church or school situations. I want to be a God-carrier to those who are hurting and need to know You. Amen.*

December 28

A Little Longer

Today's reading: Psalms 136-140

"The Lord will vindicate me; your love, Lord, endures forever—do not abandon the works of your hands" - Psalm 138:8.

David wrote of his confidence that the Lord would vindicate him and make everything right that had turned so wrong. The word vindicate is defined as "to clear, as from an accusation, imputation, suspicion, or the like." It can be difficult to trust the Lord to vindicate you, especially in this age when people regularly resort to the court system to gain the advantage or revenge over those who injure them. God is clear that vindication and vengeance are His responsibility, and not yours. In the book of Revelation, we see those who were martyred inquiring of the Lord about their vindication, and He gave them this response:

> They called out in a loud voice, "How long, Sovereign Lord, holy and true, until you judge the inhabitants of the earth and avenge our blood?" Then each of them was given a white robe, and they were told to wait a little longer, until the full number of their fellow servants, their brothers and sisters, were killed just as they had been (Revelation 6:10-11).

Are you tempted to seize control of the timetable for your vindication? Is God telling you to wait a little longer? Can you trust the Lord to clear your name, even if it happens after you are gone from the scene?

December 29

Trained for War

Today's reading: Psalms 141-145

"Praise be to the Lord my Rock, who trains my hands for war,

my fingers for battle. He is my loving God and my fortress, my stronghold and my deliverer, my shield, in whom I take refuge, who subdues peoples under me" - Psalm 144:1-2.

We know David as a king, psalmist, prayer champion, and poet, but he was also a king warrior, who was trained for battle by God Himself. In the midst of all his battles, David acknowledged that God was everything he needed – fortress, stronghold, deliverer, shield, refuge, and loving battle Companion, who taught David how to take the offensive. God wants to be all that for you, but you must be willing to engage the battle and allow God to train you to be aggressive, not expecting God to do for you what only you can do for yourself. David had mighty men around him, and one of them fought so long and hard that his hand was stuck to his sword:

> Next to him was Eleazar son of Dodai the Ahohite. As one of the three mighty warriors, he was with David when they taunted the Philistines gathered at Pas Dammim for battle. Then the Israelites retreated, but Eleazar stood his ground and struck down the Philistines till his hand grew tired and froze to the sword. The LORD brought about a great victory that day. The troops returned to Eleazar, but only to strip the dead (2 Samuel 23:9-10).

God brought the victory, but Eleazar stood his ground and fought. What do you think your part is in the spiritual battle in which you are presently engaged? Are you doing your part, or waiting on God to do your part – which He won't do?

December 30

Membership Has Its Privileges

Today's reading - Psalms 146-150

"Extol the Lord, Jerusalem; praise your God, Zion. He

strengthens the bars of your gates and blesses your people within you. He grants peace to your borders and satisfies you with the finest of wheat" - Psalm 147:12-14.

God is not only concerned for the individual, singular *you*. He is also concerned for the corporate *you*, which in modern terms is the local church. Paul wrote 13 epistles, four to individuals, and nine to churches outlining both theological issues, but also explaining expected behavioral norms for the body of Christ in general. In today's verses, we see this pattern continue, for the psalmist was addressing Jerusalem as a whole, describing how the Lord would bless the residents of the city with security, peace and food. There was a credit card company who had a slogan that stated, "Membership has its privileges." The same can be said for involvement in a local church, where you are expected to contribute your finances and spiritual gifts in return for God's blessings. Paul wrote this about your involvement in the church: "What then shall we say, brothers and sisters? When you come together, each of you has a hymn, or a word of instruction, a revelation, a tongue or an interpretation. Everything must be done so that the church may be built up" (1 Corinthians 14:26). Are you coming together with other believers for prayer, worship and Word ministry? Are you acting in the best interests of your church, building up the body of Christ through your presence? What blessings have you received for doing so?

DECEMBER 31

THOUGHT GUIDANCE

Today's reading: Psalm 119

"Direct my footsteps according to your word; let no sin rule over me" - Psalm 119:133.

Psalm 119 contains many verses that make wonderful prayers you can pray for yourself. Today's verse is a good example. The writer was asking God to guide him and keep sin from having dominion over him. Who should *not* be praying that prayer? God is able to guide your steps, and you will not even be conscious that He is doing so. What's more, He is protecting you from things so subtly that you are often not aware of His protection. The Amplified Version of Proverbs 16:3 is a wonderful paraphrase of how God will often guide you: "Roll your works upon the Lord - commit and entrust them wholly to Him - and He will cause your thoughts to be agreeable to His will, and so shall your plans be established and succeed." Have you made a commitment to do God's will *before* you know what it is? Then you can count on God directing your steps by directing your thoughts. What ideas do you have that you can assume are from the Lord because they have been present in your mind for many years and do not violate any principle in God's word, and upon which you need to act in the coming year?

Scripture References

GENESIS

1:28	July 2	4:2b-8	September 22
2:8-9	August 13	4:6-7	May 9
2:19-20	October 28	11:6-7	June 13
3:12-13	April 11	50:20	August 21

EXODUS

12:35-36	May 21	17:1-7	May 22
14:19	October 29	20:2-3	August 1

LEVITICUS

14:19	October 29

NUMBERS

11:14-15	June 9

DEUTERONOMY

1:31-33	November 23	16:14-15	October 20
6:5	March 20	16:16-17	November 20
8:2-3	September 17	28:47-48	Novermber 13
8:3-5	February 2	32:7	April 14
8:17-19	August 5	32:35	November 11
14:26-27	December 24		

JOSHUA

1:6-7a	March 20	18:4	April 2

JUDGES

16:22, 28	October 21	16:28	April 28

1 SAMUEL

1:10-11	June 2	21:12-15	October 12
10:19	July 24	30:6b	August 15

2 SAMUEL

5:19b	August 4	5:23-24	August 4
5:22-25	March 30	23:9-10	December 29

1 KINGS

4:29-30	March 15	19:14, 18	January 7
19:14	March 3		

2 KINGS

6:15-17	September 7

2 CHRONICLES

16:9	August 11

NEHEMIAH

8:2-3	November 19	8:10b	February 17

JOB

38:1-3	February 29	40:10-12	September 6
38:27	March 7		

PSALMS

1:1-2	June 1	12:5	December 3
1:6	January 1	12:7-8	April 3
2:10-11	August 1	13:1-2	January 3
3:1-2	February 1	13:5-6	February 3
3:5-6	April 1	14:1	July 3
3:7	July 1	14:6	August 3
4:3	October 1	15:1, 3	June 3
4:4	September 1	15:4b	October 3
4:6-7	May 1	15:1, 5	November 3
4:8	December 1	16:2	July 4
5:9	November 1	16:5-6	September 4
5:12	March 1	17:1-2	March 4
6:3	August 2	18:16-19	January 4
6:6-7	May 2	18:20-22	December 4
7:8	January 2	18:25-27	May 4
7:10	September 2	18:29	November 4
8:2	October 2	18:31-34	October 4
8:3-4	April 2	18:34	February 4
8:4-6	July 2	19:7-9	April 4
9:18	February 2	20:4	June 4
10:1	November 2	20:7	August 4
10:3-4	December 2	21:1	September 5
10:14	June 2	22:1-2	April 5
10:17-18	March 2	23:4	July 5
11:1-3	May 3	23:5	March 5
11:4-5	September 3	24:1-2	January 5
12:1	March 3	25:1	February 5

PSALMS (CONTINUED)

25:5	May 5	40:6-8	August 8
25:12	June 5	41:1-3	September 9
25:14	August 5	41:7-8	February 9
25:14	December 5	42:5	May 9
25:16	November 5	42:7	October 9
26:2-3	April 6	42:9-10	June 9
27:1	July 6	43:2	July 9
27:3	October 6	43:5	March 9
27:4	December 6	44:6-7	January 9
27:8	May 6	45:1	April 9
27:10	November 6	45:7	August 9
28:3-4	June 6	46:1-3	January 10
29:3-5	August 6	49:5-6	December 10
29:10-11	January 6	49:10-11	December 10
30:5	September 6	49:12	June 10
30:6-7	February 6	49:13-14	March 10
30:11-12	March 6	49:16-17	April 10
31:3	August 7	49:18-19	May 10
31:7-8	September 7	49:20	July 10
31:14-15	June 7	50:9-10	February 10
32:5	July 7	50:14-15	September 10
32:7	October 7	50:17	August 10
33:4-5	March 7	50:21	November 10
33:10-11	January 7	51:12-13	July 11
33:16-17	November 7	51:17	August 11
34:4-7	December 7	52:7	October 11
34:8	May 7	53:3	February 11
34:17	April 7	53:4-5	December 11
34:19-20	February 7	54:6	January 11
36:9	October 8	55:12-14	March 11
37:4	July 8	55:15	November 11
37:5-6	March 8	55:18	September 11
37:7	September 8	55:22	May 11
37:8	January 8	56:3	January 12
37:21, 26	May 8	56:11	October 12
38:11	June 8	57:1	November 12
39:2-3	April 8	57:4	August 12
39:4-5	February 8	57:7-8	April 12
40:1, 4	December 8	58:1-2	March 12

PSALMS (CONTINUED)

58:6-7	May 12	75:6-7	July 15
59:9-10	February 12	76:11	October 16
59:16	June 12	77:1-2	May 16
60:5-8	July 12	77:11	June 16
61:5	May 13	77:20	August 16
62:1-2	April 13	78:1-3	February 16
62:9	September 13	78:4, 7	December 16
62:10	February 13	78:5-6	January 16
63:1	October 13	78:19-20	July 16
63:1-3	December 13	78:32	April 16
63:2-4	January 13	78:70-71	September 16
63:5	October 13	78:72	March 16
64:2-4	July 13	79:5-7	November 16
64:6	June 13	80:1-2	December 17
65:9-11	August 13	81:6-7	August 17
66:6	September 14	81:7	September 17
66:13-14	January 14	81:10-11	October 17
66:16	April 14	81:13-14	April 17
67:1-2	March 14	82:2-3	January 17
68:5-6	February 14	83:3-5	November 17
68:18	May 14	84:5	February 17
68:19	June 14	84:11	July 17
68:35	July 14	85:8	March 17
69:6	August 14	85:10	June 17
69:7-9	November 14	85:10-11	May 17
70:5	December 14	86:2	September 18
71:5	December 11	86:4	June 18
71:15, 18	November 15	86:11	March 18
71:20	October 15	87:3-4	October 18
71:24	November 15	87:5	July 18
72:1-2	March 15	89:15	April 18
72:13-14	February 15	89:15-16	May 18
73:2-3	January 15	89:19-20	January 18
73:13-14, 28	May 15	89:22	February 18
73:21-22	June 15	89:47-48	December 18
73:24	April 15	90:4	August 18
73:25-26	December 15	90:17	November 18
74:9	August 15	91:1	July 19
74:16-17	September 15	91:7	August 19

PSALMS (CONTINUED)

92:4-5	November 19	108:7-9	March 22
92:12-13	February 19	109:4-5	July 22
92:14-15	September 19	109:8-9	April 22
94:7	October 19	110:1	June 22
94:12-13	June 19	111:10	January 23
94:16-17	December 19	112:4	June 23
94:18-19	May 19	112:5, 9	April 23
95:1-2	April 19	112:6-7	October 23
95:7b-9	January 19	113:4-6	December 23
96:1-3	July 20	113:7-9	March 23
96:8	November 20	114:7-8	July 23
96:10	April 20	115:4-6	February 23
96:13	October 20	115:9-11	November 23
97:11-12	June 20	115:12-13	September 23
98:1-2	September 20	115:14-15	August 23
98:4-6	March 20	116:3-4	February 24
99:1-3	May 20	116:16	June 24
99:4	February 20	116:32-33	May 24
99:6-7	August 20	117:1-2	August 24
100:3	December 20	118:5	October 24
100:4	January 20	118:6	September 24
101:6	July 21	118:8	January 24
102:16-17	October 21	118:9	July 24
103:2	January 21	118:13-14	November 24
103:2-5	February 21	118:18	May 24
103:10	March 21	118:22-23	March 24
103:13-14	April 21	118:26-27	December 24
104:2-4	September 21	119:11	August 31
104:19-23	November 21	119:18	July 31
104:34	December 21	119:27	May 31
105:1-4	June 21	119:36	January 31
105:16-17	August 21	119:63	October 31
105:37-38	May 21	119:116	March 31
106:13-14	January 22	119:133	December 31
106:16	September 22	121:1-2	March 25
106:24-25	August 22	121:3-4	May 25
107:2-3	February 22	121:7-8	January 25
107:33-34	October 22	122:1-2	June 25
107:35-36	November 22	122:9	November 25

PSALMS (CONTINUED)

123:1-2	February 25	137:4	August 28
123:3-4	October 25	138:6	January 28
124:7-8	September 25	138:7	April 28
124:8	August 25	138:8	December 28
125:1	July 25	138:8a	March 28
125:4-5	December 25	139:1-2	July 28
126:1-2	August 26	139:7	June 28
126:3	December 26	139:14	September 28
126:4	November 26	139:17-18	February 28
126:5-6	January 26	139:23-24	March 28
127:1	March 26	141:3	March 29
127:2	July 26	141:4	September 29
128:1-2	February 26	141:5	January 29
128:5-6	September 26	141:9-10	October 29
129:1-2	October 26	142:1-2	February 29
130:1-2	April 26	143:3-7	November 29
130:3-4	May 26	143:8	April 29
130:5-6	June 26	143:10	January 29
131:1	April 27	144:1-2	December 29
131:2	November 27	144:3-4	May 29
132:1	May 27	144:12	June 29
132:2-5	December 27	145:13	August 29
132:10	February 27	146:3-4	April 30
133:5	January 27	146:7-9	September 30
134:1-2	March 27	147:3	July 30
135:5	September 27	147:6	August 30
135:8-9	October 27	147:10-11	March 30
135:14	July 27	147:12-14	December 30
135:15-18	August 27	148:7-8	May 30
135:19-21	June 27	149:3-5	June 30
136:1	October 28	149:4	January 30
136:3-5	November 28	150:1-2	November 30
136:23-24	May 28	150:3-5	October 30

PROVERBS

1:7	January 23	10:7	November 18
1:30-32	September 29	13:22	December 10
2:3-5	May 6	14:31	February 15
3:4-6	February 12	16:3	December 31

PROVERBS (CONTINUED)

18:23	April 26	22:9	March 2
18:24 (NKJV)	November 5	22:16	August 3
19:17	April 23	28:1	December 11
22:2	September 13	28:27	April 23
22:6	February 16		

ECCLESIASTES

2:24-26a	February 26	11:8-10	December 18
5:18-20	September 4		

ISAIAH

30:20-21	June 5	52:12	October 24
40:31	January 22	53:5	August 19
44:3-5	June 29	54:1-2	October 24
44:28	March 12	54:17	February 18
45:1	February 27	57:15	May 4
50:4	August 8		

JEREMIAH

9:23-24	March 25	20:9	April 8

EZEKIEL

3:1-3	May 7	11:19	March 18
8:16	September 27	21:26	November 22

DANIEL

1:18-20	March 5	8:27	October 30
6:19-23	June 23		

JOEL

2:5-6	August 26	2:25-26	November 26

JONAH

1:3	June 28

HABAKKUK

2:4	March 13	3:17	May 20

MATTHEW

1:21-23	December 27	4:18	January 5
2:9-11	December 26	5:3	June 1

MATTHEW (CONTINUED)

5:4	January 26	16:8-10	July 16
5:6	October 13	16:18-19	November 25
5:7	February 25	16:26-27	April 10
5:7	April 26	18:3	October 2
5:23-24	January 27	18:21-22	March 11
5:43-44	April 22	18:32-34	November 12
6:25	April 16	19:23	July 10
6:31-33	July 17	26:27-28	December 5
8:21-22	August 28	26:35	April 6
8:24-26	May 25	28:8	July 5
10:27	November 15	28:16-18a	June 25
10:34-49	November 6	28:19-20	March 14
11:28-30	June 14		

MARK

1:15	April 20	7:37	March 16
1:45	October 6	8:34	May 27
2:8	December 21	10:27	November 4
2:15-17	July 7	10:29-30	November 17
4:24-27	August 6	12:24	August 31
4:38-40	May 30	12:35-37	June 22
5:3-5	June 24		

LUKE

1:50-53	March 23	8:24	April 1
1:52-53	January 28	9:2	August 29
2:14	December 25	9:57-59	September 10
4:16-21	September 30	11:40-42	December 3
5:16	September 1	12:5-6	November 21
6:12	June 12	12:18-21	November 7
6:13	October 11	14:11	August 30
6:20-22	December 14	18:11-12	February 10
6:24	July 10	18:13	April 26
6:26	February 1	18:22	March 28
6:34-36	June 6	22:31-32	September 18
8:22-24	December 1	24:30-32	March 17
8:22-24	July 19		

JOHN

1:2-4	September	13:17	March 18
1:11	March 24	14:6	October 8
2:17-18	November 14	14:10-12	October 8
2:24-25	December 19	14:12-14	September 19
4:13-14	December 13	15:5	February 19
6:16-21	August 25	15:10-11	May 18
6:26-27	November 27	15:16	February 11
6:47-49	December 13	16:13	January 29
7:17	April 15	16:13	February 28
8:10-11	March 21	16:33	November 2
8:12	September 21	17:4-5	April 3
9:20-23	September 24	17:14-17	August 12
12:28-29	November 10	21:21-22	September 8
12:29b-30	August 20		

ACTS

2:42-47	October 31	14:21b-22	February 7
4:12	March 22	16:23-25	April 12
6:40-42	June 21	17:11	May 31
10:38	January 18	17:28	January 25
12:8-10	October 7	18:9-11	July 12
14:14-15	April 30	18:18	January 14
14:21-22	January 10	27:23-26	February 24

ROMANS

1:5	October 18	8:37-39	June 30
1:18-20	September 15	12:1-2	March 9
2:4	October 19	12:3	December 4
6:18	May 17	12:19	May 12
8:1-2	May 19	15:4	June 16
8:31b-35	May 29		

1 CORINTHIANS

1:27b-31	October 2	11:27-28	May 25
2:16	June 4	11:32	June 19
5:11	July 21	12:24b-26	August 14
8:9	November 3	13:4-8a	September 9
10:1-5	July 23	14:26	December 30
10:14	May 23	15:33	July 21
11:17-21	May 28		

2 CORINTHIANS

1:5-7	May 2	8:13-15	May 8
3:4-5	October 23	9:8-9	January 11
6:11	July 21	10:5	January 3
6:14-16	November 1	10:3-6	February 4
6:15-17	August 27	13:4	July 14

GALATIANS

2:9b-10	January 17	6:7-10	August 23
3:28	September 13		

EPHESIANS

2:6-7	December 23	5:5	February 13
2:10	March 1	5:18-20	September 20
4:25	February 9	5:20	January 20
4:26	January 8	5:25-30	December 17
4:29	June 3	6:10-12	September 2

PHILIPPIANS

2:6-8	June 17	3:17-19	December 2
2:13	June 11	4:4-7	June 20
2:14-15	August 22	4:6	February 21
3:10-11	May 3	4:7	July 8
3:12-14	November 24	4:11-13	July 4

COLOSSIANS

1:20	July 2	3:16	April 19
3:5	February 23	3:23-24	March 8

1 THESSALONIANS

4:13	June 15

2 THESSALONIANS

1:4-6	October 15	2:13	September 25

1 TIMOTHY

1:13-14	July 3	3:14-15	December 20
1:15-16	July 11	6:6-10	January 15
1:18-19	October 4	6:8	May 1
3:1	September 23		

2 TIMOTHY

1:7	January 3	1:16	June 8
1:12	April 29	3:12	October 25
1:15	January 24	4:14	October 9

HEBREWS

1:9	June 18	11:34b	April 7
2:17-18	July 9	12:1-3	August 9
3:7-10	January 19	12:4-5, 12	April 5
3:12-15	August 7	12:8-11	May 24
4:12-13	January 31	12:10-11	October 17
10:24-25	May 5	12:26-29	July 25
10:30	July 27	12:28-29	April 13
11:6	February 5	13:17	September 16
11:24-27	December 8		

JAMES

1:2-4	June 7	3:16	May 10
2:1-7	February 20	4:3-4	October 25
2:17	January 1	5:1-5	June 10
3:5-6	March 29		

1 PETER

2:19-20	August 16	4:12-13	March 6
2:21-23	March 4	4:16-18	November 16
3:9	September 26	5:7	May 11
3:23	January 2	5:8-9	July 1
4:1-2	August 2		

2 PETER

1:3-4	December 15	3:8	August 18
1:19-21	August 17	3:9	September 3

1 JOHN

1:5b-9	April 18	5:3-5	September 5
2:15-17	December 6		

JUDE

24-25	November 30

REVELATION

2:4-5	August 11	18:9-10	March 10
6:10-11	December 28	21:2	January 30
7:9-11	June 27	21:2-3	July 18
12:10-12	September 11	21:5	July 20
12:11	January 21		

About the Author

John Stanko was born in Pittsburgh, Pennsylvania. After graduating from St. Basil's Prep School in Stamford, Connecticut, he attended Duquesne University where he received his bachelor's and master's degrees in economics in 1972 and 1974 respectively.

Since then, John has served as an administrator, teacher, consultant, author, and pastor in his professional career. He holds a second master's degree in pastoral ministries, and earned his doctorate in pastoral ministries from Liberty Theological Seminary in Houston, Texas in 1995. He recently completed a second doctor of ministry degree at Reformed Presbyterian Theological Seminary in Pittsburgh.

John has taught extensively on the topics of time management, life purpose and organization, and has conducted leadership and purpose training sessions throughout the United States and in 32 countries. He is also certified to administer the DISC and other related personality assessments as well as the Natural Church Development profile for churches. In 2006, he earned the privilege to facilitate for The Pacific Institute of Seattle, a leadership and personal development program, and for The Leadership Circle, a provider of cultural and executive 360-degree profiles. He has authored fifteen books and written for many publications around the world.

John founded a personal and leadership development company, called PurposeQuest, in 2001 and today travels the world to speak, consult and inspire leaders and people everywhere. From 2001-2008, he spent six months a year in Africa and still enjoys visiting and working on that continent, while teaching for Geneva College's Masters of Organizational Leadership and the Center for Urban Biblical Ministry in his hometown of Pittsburgh, Pennsylvania. John has been married for 38 years to Kathryn Scimone Stanko, and they have two adult children. In 2009, John was appointed the administrative pastor for discipleship at Allegheny Center Alliance Church on the North Side of Pittsburgh where he served for five years. Most recently, John founded Urban Press, a publishing service designed to tell stories of the city, from the city and to the city.

Keep in Touch with John Stanko

www.purposequest.com

www.johnstanko.us

www.stankobiblestudy.com

www.stankomondaymemo.com

or via email at johnstanko@gmail.com

John also does extensive relief and community development work in Kenya. You can see some of his projects at www.purposequest.com/contributions

PurposeQuest International
PO Box 8882
Pittsburgh, PA 15221-0882

Additional Titles by John W. Stanko

A Daily Taste of Proverbs

A Daily Dose of Proverbs

What Would Jesus Ask You Today?

The Price of Leadership

Changing the Way We Do Church

Unlocking the Power of Your Creativity

Unlocking the Power of your Productivity

Unlocking the Power of Your Purpose

Unlocking the Power of You

Life Is A Gold Mine: Can You Dig It?

These titles, and more by John W. Stanko, are available in paper or Kindle versions at www.amazon.com